BARRON'S

American Sign Language

A Comprehensive Guide to ASL 1 and 2

DAVID A. STEWART, ED.D. AND **JENNIFER STEWART, M.S.ED.**

Formerly of Michigan State University   Henry Ford College

Dedicated to the memory of my brilliant father, the original author of this book.
May your legacy and teachings continue to live on forever.

Acknowledgments

Thank you to my father, who brought the joy of ASL and Deaf Education to thousands of students by radiating a contagious passion and determination in all he accomplished. Thank you to my wonderful family, especially my mother, for encouraging my journey. Thank you to the many ASL educators, colleagues, ASL instructors, interpreters, and educating members of the Deaf community who provided feedback on the content and to my editor, Angela Tartaro. A special thank you to my loving partner John and my son David for supporting me through it all.

Published by Kaplan, Inc., d/b/a Barron's Educational Series
750 Third Avenue
New York, NY 10017
www.barronseduc.com

ISBN: 978-1-5062-6382-3

10 9 8 7 6 5 4 3 2 1

Kaplan, Inc., d/b/a Barron's Educational Series print books are available at special quantity discounts to use for sales promotions, employee premiums, or educational purposes. For more information or to purchase books, please call the Simon & Schuster special sales department at 866-506-1949.

CONTENTS

About the Authors

David A. Stewart, Ed.D.

David Stewart was a professor and director of the Deaf Education program at Michigan State University, where he prepared teachers to teach Deaf and hard-of-hearing children and oversaw the American Sign Language program. Prior to attending graduate school and becoming a professor, Stewart taught Deaf and hard-of-hearing children in a School for the Deaf. He wrote extensively about the use of American Sign Language in the classroom and the critical role it has in the identity of the Deaf community. He is the author of seven books and more than sixty academic publications related to ASL, sociocultural aspects of the Deaf community, ASL Interpreting, and the education of Deaf and hard-of-hearing children. Stewart was also the American Sign Language content expert behind the Signing Online program. As a Deaf individual, Stewart has had long ties with the Deaf community and its members, and he served on the board of trustees for many years at Gallaudet University. Stewart's teachings continue to play an integral role in paving the way for Deaf education and the pedagogy of ASL education everywhere.

Jennifer Stewart, M.S.Ed.

Jennifer Stewart serves as the ASL program coordinator and is a tenured professor of the American Sign Language program at Henry Ford College, where she helped develop the course curriculum for the Certificate of Deaf Studies. Professor Stewart obtained her associate of applied science in ASL Interpretation for the Deaf and a Deaf Studies Certificate from Sinclair Community College. While working as an ASL interpreter, she continued her education and received her bachelor's degree in ASL Interpretation for the Deaf from Siena Heights University. Recognizing her passion for teaching, Stewart graduated with a master's degree in Education–Special Education and a teaching certificate for Deaf and hard-of-hearing students from Saint Joseph's University. Stewart is also an ASL instructor and curriculum advisor for online ASL instruction, has worked internationally as an ASL interpreter, is an active member of the American Sign Language Teacher's Association (ASLTA), and is a collegiate-level ASL Club advisor.

Contributors

Jessica Marie Minor, M.A., Doctoral Student

Jessica Marie Minor is a tenured professor in the Interpreter Education program at Sinclair College in Dayton, Ohio, where she has been teaching ASL since 2001. She has been honored nationally by Sinclair College with the NISOD award for excellence in teaching. Professor Minor earned a B.S. in Special Education from the College of Charleston in Charleston, SC, an M.A. in Deaf Education: Family Centered Early Education from Gallaudet University in Washington, D.C., and she is currently a doctoral student in the Educational Leadership program at the

University of Dayton. Minor has presented at the Conference of Interpreters of the Deaf (CIT), has been the keynote speaker for the Ohio chapter of the Registry of Interpreters for the Deaf (OCRID), and has presented workshops for the Ohio Association of American Sign Language Teachers (OASLTA). She has also worked internationally and nationally as a support service provider for the deaf-blind. Her educator experience includes ASL instruction, interpreter training instruction, and curriculum design. Minor was a former Miss Deaf South Carolina and a graduate assistant to Dr. I. King Jordan. She enjoys socializing with the Deaf community and signing books with her children.

Otis T. Newsome, Jr.

Otis T. Newsome, Jr., also known as Tyrone, is a former ASL instructor at Sinclair College and a former board member at the Deaf Community Resource Center in Dayton, Ohio. He currently works as a Sign Language mentor in Sinclair College's ASL Interpreting program. His educator experience includes ASL instruction, interpreter training instruction and mentorship, involvement with the Deaf Adventure Camp and OYO Deaf Camp as a camp counselor, and continuing advocacy for Deaf education. Newsome also played basketball with a Deaf league called Central Athlete Association of the Deaf (CAAD).

Becky Craft

Becky Craft is a board member and treasurer at the Deaf Community Resource Center in Dayton, Ohio, where she has resided as an active member of the Deaf community for more than twenty years. She is also an office administrator at Interpreters of the Deaf LLC, as well as a freelance Deaf interpreter. Her educator experience includes ASL instruction, interpreter training instruction and mentorship, and continuing advocacy for Deaf education.

How to Use This Book

What Will You Learn?

Learning objectives are listed at the start of each chapter. These will help guide and track your learning and allow you to easily return to topics that you want to review again.

ASL Tips appear throughout the book to provide helpful information and advice on the surrounding topics.

Chapter Review and Practice Activities are included to track and reinforce what you've learned. If answers are required, they can be found in the Appendix.

All About ASL

Chapters 1 and 2 cover the history of ASL, the physical and spatial aspects of signing, and Deaf culture and community. Both chapters include a **Chapter Review** with questions on what you've learned. Once you have a sound understanding of where ASL comes from, you will be on your way to signing successfully!

A Solid Foundation

Chapters 3, 4, and 5 cover grammar, fingerspelling, and numbers. You'll learn the ten grammar rules, the importance of facial expressions and nonmanual signals, how to sign numbers and addresses, and how to fingerspell—including the fully illustrated ASL alphabet! Each chapter also includes a **Chapter Review**. These topics are the basic foundations of learning ASL. Review them carefully before continuing on your ASL journey.

The Lessons

Chapters 6–15 include ASL lessons on important topics, such as conversational ASL, role shifting, directional verbs, health, and much more. Each chapter is heavily illustrated with ASL signs to enhance learning. Lessons include:

- **Dialogues** with illustrated signs for each sentence. The dialogues are short authentic sentences that you might have in daily encounters. Different names are used so you can practice fingerspelling names other than your own. The dialogues are used to show how grammar rules are applied to the formation of ASL sentences. Studying and practicing the dialogues will teach you how the hands, face, body, and the space around you are manipulated to form sentences in ASL.

- **Breaking Down the Dialogue** feature that shows you which ASL grammar rule best fits each sentence. The term *best fits* is used because in some instances more than one rule applies; however, the rule that is the focus of the sentence is the only one that is analyzed.

- **What's the Sign?** section that explains the particular ways in which some of the signs in the dialogue are used.
- **ASL Synonyms** for signs that are also used to mean different things. For example, the sign START can also be used to mean BEGIN, ORIGINATE, ORIGINAL, and INITIATE.
- **ASL Signs**, aside from those illustrated in each dialogue, throughout to enhance your ASL vocabulary.
- **Practice Activities** that follow each lesson. They break down the lessons into sections that you can practice until you have mastered them. You will also be prompted to practice signing the entire dialogue in each lesson. Practice with a partner so that you can get used to using facial grammar and the signing space. You should also practice signing the dialogues by yourself in your own "space" so that you can slow down the signing without feeling any pressure to complete a sentence.
- **Grammar Practice** boxes in applicable lessons to test your knowledge. Answers are provided in the Appendix.

 Online Video Practice

Watching someone sign is a critical element in learning this visual language. It helps you see that ASL is composed of not only signs, but facial expressions, natural expressions, and gestures.

Barron's American Sign Language provides **Video Quizzes** and a **Final Exam** online for optimal learning. If a chapter includes a video quiz, you will be prompted to visit the Barron's Online Learning Hub:

online.barronsbooks.com

Register now and begin your language-learning journey with Barron's!

Note: *Your online ASL Teacher who signs in the videos is Deaf. He has his own particular signing style, just as you have your own speaking and communication style. Review the signs in the book carefully and study his gestures and facial expressions—you'll be mastering ASL in no time!*

Note to the Student

Barron's American Sign Language is designed to give you comprehensive knowledge of ASL. Here are important tips to follow while learning from this book:

- ***Think visually***. American Sign Language (ASL) is understood by seeing it because all information in ASL is visual. How you make a sign is important, but just as important are the facial expressions and body movements you use when signing.

- ***Learn the ten basic ASL grammar rules***. You will see examples throughout the book of how these grammar rules are used in dialogue. Most of the rules are frequently repeated to help you gain greater familiarity with them.

- ***Master signing the dialogue practice activities***. Each lesson has a dialogue, and they become progressively more difficult throughout the book. Practice signing each dialogue until you are comfortable with the signing. You can do this best with a partner or with a fluent ASL signer. VOICES OFF! To determine who signs which part, fingerspell the various practice dialogue names. If you are alone, practice signing in front of a mirror or record yourself. This practice will help you develop fluency in your signing.

- ***Follow all suggestions for further practice***. These suggestions ask you to develop your own dialogues and practice signing them. Do not rely on learning only from the dialogues in this book. Create your own dialogues based on what you've learned and add some personal touches. The goal is for you to be able to sign comfortably about yourself and about the world around you.

- ***Create ASL sentences and write the English translations of these sentences***. Translation is important for learning the differences between ASL and English grammar, because in ASL you do not sign each word you say in English.

- ***Learn the different meanings of some ASL signs***. A list of these signs and their alternative meanings is presented in some chapters. Some are signed the exact same way but have different meanings. This is based on context. For example, the sign for NICE and CLEAN may look the same, but we use context to know which word the signer means to convey.

- ***Learn about Deaf culture***. Deaf culture is full of history, music, poems, humor, sports, memberships, activities, education, organizations, language, and so much more. The language of Deaf individuals does not exist without the rich culture it encompasses.

- ***Communicate with Deaf people***. Try to communicate with Deaf people if possible. Doing this will help you learn more about ASL and help you expand your vocabulary of signs. Learning and practicing ASL with native Deaf users is the best way to develop your skills.

All About American Sign Language

What Is ASL?

American Sign Language, or ASL, is the language of the American Deaf community. It is used in North America, and it is the only complete and natural sign language recognized by the Deaf community. This is a simple definition. Once it is understood that ASL maintains grammatical structure, syntax, and rules entirely separate from English grammar, we can begin to understand how to use it properly—the way the American Deaf community intends.

As you venture through this book, you will notice that ASL grammar is not only comprised of signed words or concepts, but it heavily involves the use of facial grammar to give information or meaning to signs. Facial grammar, including eye contact, facial expressions, eye gazing, and head movements are part of the unique grammatical structure of ASL. Because of this, and many other reasons, the visual language of ASL is fascinating for nonsigners to observe and quickly becomes a desired language to learn.

Is ASL a Universal Language?

One of the most common assumptions is that ASL is a universal language, but, if we break it down, then you will begin to understand that it is not—and how could it possibly be? If someone assumed English is a universal language, you may chuckle at that assumption. The same could be said about the visual language of North Americans. British Sign Language (BSL), Australian Sign

Language (Auslan), Arabic Sign Language, Japanese Sign Language, and Ukrainian Sign Language are only five of the approximately 135 known sign languages used across the globe.

It should also be clear that if you wish to communicate with Deaf people from other countries, then you must learn their sign language because ASL is only commonly used in the United States and in all provinces of Canada (other than Quebec where Language des Signes Québécoise is the dominant sign language). Thus, British Sign Language is as Greek to Deaf Americans as Mexican Sign Language is to Deaf Brazilians. The World Federation of the Deaf created a standardized system of signs to meet the needs of Deaf people throughout the world to promote understanding. The sign system Gestuno, now called International Sign Language, was created by the World Federation of the Deaf in 1975 utilizing signs commonly used by Deaf people across the world and those which occur in a naturally spontaneous manner (*World Federation of the Deaf, 1975*). International Sign Language is often used at worldwide conferences, such as the Annual World Federation of the Deaf and International Congress on the Education of the Deaf to facilitate communication.

English Gloss

ASL is an expressive and receptive language only. Because of the spatial and gestural qualities of ASL, there can be no convenient written form of ASL. What we can do is write English glosses of ASL signs. An English gloss is the best approximation of the meaning of a sign. It gives us a way of laying out ASL so that it can be studied and discussed, but it is not a written form of ASL. In this book, English glosses are set in uppercase lettering. For example, the English sentence "What are you doing tonight?" is written in English gloss using ASL signs and reads, "TONIGHT, YOU DO-what?" When signed in ASL, the sign TONIGHT is signed first, to indicate time, then the subject YOU is signed, the verb DO, and finally the question WHAT, which is commonly placed at the end of the sentence. This method of ordering sentences with the subject first, object next, and verb at the end is not found in English.

History of ASL

The first school for the Deaf was founded in America in 1817. It is a landmark in the history of American Sign Language. Located in Hartford, Connecticut, and now known as the American School for the Deaf, the school brought together two main sources in the development of ASL signs and grammar.

The first source was the school's founders and first two teachers, a Deaf Frenchman, Laurent Clerc, widely considered the father of ASL, and an American, Thomas Hopkins Gallaudet. Clerc was born hearing, but at age one, he fell into a fire resulting in a loss of hearing and sense of smell. The side of his face that was burnt gave him a distinguished look, and later his "name sign" was based on his scar. As an adolescent, Clerc attended the Royal Institution for the Deaf in Paris. From an early age, he excelled in his studies and went on to become a sign language instructor at the Royal Institution for the Deaf.

ASL TIP

Martha's Vineyard Sign Language (MVSL)

Martha's Vineyard Sign Language (MVSL) was once widely used on the island of Martha's Vineyard from the early 18th century to 1952. Deafness was prevalent on Martha's Vineyard due to hereditary reasons. MVSL was used equally by both Deaf and hearing residents, allowing Deaf people to be independent because there was no language barrier.

Thomas Hopkins Gallaudet was studying to become a minister when a young Deaf girl, Alice Cogswell, came into his life. While getting to know her, he recognized her intelligence and became frustrated with the lack of schools to accommodate and educate Deaf children in America. With her as his inspiration, a journey to England began in search of how to teach Deaf students. While in England, the schools for the Deaf that he explored used only oral language, so he traveled to France, where he observed Laurent Clerc, who was teaching his Deaf students using sign language. Clerc invited him to learn sign language at the Royal Institution for the Deaf. Clerc was his teacher and the two of them quickly connected through discussions about deafness, sign language, and education. Gallaudet asked Clerc to come to America with him to open a school for the Deaf. A year after they arrived, the first school for the Deaf was founded.

The second source of ASL was the Deaf students in attendance at the school. They came at a time when schooling was not mandatory, and most of the population lived in farming communities. For some of these children, the school marked the first time they were in the company of other Deaf people, so the signs they used were mainly created at home. But other Deaf children, and especially those with Deaf parents, introduced to the school signs native to America—signs that were used in the Deaf community. For about the next sixty years, this pattern was repeated in other states where schools for the Deaf were springing up, many of them employing Deaf teachers who had graduated from other schools for the Deaf. The work of these early pioneers of education had a lasting influence on the shape of ASL as we know it today.

Gallaudet University

Gallaudet University, located in Washington, D.C., is the first higher education institution to service Deaf and hard-of-hearing students in all programs and subjects. The University is bilingual, using ASL and written English for instruction.

Signing as a Choice of Communication

I taught ASL to over two thousand students, and my strongest impression of this language can be summed up in a simple observation: Once students have tasted the excitement of communicating with their hands, they never lose their appetite for learning more about signing. I have not met a sign language teacher who has observed otherwise. Not all students learn to sign well nor do they all continue in their study of signing. But once their curiosity is piqued, they continue to have an interest in signing. I was asked by a student if I signed in my dreams. Whether Deaf people sign in their dreams is a moot question, so I flipped it around and told her to tell me how she dreams after she becomes a fluent signer. Such is the nature of learning about sign language.

For many of you, ASL is a new language that forces you to confront your prejudices about communicating with your hands and facial expressions. You might wonder about what you can talk about in signs. Would you wonder about this if you were learning to speak Spanish? Probably not. But ASL is not just a different language—it is a different medium for talking, and this fact may make you hesitant and perhaps even suspicious about what you can and cannot say in ASL. You are in good company because Deaf people wonder how it is possible to talk in speech about such things as the destructive force of tornadoes and the tender moments of a child playing alone. To Deaf people, the picture of communication painted by vowels and consonants and pitch and loudness pales in comparison to the vibrant images that jump off the fingers and hands, face, and body of a person signing.

Being able to communicate with your hands should not be a surprise because you have been doing it for years, albeit to a far lesser extent than Deaf people. From the earliest days of human communications, people have relied on symbols created by the hands to communicate with other groups of people they encountered as they followed a herd of animals or moved across the continent in search of food and shelter. Native Americans used signs for intertribal communications because mastering many spoken dialects is difficult. Hunters in the African savanna still use signs to help them hunt better. It is hard to imagine a hunter yelling, "Sneak up on the wildebeest on your left!" A neon sign could hardly be more invasive. Yet it is easy to imagine hunters and others using natural gestures and created signs to communicate.

For Deaf people, signing is necessary for communication. How did Deaf people living 3,000 years ago in Athens communicate with one another? They used sign language, the same way they communicate today. Then why, until recently, did so many hearing people know so little about signing? There are at least three reasons for this. First, Deaf people make up just a small fraction of the population in any area. Therefore, many hearing people never encounter a Deaf person in their walk through life. Second, speech is the dominant form of communication in society and gets the most attention. Third, Deaf people tend to socialize with one another and with hearing people who know how to sign.

Given these reasons for why hearing people know so little about signing, it is reasonable to assume that if you know someone who communicates with the hands, you know someone who is Deaf. Or is it? Consider how much gestural and nonverbal communication you encounter in your everyday conversations. A stare ("Don't do it"), an affectionate smile ("I am comfortable around you"), pushing the hand quickly to the side ("Get rid of it"), brushing the index finger back and forth across the chin ("I'm thinking about it"), and placing the hand on the forehead ("I don't believe this happened") convey information. They are not random acts unrelated to a conversation taking place. In fact, we use nonverbal communication so naturally that we don't talk about these gestures other than to say, "Don't talk with your hands." But we do talk with our hands, and for Deaf people it is the most natural way of talking.

ASL Awareness

Awareness of ASL has been growing since Professor William C. Stokoe, Jr., of Gallaudet University, known as the father of ASL linguistics, published his research on the linguistics of ASL about sixty years ago. His first paper, published in 1960, is titled "Sign Language Structure." This was followed by the first dictionary of ASL in 1965, *Dictionary of American Sign Language on Linguistic Principles*. Stokoe compiled the dictionary with two Deaf colleagues at Gallaudet, Carl Croneberg and Dorothy Casterline. In 1971, Stokoe established the Linguistic Research Laboratory at Gallaudet. Stokoe's work had a profound impact on ASL awareness in the United States and throughout the world, and we've even come a long way since then.

ASL courses in high schools and colleges are booming. The television and movie industry has discovered the value of including Deaf actors and actresses in films. The series *Switched at Birth* and various thriller movies, such as *The Quiet Place*, have starred Deaf actors and actresses in the main roles. The effect is that ASL is steadily working its way into households across the nation. Sign language interpreters are also indirectly promoting exposure to ASL whether they are interpreting in schools, for national emergencies, in a doctor's office, at a music festival, or for the President on the campaign trail. An interpreter's visibility translates to ASL visibility. Just how effective is the movement to create greater awareness of ASL with Deaf actors/actresses, ASL interpreters, and ASL being offered for language credit in schools? Answer this question yourself by thinking about your first encounter with signing and the reason why you are reading this book.

ASL for All

Although ASL is the language of Deaf individuals, it is for all people: Deaf/deaf, hard of hearing, hearing, babies, children, parents, grandparents, and people with varying abilities and speech or communication difficulties. Any and all people can benefit from the use of a visual language.

The Beginning of Signs

At some point, you will wonder where in the world signs came from. Compared with the study of other languages, the study of sign language is relatively new, with ASL being the most widely studied sign language in the world. But even ASL has had only sixty years under the microscope of psycholinguists and sociolinguists, who are seeking to determine its roots, map out its grammar and vocabulary, and survey its linguistic versatility in all phases of communication. Although we have learned much, we still have much more to learn.

It was mentioned earlier that even though ASL did not only begin with the schooling of Deaf children, schools for the Deaf have helped spread its use. Moreover, because Deaf communities tend to form around schools for the Deaf, there is a close association among ASL, schools for the Deaf, and the Deaf community.

As with any language, we want to know about its roots. We also want to know why we use a particular word and where this word comes from. Sign language is no exception, and like gazing at the stars, we are curious about whether any of the signs used almost 200 years ago are still used today. Some of them are, such as the signs HELP, OTHER, and SEARCH-FOR, which are similar to signs in French Sign Language. As you now know, ASL came to America with the help of Laurent Clerc from France; therefore, many signs are derived from French Sign Language. The ASL noun-adjective grammar structure creates phrases such as SHIRT BLUE and BIRD YELLOW, the same sort of structure used in French Sign Language. Sign language used in other countries may also have influenced the development of ASL, but we are just learning about the nature of this influence.

A Versatile Language

We can say that ASL is a versatile language, which is something we say about English. Many words were introduced to English by speakers from other languages: The word *skunk* comes from the Native Americans, *patio* comes from Spaniards, *corral* comes from people in southern Africa. Surprisingly, ASL is flexible enough to borrow from English. The sign OK is made by fingerspelling O-K. Signs for many countries are typically taken from the native sign language used in that country, as you will see in Chapter 15.

Deaf people create new signs as necessary to accommodate changing lifestyles, the influence of technology, and the evolving world we live in. Signs of recent origin are SELFIE, VIDEO-CHAT, and HASHTAG. Creating new signs is a part of ASL's evolution. It is also a part of Deaf culture. It is unthinkable that you will wake up one day speaking words that you have invented. Likewise, you should not think that learning ASL is an invitation to make up signs. The signs you need for communicating are there already. Your goal is to learn them.

SELFIE   VIDEO-CHAT   HASHTAG

The Physical Dimensions of ASL: The Five Parameters

ASL is a visual-gestural language. It is visual because we see it and gestural because the signs are formed by the hands. Signing alone, however, is not an accurate picture of ASL. How signs are formed in space is important to understanding what they mean. The critical space is called the signing space and extends from the waist to just above the head and to just beyond the sides of the body. This is also the space in which the hands can move comfortably. As you will learn in this book, the signing space has a role in ASL grammar. Two or more concepts can be simultaneously expressed in ASL. This feat cannot be accomplished in a spoken language because speech is temporal in that one word rolls off the tongue at a time. One further dimension of ASL is the movement of the head and facial expressions, which help shape the meaning of ASL sentences.

How Are Signs Formed?

The five parameters below come together to create a sign.

1. *Handshape* is the shape of the hands when the sign is formed. The handshape may remain the same throughout the sign, or it can change. If two hands are used to make a sign, both hands can have the same handshape or be different.

2. *Orientation* is the position of the hand(s) relative to the body. For example, the palms can be facing the body or away from the body, facing the ground, or facing upward.

3. *Location* is the place in the signing space where a sign is formed. Signs can be stationary, such as THINK and LOVE, or they can move from one location in the signing space to another, like the signs LONG and EXCITED.

THINK   LOVE   LONG

EXCITED

4. ***Movement*** of a sign is the direction in which the hand moves relative to the body. There is a variety of movements that range from a simple sliding movement, such as NICE, to a complex circular movement, TRAVEL-AROUND.

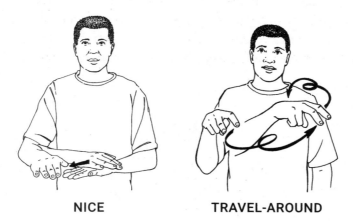

NICE   TRAVEL-AROUND

5. ***Nonmanual markers*** add to signs to create meaning. They consist of various facial expressions, head tilting, shoulder movement, and mouth movements. With a nonmanual marker, the meaning of the sign can change completely. Nonmanual markers will be discussed in more depth in Chapter 3: ASL Grammar.

ASL TIP

Important Note on the Five Parameters

If any one of these five parameters change, the entire meaning of the sign changes. Let's take the sign for MOTHER and change the *location* from touching the chin to touching the forehead, and keep the rest of the parameters the same (the movement, orientation, handshape, and nonmanual markers). Now the sign is FATHER. One parameter change is critical in disrupting the meaning of the sign.

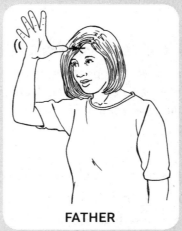

MOTHER   FATHER

Iconic Signs

Some signs are *iconic* in that their meanings can be guessed from the sign alone. When a student sees an iconic sign, they may think, "I could have guessed that's what that sign meant!" However, a majority of signs are not iconic, and their meanings must be learned. There is usually a reason, however, for why a sign has taken the shape it has. In the sign LEARN, the movement of the hand represents taking knowledge from a book and inserting it in the brain.

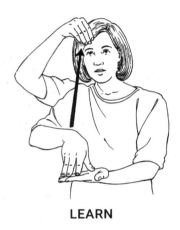

LEARN

Cultural Importance

ASL gives us access to Deaf culture. Learning ASL is not simply about learning another language. It is also about access. Even though we can learn something about any culture from reading about it, we acquire a deeper understanding when we can experience the culture or hear firsthand accounts from the people who are a part of the culture.

TIP

How to Appropriately Get a Deaf Person's Attention

There are a few common and appropriate ways to get a Deaf person's attention. Using your best judgment, you can decide which way is the most appropriate in a particular given situation.

- Gently tap the person's shoulder
- Flick the lights
- Wave gently (a low, light wave within the person's eyesight)
- Get in the person's line of vision and make eye contact
- Stomp on the floor close to the person's feet

ASL is one of the defining characteristics of the Deaf community. Although groups exist within the community, such as the Black Deaf community and LGBTQAI+ Deaf communities. Deaf community members are bound instead by their language: ASL. To learn more about Deaf culture and to tap into the resources of the Deaf community, you need a solid grasp of ASL.

ASL TIP

Name Signs

Name signs or *sign names* are signs that represent your name in ASL. A name sign can only be given to you by a Deaf person, and the gift of a name sign carries a linguistic and cultural importance. The sign chosen to represent you is typically based on a personal characteristic, hobby, or unique personality trait, much like a nickname in English.

Chapter Review

1. Write down the top five reasons why you are learning ASL. Compare your reasons with others who are learning ASL. Compile a list of the most common reasons.

2. Schools for the Deaf are closely associated with ASL because they bring together large numbers of Deaf students who use ASL as their major language of communication. When these students leave the school, they spread their knowledge of ASL to other Deaf people as well as to nondeaf people. Look up the names of the public or private schools for the Deaf in your state, province, or region and list them. How close do you live to one? Find answers from the Internet.

3. What is ASL, and who uses it to communicate?

4. Name two out of the five given ways to get a Deaf person's attention.

5. Name the main sources of influence on the early development of ASL.

6. Describe the five parameters used to create a sign.

7. What is a sign name/name sign and who can give you one?

Deaf Culture and the Community

The Deaf Community

Many hearing people view the world of the Deaf as a place where people don't hear—where silence is a loud reminder of the difference between the two groups of people. But for Deaf people, silence is not the focus. What is important to us is that we obtain a lot of pleasure by being with other Deaf people. We relish the tales about other Deaf people's experiences in the Deaf community. We take great pride in the Deaf community's activities and the accomplishments of fellow members. We treat each other with care and understanding— almost like we are all members of the same family (and in a sense we are). Each of these behaviors is a reason why there is a Deaf community, why Deaf people have their own clubs, sports, music, poems, folktales, stories, organizations, and much more.

ASL TIP

Self-identification

Self-identification is valued by people from all cultures and backgrounds, and the Deaf community is no different. It is important to keep in mind that how one deaf or hard-of-hearing person identifies may not be how another deaf or hard-of-hearing person identifies. Therefore, the choice to identify as Deaf, deaf, hard of hearing, or none of the above is personal. The following is a list that will help you understand each identifier.

Offensive terms to avoid are "deaf-mute," "deaf and dumb," or "hearing-impaired."

"Big D" Deaf

Those who use *Deaf*:

- identify as culturally Deaf and part of the Deaf community
- take pride in Deaf identity
- may have an auditory device, such as a cochlear implant, hearing aid, or FM system
- may have a more severe hearing loss
- use sign language as their primary source of communication
- most likely attend a Deaf school/program
- feel more comfortable in the Deaf world

"Little d" deaf

Those who use *deaf*:

- do not typically associate as members of the Deaf community
- may have an auditory device, such as a cochlear implant, hearing aid, or FM system
- may refer to hearing loss as a medical condition
- may not use sign language as their primary choice of communication
- may attend a mainstream school
- may feel more comfortable in the hearing world

Hard of hearing (HoH)

Those who use *HoH*:

- do not associate as members of the Deaf community
- have hearing loss but may have residual hearing
- possibly use an auditory device, such as a hearing aid or FM system, to access sounds

- refer to hearing loss as a medical condition
- may not use sign language as their primary choice of communication
- may attend a mainstream school
- feel more comfortable in the hearing world

Unsure on what to use?

Ask the person how they self-identify.

Who Are Deaf People?

Deaf people are a group of people who have a hearing loss, use a sign language as their primary means of communication, and have shared experiences associated with the hearing loss and the use of sign language.

There is no way that you can point to a person sitting and reading a magazine in a lobby whom you have never met before and say, "That person is Deaf." Even if the person is wearing hearing aids, we don't know which community the person identifies with. Similarly, it is not important whether the person is European, African-American, Asian, or of some other ethnic origin. Age is not relevant, and neither is the social class or gender of the person. The Deaf community is not shaped by any of these characteristics. In fact, having a hearing loss does not mean that a person is a member of the Deaf community, although it is certainly an important requirement.

The pivotal mark of a Deaf person is how this person communicates. A Deaf person uses sign language, which in America and most of Canada is ASL. This does not mean that the person cannot use other forms of communication, such as writing and speaking. Rather, ASL is the linguistic trademark that sets Deaf people apart from the communication behavior of all other groups of people. It is the reason we say that Deaf people represent a linguistic minority. It is also why some people who are deaf do not see themselves as belonging to the Deaf community. We use the lowercase spelling of deaf to refer to a person or a group of people who have a substantial degree of hearing loss. Having a hearing loss does not mean that a person automatically knows how to sign. If a deaf person does not know sign language, then that person will not be able to access the varied cultural experiences associated with the Deaf community. Communication is basic, and ASL is the communication of the Deaf community.

Can a nondeaf person who is fluent in ASL be a member of the Deaf community? No. Deaf people do not view nondeaf people as members of their community because nondeaf people lack a third critical characteristic, which is shared experiences. If you have normal hearing, then you will never have the experiences of a life that is centered on seeing. However, one group of hearing people is often accepted into the Deaf community, but may not be considered part of the Deaf culture, as they are not Deaf themselves. Often referred to as CODA, Children of Deaf Adults, they are brought up in the Deaf community and learn the language and cultural customs because their parents are Deaf and participate in that community.

Let's put all of this in perspective. Let's say you have a young friend who acquired a hearing loss and was fitted with hearing aids. Would we say that he was Deaf? No, we would say that he is hard of hearing because speaking is still his main means of communication. If his hearing continues to deteriorate, then we might say that he is becoming deaf; that is, he is acquiring a substantial degree of hearing loss. What if his difficulty with hearing leads him to learn to sign ASL, which becomes his primary language of communication, and he begins participating in some activities in the Deaf community? Would we then say that he is Deaf? We would probably say, "Friend, welcome to the club."

Where Is the Deaf Community?

The Deaf community has no geographical boundaries. There are Deaf clubs in many cities, but the clubs are just a part of the larger community of Deaf people. We can talk about the Deaf community in very broad terms like "the Deaf community in America," or we can talk about it in more local terms like "the Deaf community in Phoenix." In both instances, we are talking about a group of Deaf people and the things they do in life.

Just as we cannot draw a map outlining the boundaries of the Deaf community, we cannot put our finger on the precise number of Deaf people in the United States. This information does not exist. Estimates seem to peg this number at about a half million.

Deafness can be present at birth, acquired soon after birth, or occur much later in life. Those who become deaf later in life are referred to as late-deafened adults. Most late-deafened adults do not readily learn to sign, especially if they become deaf after their school years. Therefore, the biggest group of signers are those born deaf or who become deaf early in life. And where do they learn to sign? Only about 10 percent of all Deaf people have at least one Deaf parent. These children then have someone who teaches them ASL and helps them develop their cultural identity with the Deaf community. But most Deaf people do not come from Deaf families. Approximately 90 percent of all Deaf people have hearing parents, most of whom do not expose their children to people and events in the Deaf community. A majority of hearing parents never learn to sign. Therefore, Deaf people who have hearing parents will likely have developed their ties with the Deaf community away from home, learning ASL from other Deaf children they meet in school programs, especially in schools for the Deaf.

What's Important in the Deaf Community?

By coming together and forming their own community, Deaf people have created their own Deaf culture. A *culture* is all that a group of people do and includes their beliefs, values, customs, activities, and language. Many things that Deaf people do are the same as what occurs in nondeaf communities. They work, own homes, get married, raise families, play sports, watch videos, and so forth. They eat, dress up, and celebrate the same kinds of holidays, as do most other people in America and Canada. But we define Deaf culture by looking at what's different in the Deaf community. Deaf people have a strong identity with Deaf culture because they embrace these differences. Descriptions of six important differences follow.

American Sign Language

The language Deaf people use is the foremost characteristic of the Deaf community. Knowing ASL opens the doors to meeting other Deaf people and to learning about the Deaf community. ASL cannot be written; therefore, knowledge of it is essential if a person is to learn about the history of a Deaf community, its folklore, its traditions, and, as the case might be, its dark secrets. Although there are some written accounts about Deaf culture, experiencing a culture firsthand is much more rewarding and informative than having secondhand knowledge about it. One way the Deaf community is preserving and documenting the linguistic forms of ASL is through several media sources. There are also several online resources that provide an outlet for the Deaf community to share their vlogs, stories, and comments and connect with other Deaf community members. In addition, social media/networking sites, such as Facebook, Instagram, and Twitter—used by scores of people who are hearing, Deaf, or hard of hearing—also provide a means for the Deaf community to preserve their language, socialize, connect with other Deaf people, give their opinions, and simply have fun. The possibilities are endless!

Socialization

An elderly Deaf man told me about how he would catch a train in the 1940s for a four-hour ride to visit the Deaf club on the weekends. Another Deaf man said that before he got a TTY (a device that allows communication on the phone by typing on a keyboard) in the late 1970s, he and his wife would drive up to three hours to visit their Deaf friends in other cities. They would make the arrangement by exchanging letters, but sometimes a visit would be a spur-of-the-moment adventure with no guarantee that their Deaf friends would be home. Whether in Deaf clubs, community events, restaurants, or homes, Deaf people feel a strong need to socialize with each other. They crave the social contact that is absent from their home life, school, and workplace when no one else signs in these places. Socializing among themselves keeps Deaf people abreast of news in the Deaf community and provides emotional support.

Organizations and Clubs

Given the importance of socializing, it is only natural that Deaf people would have their own clubs and organizations. The first known organizations to form in the United States were alumni associations established by graduates of schools for the Deaf. Schools for the

Deaf foster a bond between their students and forge strong ties with Deaf people across the state. Alumni associations provide a means for Deaf people to maintain contact with each other as well as to help the schools that brought them together. Deaf clubs are another natural offspring of schools for the Deaf, and many of them are founded in the same city in which the schools are located. Other groups are devoted to providing opportunities for community members, such as sports and recreation and activities for senior citizens.

Schools for the Deaf

The hub of many Deaf communities is often a residential school for the Deaf. Almost every state and province has at least one. Children either attend these schools and stay in the dormitories, going home every weekend, or they commute to the school on a daily basis. There are also day schools for the Deaf where all students are commuters. Since the founding of the first school in Hartford in 1817, residential schools have played a prominent role in defining the Deaf community. Children growing up together in a residential setting develop lifelong friendships. Indeed, many Deaf people will say that the older Deaf students and the adults—and especially the Deaf adults—who cared for them in the residences were like family to them. Schools for the Deaf are a haven of Deaf culture, offering a lifestyle that cannot be replicated elsewhere.

ASL TIP

A Note on Humor

Humor is an important part of Deaf culture. Deaf people, much like members of other minority communities, sometimes use humor to help cope with pain from any injustice or prejudice they face. Humor and jokes are used to pass on information about Deaf history and can be found in art, language, and storytelling from generation to generation.

Deaf Pride

Deaf people live in a world that is largely made for people who can hear and speak. Consider how you would feel if you were Deaf and had to deal with the following: dialogue in a movie, negotiations with a car salesperson, inspecting a house with a realtor, the weather forecast in the event of an impending storm and having only a radio in the house to learn about it, going through customs at an international airport, filing an accident report with the police, indicating that you were overcharged by a cashier, and giving directions to a person who is lost. These are just a fraction of the situations that Deaf people encounter in their day-to-day interactions in society. The fact is, however, that Deaf people do get along in many of these situations, and it is this success in the face of such strong communication barriers that instills them with pride. Their many responses to these situations may be a result of on-the-spot ingenuity or technological adaptation that you will read about later in this chapter. Whatever their response, Deaf people are proud of their place in society. They are proud of their history and of their culture, which is how they have adjusted to society. Quite simply, many Deaf people are proud to be Deaf and would want it no other way. This pride is one of the reasons why Deaf people tend to hug one another during greetings and why many of them will marry another Deaf person.

Many other aspects of the Deaf community make Deaf culture a distinctive and desirable choice in life. These aspects are all woven together with the linguistic thread of ASL.

Technology and Other Adaptations

Many of the technological advances for the majority in our society have penalized Deaf people. This irony emerges most clearly in telecommunications. The invention of the telephone made it difficult for Deaf people to compete in the labor market. Radio became an important means of broadcasting information, whether commercial, political, governmental, or whatever, further cutting off Deaf people from the larger society surrounding them. Television did little to improve the situation, though it embraced the technology that could have (and to some extent does) include Deaf people. Talking pictures were a blow to the entertainment and education of Deaf people; they could enjoy the "silents" on par with the rest of the audience. But Deaf people and their supporters have not passively accepted the status quo. They have taken steps to reduce the handicap the new technologies have imposed.

—*Jerome Schein*
At Home Among Strangers

Written more than 20 years ago, this account of everyday struggle was not uncommon for Deaf individuals. Only in recent years have technological developments arisen that help rather than hamper the lives of Deaf people. I am reminded of this each time I stay in a hotel. In the past, when I had to wake up early in order to catch a flight home, I would ask the hotel staff to come into my room at a certain time and turn the light on. One morning, I happened to wake up thirty minutes after the time I had asked to be awakened. I noticed a sheet of paper that had been slipped under the door with the message, "It is 4:30 A.M., time to wake up. The hotel management." More amazing is the fact that I had heard the same story from other Deaf people and so I had warned the staff about the necessity of actually turning on the light. Today when I stay at a hotel, I set an alarm that vibrates under my pillow. I make calls on a TTY to confirm that my flight is leaving as scheduled. I answer the door or the telephone when a light flashes in the room. I hope the flashing light for the fire alarm never goes off. I then nod off to sleep watching a late-night movie that is fully captioned. Now, Deaf people have technology at their fingertips that was unimaginable

20 years ago. FaceTime, text messaging, and alarm systems are considered to be new advances for the Deaf community, and all these little wonders are provided at no extra charge by hotels. Let's explore these technological wonders.

Telecommunication Technology

TTY

Although a TTY is old technology, it is important to learn about its existence and the major impact it had on the Deaf community. Telecommunication technology had its first major impact on the Deaf community with the introduction of the *teletypewriter*. Known as a TTY, this device was invented in the 1960s by Robert Weitbrecht, a Deaf physicist and electrical engineer. The principle of the TTY is that signals are sent over a normal phone line that are translated to letters and symbols that can be read either off a scroll of paper and/or an LCD display. The TTY itself looks like a keyboard similar to that used with a computer but smaller. A regular telephone handset is rested on a coupler on top of the TTY. Pressing the keys produces a series of tones, which are the signals that are received and sent after a number has been dialed and a connection with another TTY is made.

Videophones

Videophones are the current generation of telecommunication access for Deaf people. These systems have a camera mounted on top of a screen or a built-in camera so that two people can communicate using sign language. One Deaf individual calls another Deaf individual simply by dialing the number as is done on a phone. Instead of a noisy ringer, videophones will have flashing lights that indicate a call is coming through. It is safe to say that almost every Deaf household has one. A common spot for a videophone is anywhere an individual spends a lot of time, whether it be in the kitchen, living room, basement, or all three.

VRS

Telecommunication access for Deaf people also involves the Video Relay System (VRS), which is a form of the Telecommunication Relay Service (TRS). These services assist people with hearing loss to communicate with the hearing community through video equipment and a communications assistant (CA), who is a qualified ASL interpreter, thus enabling Deaf or hard-of-hearing people to communicate through sign language, rather than through a typed text. With this system, the Deaf person calls the CA using a television or computer with video conferencing equipment, such as a videophone, and a high-speed Internet connection. The CA relay operator makes the call to the hearing person and relays the conversation to each person in either sign language (to the Deaf person) or voice (to the hearing person). With the use of the VRS, Deaf people can communicate in their own language, rather than having to type their messages. Several service providers offer equipment free of charge for Deaf or hard-of-hearing people; however, the Internet is necessary. Deaf or hard-of-hearing people are responsible for paying for high-speed access; therefore, VRS is not the reality for all.

Smartphones

There are additional means for Deaf people to communicate face-to-face with other video-phones and webcams. Further, the latest and current technology allows video conferencing through smartphones, which enable Deaf people to communicate "on the go," rather than in their homes, through the VRS or videophone. FaceTime, WhatsApp, Zoom, Skype, and Google Duo/Hangouts are just a few of many smartphone technologies that are easy to access and used by just about every Deaf or hard-of-hearing person today. Smartphones provide an instant connection among Deaf people and the outside world. Now that smart-phones exist, and most of you reading this have never lived life without one, it is hard to imagine a world without them. As you are learning about how far technology for the Deaf has come, take a second to imagine a world for Deaf people when these devices didn't exist. For many Deaf people, the world pre-smartphone was a very dangerous place with no way to get help in case of an emergency.

VRI

Another form of communication technology is Video Remote Interpreting (VRI). This is used when a Deaf person and a hearing person are in the same room with a TV and video equipment connected to a high-speed Internet service. An interpreter from a remote call center appears on the TV, and the Deaf person signs to the interpreter as the interpreter voices the message to the hearing person. The key difference between VRS and VRI is that with a VRS call, the interpreter is interpreting a normal telephone call made by one party to the other. VRI is useful for emergencies or whenever in-person interpreter contact is not available.

CapTel

The Captioned Telephone (CapTel) is a telephone with a screen that displays every word the other party says throughout the conversation. It is used by Deaf and hard-of-hearing persons who prefer to use their voice when making a call. CapTel users can listen to the caller and can also read written captions in the CapTel display window.

Captioned Films and TV

Another telecommunication technology device that has had a significant impact on the lives of Deaf people is *captioning* or *subtitles* of television and social media programs and videos. Captioning allows viewers to read the spoken dialogue on a screen. To read the captions, however, the captioning option on a television set must first be turned on, which is why this technology is often referred to as closed captioning or closed captions. In the past, a special decoder unit had to be attached to a television for the closed captions to be made visible on the screen. In 1993, Congress passed the Television Decoder Circuitry Act, which requires all televisions with a screen thirteen inches or larger to have the capacity to display captioning. The captioning itself is usually done prior to being shown on television or placed on a video. Real-time captioning also occurs and is used with major sports programs and other live broadcasts. A number of companies are in the captioning business, and together they caption all prime-time network programs and many daytime and late-night programs, including news, various sports, State of the Union addresses, and many other programs. Even hearing people use captions, as not everything that is said on TV is easily understood.

Alerting Devices

Alerting devices make Deaf people aware of sounds that are in the environment. There are various types of alerting devices, and they all operate on the principle of making the occurrence of sounds visible (lights flashing) or tactile (vibration). The first and most popular types of alerting devices are those adaptations where lights flash when a doorbell or telephone rings, an alarm goes off, a dog barks, or some other sound signal occurs. Video monitor alert systems are also popular, especially among parents and families, as they can connect to smartphones. The advancement of this technology is such that an entire house can be wired for Deaf people. This setup allows a Deaf person to control where in the house the lights will flash and when—for example, when the phone rings. Obviously, a light flashing in the living room is of no use to a person who is sleeping in an upstairs bedroom or is downstairs in the workshop. Schools for the Deaf and institutions such as Gallaudet University and the National Technical Institute for the Deaf have visible fire alarms throughout their campuses.

The alerting principle of a flashing light has been applied to tactile technology. Bed alarms that vibrate—for example a gadget placed under a pillow—are available. Another type of tactile signal is air blowing from a fan. This type of signal is used by deaf-blind people.

Computer Technology and Social Media

Deaf people are riding the wave of advances in computer technology. The major benefit they receive from this technology is the same that nondeaf people receive—convenience. The Internet provides the greatest access for Deaf people to reach out to one another. Smartphones allow people to send online videos of themselves. This is a boon to those people who wish to use ASL to converse with someone online. Another example of the value of the Internet is seen with social media. Social media connects over 2.95 billion people worldwide. Billions of people turn to social media for fast-information learning, sharing of personal and nonpersonal information, and making personal connections. For Deaf people, this is no different. In fact, you and I may take social media for granted, but a Deaf individual may value its importance because of the connections and information that are otherwise missed without the fast-streaming service social media provides.

Sign Language Interpreting

A sign language interpreter transmits messages from ASL to English and from English to ASL. To do this, interpreters must be fluent in both languages. They must also understand the culture of the speakers of both languages. Their work is indispensable to facilitating the interactions between Deaf and hearing people. Sign language interpreting became an official profession with the formation of the Registry of Interpreters for the Deaf in 1964. Since this time, the availability of interpreters has given Deaf people better access to communication in many places that hearing people have always taken for granted. Such places include public schools, training facilities for jobs, the workplace, medical and dental offices, courts of law, tours on cruise ships, national park lectures, and many more. There is a need for more interpreters now because of the Americans with Disabilities Act (ADA). Under the ADA, people who are Deaf or hard of hearing are entitled to the same services law enforcement provides to anyone else. They may not be excluded or segregated from services, be denied services, or otherwise be treated differently than other people.

ASL TIP

Virtual Interpreting

Sign language interpreting is an adaptation to a hearing world. Or, if we look at it from the Deaf perspective, it is an adaptation by hearing people that allows them access to the Deaf world. It is included in this chapter because the day has arrived when some interpreters will work without leaving the confines of their homes or offices. Using VRS or VRI, a Deaf person or an agency with a videophone dials an interpreter at home who also has one. The videophone transmits sounds in addition to videos. Thus, a Deaf person and a hearing person sit in front of the videophone where the Deaf person signs to the camera and the hearing person speaks to a microphone. The interpreter at the other end of the line interprets what is being signed or spoken.

Real-time Reporting

The technology of court reporters is being used in classrooms and meetings to provide Deaf people with a transcription of all that is being said. The technology setup requires a stenographic machine, a laptop computer, and software to convert stenographic symbols to print on the screen. The real-time reporter types everything being said, and the Deaf person is able to read this on the computer screen. Modification of this setup includes using television monitors with the words being printed against the background of a video of the speaker, including that of the Deaf person when she or he is talking. C-print has also been created where a regular keyboard on a laptop can be used instead of a stenographic machine. Automatic c-printing has been added to some platforms for virtual meetings like

Microsoft Teams and a few others. Whatever the setup, real-time has given Deaf people another option for accessing spoken information that can be used in place of sign language interpreters or alongside of them.

Smartphone Technologies

Smartphone technology has provided texting, which is an invaluable tool for the deaf and a silent, convenient, and more confidential means of communication for all people. Shortly after texting became available in the late 1990s, it spread through the Deaf community very quickly and has become a way of life for most Deaf members. Texting has become one of the primary means of convenient and fast communication, opening up access for socializing, conducting business, signaling emergencies, and so on for Deaf and hard-of-hearing people. In some U.S. cities, 911 accepts text messages to alert emergencies.

With a smartphone, a Deaf person can also make, break, or change appointments or even conduct personal business at any time without the intervention of an interpreter or other third party. Similarly, videophones yield visual conversations for those wishing to communicate in sign language. These technologies allow one to see who's available to exchange messages whenever and wherever they happen to be.

Other Technologies

ALD

Assistive listening devices (ALD) amplify sounds and include hearing aids, telephone amplifiers (usually through bluetooth), and infrared transmitters and FM transmitters used to amplify sounds without interference from extraneous environmental noise. Although these devices are a part of Deaf culture, they are not crucial to a person functioning or socializing in the Deaf community. Their value stems only from the access to sounds that they provide some Deaf people, wherever they might be. What is important to know about ALD is that they do not make a Deaf person hear normally in a way that eyeglasses help many people see normally. Hearing aids help some people hear some sounds, but the benefit is highly individual and most Deaf people do not use them. The major group of people who use ALD are hard-of-hearing people and late-deafened adults.

Cochlear Implants

A cochlear implant is an electronic device that is implanted into a person's inner ear to deliver a sensation of hearing for profoundly Deaf persons who do not benefit from regular high-powered hearing aids.

The first cochlear implant system was created in the 1970s. Today, thousands of people in the world use cochlear implants. Although originally intended for late-deafened adults, cochlear implantation rates continue to explode, and infants as young as six months old are now using implants. Unlike hearing aids and ALDs that amplify sounds, a cochlear implant does not make sounds louder. Instead, it directly stimulates the surviving auditory nerve fibers in the cochlea, enabling the individual to perceive sound. The device consists of a receiver, a thin cord, and a transmitting coil that acts like the hair cells of the cochlea. The speech processor of the implant codes the sounds picked up from the environment by a microphone worn outside the body. A cochlear implant does not restore normal hearing; it provides an artificial form of hearing. The sounds people hear with cochlear implants can be quite different from sounds they might *remember* hearing before becoming Deaf.

Deaf Organizations

National Association of the Deaf

The National Association of the Deaf (NAD) is a national advocacy group that works with its state affiliations to improve the lives of Deaf people. The NAD was formed in reaction to hearing people denying the use of ASL in the education of Deaf children, and even though ASL is the focus of many of its activities, the NAD also works to improve the social conditions of Deaf people and promote the integrity of the Deaf community. It sponsors biennial conventions that are attended by thousands of Deaf people from all over the country and other parts of the world. The convention serves to remind Deaf people about their heritage and accomplishments, as well as to focus their attention on the critical issues of the times. The convention includes a Miss Deaf America pageant; presentations and workshops relating to education, rehabilitation, the workplace, technology, and other matters; exhibits promoting recent technological developments, publications, videos, and information about other events of interest to Deaf people; banquets; and theatrical performances. It is the grandest show of Deaf people in America, many of whom use the occasion as an opportunity to reunite with friends and former classmates.

Junior National Association of the Deaf Youth Program

The NAD sponsors a Junior NAD program for school-age Deaf children. The purpose of the program is to develop leadership skills in Deaf students who will then use these skills to build stronger Deaf organizations wherever they might one day settle. Typically, schools for the Deaf are the home base for most Junior NAD programs. Each year, selected members from each state's Junior NAD chapter are invited to a summer leadership program. Here they meet adult Deaf leaders and learn about key issues in the Deaf community and what they can do to preserve and promote Deaf culture in their homes and communities.

Beginnings for Parents of Children Who Are Deaf or Hard of Hearing, Inc.

Beginnings is a nonprofit organization that provides emotional support and access to information for families with Deaf or hard-of-hearing children. These services are also available to Deaf parents who have hearing children. The goal of this organization is to help parents feel supported, informed, and empowered as they make decisions about their Deaf or hard-of-hearing children. Beginnings is also committed to providing technical assistance to professionals who work with these families so their children can achieve full participation in society.

Gallaudet University Alumni Association

Gallaudet University is the only liberal arts university for the Deaf in the world. It is world renowned and has been referred to as the mecca of the Deaf community. Given this status, it is not surprising that its alumni exert much influence on the activities of Deaf communities. The primary goals of the Gallaudet University Alumni Association (GUAA) are to increase the influence and prestige of Gallaudet University and to promote the welfare of Deaf people, particularly in the area of education. Many GUAA members are prominent in their local Deaf communities. The GUAA also awards scholarships, and one such recipient, I. K. Jordan, went on to become the first Deaf president of Gallaudet University in 1988.

National Theater of the Deaf

The National Theater of the Deaf (NTD) was founded in 1967 and is not an organization of Deaf people in the same sense as the NAD and National Fraternal Society of the Deaf (NFSD) which was an insurance business established in 1901. Its purpose was to provide insurance to mainly Deaf members, to serve as an advocate for the Deaf, and to provide community service and recreational opportunities through divisional activities. It is a nonprofit group of Deaf and hearing actors who perform across the United States and other parts of the world. Their value to the Deaf community is that their performances are in ASL, which has helped introduce many hearing people to sign language as well as inspire many Deaf children to take pride in their language and culture. Skits that aim to educate people about Deaf culture and to illustrate the experiences of Deaf people in their daily living are a part of their repertoire. The skits are also used to attack the negative stereotypes that nondeaf people have about Deaf people and, in the language of the stage, show that Deaf and hearing people are not all that much different.

United States of America Deaf Sports Federation

Formerly known as the American Athletic Association for the Deaf, the USA Deaf Sports Federation (USADSF) was founded in 1945 to promote athletic competitions among Deaf athletes. The USADSF provides year-round training and competition that promote physical fitness, sportsmanship, and self-esteem as well as develop elite-level athletic skills in a variety of sports at the state, regional, national, and international level. While the USADSF focuses on Deaf athletes competing against one another, it also provides opportunities for competition with nondeaf peers. This type of competition is desirable for at least three reasons. First, both groups of people are competing on equal grounds with the use of signing and the use of hearing giving no team an advantage. Second, the competition is an opportunity to increase awareness of the Deaf community among hearing people. Third, the competition prepares the athletes for competition at higher levels where the competitors are all Deaf.

The USADSF recognizes that not all its athletes will know how to sign when they first begin competing on a Deaf team. Indeed, USADSF actively fosters social interactions among athletes and their supporters. As a result, many athletes who do not know ASL when they first get involved in Deaf sports activities may come to learn it and develop a fondness for the Deaf community. The USADSF also selects and prepares athletes for competition in the Deaflympics. The Deaflympics is a quadrennial event with Summer and Winter Games. The Games are held all over the world, and the competitions are of high caliber with some of the Deaf athletes also representing their countries in the Olympics.

There are also several national organizations for specific sports that are affiliated with the USADSF, including the U.S. Deaf Team Handball Association, U.S. Deaf Skiers and Snowboarders Association, and USA Deaf Basketball.

The World Recreation Association of the Deaf

The World Recreation Association of the Deaf (WRAD) was incorporated in 1985 to promote greater participation of Deaf people in recreation and leisure activities. There are activities that are suitable for all ages, including walks through city parks, camping excursions in national parks, Caribbean cruises, skiing, beach parties, paint pistol war games, and scuba diving. The goal of all activities is accessibility, and arrangements are made for sign language interpreters who ensure that the Deaf people are able to take advantage of all that an activity has to offer. The activities of the WRAD are open to hearing people as well, and there are WRAD organizations in other countries including Turkey, Colombia, France, and South Africa.

World Federation of the Deaf

The World Federation of the Deaf (WFD) works to ensure equal rights for the approximately 70 million Deaf people around the globe. By promoting human rights and access to sign language, the WFD is improving the lives of millions of Deaf people who face inequality every day. It collaborates with Deaf leaders and policymakers to implement human rights mechanisms. The WFD also takes direct action by providing human rights training and representing deaf people's interests on a global scale.

World Federation of the Deafblind

The World Federation of the Deafblind (WFDB) aims to improve the quality of life of people with deaf-blindness worldwide. The WFDB's main objectives are to achieve equal rights and opportunities for deaf-blind individuals in all areas of society, increase international solidarity among organizations of people with deaf-blindness, and act as a worldwide forum for knowledge and experiences in the area of deaf-blindness.

National Black Deaf Advocates

National Black Deaf Advocates (NBDA) is the official advocacy organization for Black Deaf and hard-of-hearing Americans. NBDA has been at the forefront of advocacy efforts for civil rights and equal access to education, employment, and social services on behalf of Black Deaf and hard-of-hearing Americans for more than thirty years.

National Council of Hispano Deaf and Hard of Hearing

The National Council of Hispano Deaf and Hard of Hearing (NCHD) strives to ensure equal access of the Hispano Deaf and hard-of-hearing community in areas of social, recreational, cultural, educational, and vocational welfare. The NCHD offers a national awareness and advocacy program to educate the Deaf and hard-of-hearing communities, as well as programs and organizations that address the needs and issues facing Deaf Hispano individuals.

National Asian Deaf Congress

The National Asian Deaf Congress (NADC) is a nonprofit organization. Its goal is to define and address the cultural, political, and social issues experienced by Asians who are deaf or hard of hearing. The NADC also strives to provide education, empowerment, and leadership for its members and organizations that represent various geographic regions, languages, religions, cultures, and generations.

Sacred Circle (Intertribal Deaf Council, Inc.)

Sacred Circle is a nonprofit organization for Deaf, deaf-blind, hard-of-hearing, and late-deafened American Indian, Alaska Native, and First Nations individuals and their families. Non-Natives who are hearing or Deaf or hearing Natives are also welcome to participate as associate members.

Canadian Association of the Deaf

The Canadian Association of the Deaf (CAD) is a national consumer organization for Deaf Canadians. It advocates in much the same way that the NAD does for Deaf Americans.

As a consumer organization, it functions as a research and information center, an advisory council on legislative matters relating to the well-being of Deaf people, a self-help society, and a community action organization.

Over the years, the association has undertaken a number of activities that have ranged from speaking against Deaf peddlers in the 1940s, establishing a Canadian Deaf Information Centre in the 1960s, sponsoring National Education Workshops to address issues relating to the use of communication in the education of Deaf students in the 1970s, hiring a full-time staff person in the 1980s, and establishing a Hall of Fame in 1991. It is actively involved in ensuring that Deaf Canadians are represented in legislative matters relating to employment, education, human rights, and technology.

Canadian Deaf Sports Association

The Canadian Deaf Sports Association (CDSA) promotes the physical fitness of Deaf persons by creating opportunities for participation in a variety of amateur sports and recreation activities. A primary goal for the CDSA is to select and prepare athletes to compete in the World Games for the Deaf, a competition that the CDSA has participated in since 1965. The CDSA hosted its first and only World Winter Games for the Deaf in 1991, in Banff, Alberta. The Summer and Winter Games are quadrennial events and occur two years apart from each other.

Chapter Review

1. What are the three characteristics that best describe members of the Deaf community?

2. How can a person have a hearing loss and not belong to the Deaf community?

3. How do Deaf children who have nondeaf parents usually learn ASL?

4. Describe how the language you speak, the people you hang around with, and the schools you went to influenced your involvement in your community.

5. What does the term "Deaf pride" mean to you?

6. Through online research, compile a list of organizations of the Deaf in your state.

7. Select one of the organizations on your list and dive deeper to gather information about the types of activities it is involved in.

8. Why was the founding of the National Association of the Deaf an important event?

9. Imagine that you are a reporter writing a story about an organization for the Deaf. Write five questions that you would want to ask about this organization and explain the reasons why.

CHAPTER 3

ASL Grammar

Learning Objectives

In this chapter, you will learn:

- The ten rules of ASL grammar and when to use them
- Facial grammar rules and when to break them
- How to use facial grammar to communicate properly

ASL has visual, spatial, and gestural features that combine to create some grammatical structures that are unparalleled in the world of spoken languages. As you learn about ASL grammar, look for similarities with English and other spoken languages, but also prepare yourself for a journey through new linguistic territory. In particular, the spatial qualities of ASL grammar allow a signer to express more than one thought simultaneously—a characteristic that cannot be duplicated in English. Facial grammar, or nonmanual signals, is also a significant component of ASL.

Facial Grammar

ASL Is Much More Than Signs

What's in a sign may not be what's in the mind. To capture the sense of what a signer is signing, you must read the signer's face and body. When you listen to someone speak, you listen not only to the words but also to how the words are spoken. The tone of the voice, the rise and fall of the pitch, the length of the pause, and the steadiness of voice are all features that you latch onto with little effort in your spoken communication.

These traits are nonexistent in signing, but they do have parallel traits that are crucial to ASL's grammar. The raised eyebrow, the tilted head, the open mouth, hunching of the shoulders, and a sign held slightly longer than others shape the meaning of the signs that are made by the hands. We call these nonmanual signals (NMS) *facial grammar*, which allows you to use facial expressions, your body, and gestures to add meaning and additional information to your signing. Mastering ASL cannot occur without a mastery of facial grammar.

Maintaining Eye Contact

ASL is a visual language, and eye contact is the starting profile of any two people who are about to sign to each other. You cannot understand signing if you are not watching someone sign. That's the easy part. What is harder to learn is how to maintain eye contact even when you are signing. That is, even when you have someone's attention, you must continue to look at this person while you are signing.

You achieve eye contact with someone by drawing their attention to you. Deaf people will lightly tap a person on the shoulder to indicate that eye contact is desired so that a conversation can begin. Looking away from someone can mean several things. Perhaps you are finished with a conversation. Or it may be that you are distracted by something. Or, just as likely, your eyes are being called upon for a role in structuring an ASL sentence.

Breaking Eye Contact

Eye contact is not always maintained throughout a conversation. The eyes will gaze elsewhere, but only if such movement is relevant to what is being signed. Eye contact and eye gazing send several signals to the other person. These signals are influenced by the signs that are made as well as by the facial expressions that accompany the signing. Some grammatical signals are associated with the eyes and an example of each follows.

Ask a particular type of question. The sentence "Are you ready?" is translated as YOU READY? in ASL. In the absence of any nonmanual signals from the face, signing YOU and READY would give us the sentence "You are ready." To indicate that a question is being asked, the signer looks directly at the person, raises the eyebrows, and tilts the head slightly forward. Nonmanual signals for other types of questions require a different set of facial expressions and body movement.

Draw attention to a particular place in the signing space in which a person or thing has been established. ASL signing relies heavily upon establishing reference places in the signing space. After establishing a reference place, the signer can point to it or look at it to draw attention to the referent that is in that place. In this way, the eyes can incorporate referents that are in the signing space into a sentence.

Highlight key information in a sentence. Eye contact accompanied by a raised eyebrow, the head tilting forward, and a sign held slightly longer than other signs can indicate the topic of a sentence.

Reinforce the direction in which certain signs might be moving. A signer can make the sentence "I watched him walk past me" by simply gazing from the right to the left side of the signing space. This is called an *eye-gaze.*

Reveal emotions about a topic. Adjectives such as *surprised* and *suspicious* can be expressed by opening the eyes wide or by narrowing them.

Each of these examples are mentioned here to emphasize the importance of the eyes in enhancing meaning when signing.

Common Types of Nonmanual Signals

Questions

1. Did you see the game last night? (LAST NIGHT, GAME SEE FINISH YOU?)
2. What time did you arrive home yesterday? (YESTERDAY, YOU HOME ARRIVE, TIME?)

LAST   NIGHT   GAME

SEE   FINISH   YOU

YESTERDAY

YOU

HOME

ARRIVE

TIME

Both of these sentences ask questions. Asking a question calls for a particular kind of non-manual signal. To know what type of nonmanual signal to use, you must first know what type of question you will ask. Sentence 1 asks for a yes or no response and is called a yes/no question. Sentence 2 is a wh-question and asks for information about something.

Eye Contact

For all types of questions, the signer *maintains eye contact with the person to whom she or he is signing*.

YES-NO-QUESTION

Yes/No Questions

For yes/no questions, the signer uses the following nonmanual signals:

(1) *raises the eyebrows* and (2) *tilts the head forward*.

If the question is short, then the signer can raise the eyebrows and tilt the head throughout signing the question. This is the case with the following questions:

FINISH YOU? (Are you finished?)

FINISH   YOU

SEE FINISH YOU? (Have you seen it?)

SEE   FINISH   YOU

TIRED YOU? (Are you tired?)

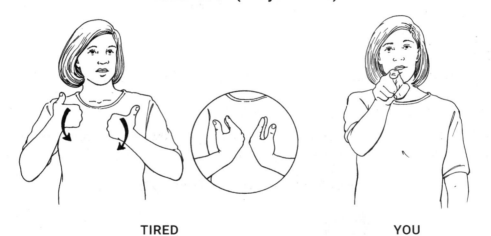

TIRED   YOU

YOU HUNGRY? (Are you hungry?)

YOU   HUNGRY

If the question is long, then the signer usually adds the nonmanual signal at the end of the sentence while signing those signs that are directly associated with asking questions.

In the following sentences, the nonmanual signals should be added while signing the underlined phrases.

LAST-WEEK, MOVIE <u>SEE FINISH YOU</u>? (Did you see the movie last week?)

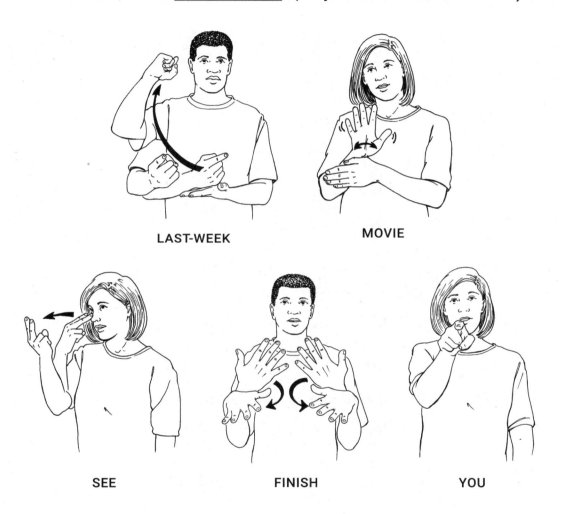

LAST-WEEK

MOVIE

SEE

FINISH

YOU

TOMORROW, SCHOOL GO-to <u>WANT YOU</u>? (Do you want to go to school tomorrow?)

TOMORROW   SCHOOL   GO-TO

WANT   YOU

YOUR SCIENCE BOOK, <u>HAVE YOU</u>? (Do you have your science book?)

YOUR   SCIENCE

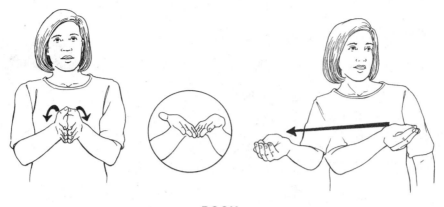

BOOK

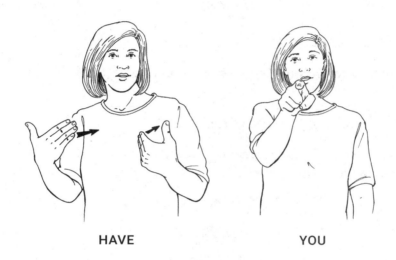

HAVE   YOU

ME LEAVE NOW, <u>DON'T-MIND YOU</u>? (Do you mind if I leave?)

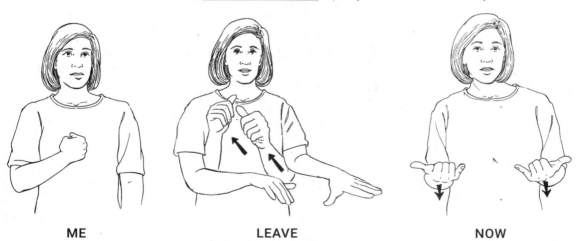

ME   LEAVE   NOW

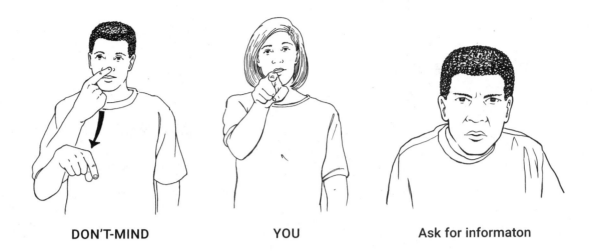

DON'T-MIND   YOU   Ask for informaton

Questions Seeking Information

For questions that ask for information such as wh-questions, the signer uses the following nonmanual signals:

(1) *squeezes the eyebrows* and (2) *tilts the head forward.*

If the questions are short, then the signer can make the nonmanual signals throughout the question as in the following examples:

TIME? (What time is it?)

TIME

DO-what YOU? (What are you going to do about it?)

DO-WHAT   YOU

YOU LIVE WHERE? (Where do you live?)

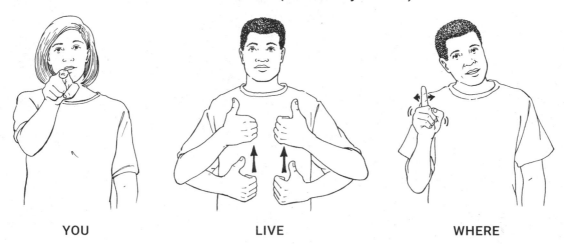

YOU   LIVE   WHERE

YOU EAT WHAT? (What did you eat?)

YOU   EAT   WHAT

WHAT

ASL TIP

WHAT

There are three signs for WHAT. These two shown here are the most common signs for WHAT. Fingerspelling W-H-A-T quickly with a twist toward your body is also used as the sign for a shocked expression, "WHAT!?"

If the question is long, then the signer should add the nonmanual signals at the end of the sentence and especially on the sign that is asking the question. Nonmanual signals are typically added while signing the underlined phrases in the following sentences:

PAST MONDAY, YOU SWIM <u>WHERE</u>? (Where did you swim last Monday?)

PAST (BEFORE)   MONDAY   YOU

SWIM   WHERE

BEFORE, YOU ENGINE FIX HOW? (How did you fix the engine before?)

BEFORE   YOU   ENGINE

FIX   HOW

> **ASL TIP**
>
> **HOW**
>
> There are three known variations for the sign HOW. As you go through this book, remember, signs are *regional*. Just like POP and SODA, the sign used depends on where you live.

YOUR ASL CLASS, STUDENT <u>HOW-MANY</u>? (How many students are in your ASL class?)

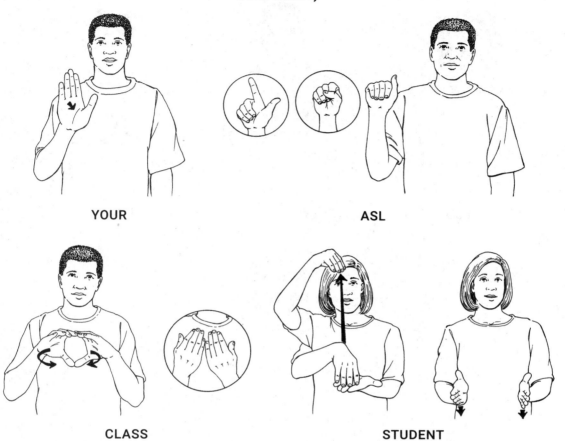

YOUR   ASL

CLASS   STUDENT

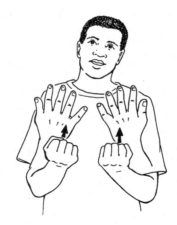

HOW-MANY

YOU WORK FINISH, <u>TIME</u>? (What time does your work finish?)

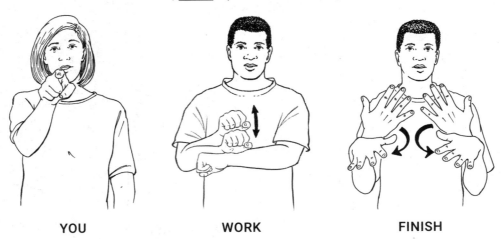

YOU   WORK   FINISH

TIME

Rhetorical Questions

I will meet you next week on Thursday. (me-MEET-you WHEN? NEXT-WEEK THURSDAY.)

ME-MEET-YOU WHEN NEXT-WEEK

THURSDAY

I arrived late because my car broke down. (ME ARRIVE LATE WHY? MY CAR BREAK-DOWN.)

ME   ARRIVE   LATE

WHY   MY

CAR   BREAK-DOWN

Both of these sentences are examples of rhetorical questions. The signer asks a question and then answers it. No question is being asked to someone else. ASL rhetorical questions are not translated as questions in English. When signing a rhetorical question, the signer must use the appropriate nonmanual signals to indicate that a question was asked and that she or he will answer it. For rhetorical questions, the signer does the following:

(1) *maintains eye contact*, (2) *raises the eyebrows*, (3) *tilts the head forward*, and (4) *holds the last sign of the rhetorical question slightly longer than the other signs.*

Even though this last feature is not a facial expression, the time during which the sign is held is still a part of the nonmanual signals that the signer is sending. The signer typically relays the nonmanual signals while signing the entire rhetorical question, which tells the *addressee* (the person to whom the signer is signing) that what is being signed is a rhetorical question. Examples of rhetorical questions are underlined in the following:

<u>ME GO-to WORK TIME</u>? NOON. (I go to work at twelve o'clock.)

ME   GO-TO   WORK

TIME   NOON

<u>YOU LINE-UP FOR-FOR? MOVIE FINISH NOT-YET.</u>
(Why are you lining up? The movie isn't over yet.)

YOU   LINE-UP   FOR-FOR

MOVIE

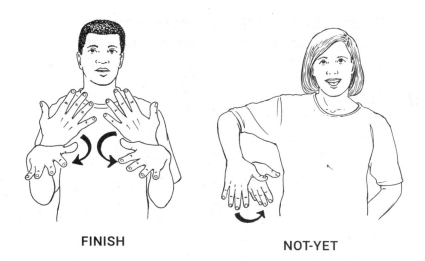

FINISH

NOT-YET

ME GO-to SEATTLE HOW? FLY. (I am flying to Seattle.)

ME

GO-TO

SEATTLE

HOW

FLY

ME HOMEWORK FINISH WHAT? GEOGRAPHY.
(I have finished my geography homework.)

ME   HOMEWORK

FINISH   WHAT   GEOGRAPHY

Notice that the nonmanual signals for rhetorical questions are the same whether a yes/no question or a question seeking information is asked.

Topicalization: Topic/Comment Sentences

BOY THERE COLOR BROWN HAIR, MY SON.
(That boy with the brown hair is my son.)

BOY	THERE	COLOR

BROWN	HAIR

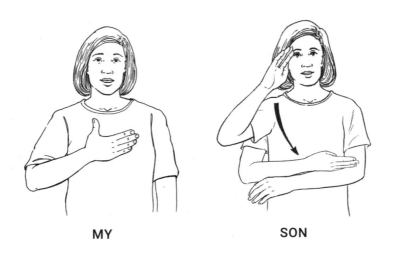

MY   SON

YOU TAKE-UP MATH, ME SHOCKED. (I am shocked that you are taking math.)

YOU   TAKE-UP   MATH

ME   SHOCKED

Both of these sentences are examples of a common ASL sentence structure known as topic/comment. The signer describes a topic and then makes a comment about it. The nonmanual signals consist of the following:

(1) *maintain eye contact with the person being addressed* provided the eyes are not needed for relaying other grammatical information, (2) *raise the eyebrows and tilt the head slightly forward* when signing the topic, (3) *hold the last sign of the topic a little longer than the other signs*, and (4) *pause slightly between signing the topic and the comment.*

When the comment is signed, the signer reverts to a neutral signing posture and facial expression or uses eye gazing, facial expressions, and body posture suitable to the intended meaning of the comment.

The four parts of the nonmanual signals are conveyed during the signing of the topic, which is underlined in each of the following sentences:

<u>you-HELP-me STUDY ASL</u>, ME HAPPY.
(I'm happy when you help me study ASL.)

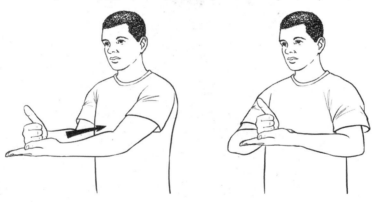

you-HELP-me

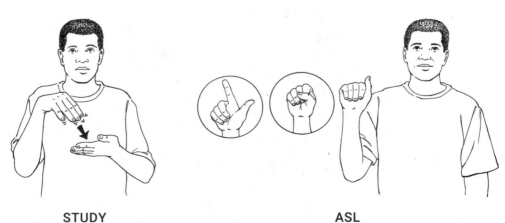

STUDY   ASL

ME   HAPPY

STORY ABOUT THREE PIGS, EXCITING.
(The story about the three pigs is exciting.)

STORY

ABOUT   THREE

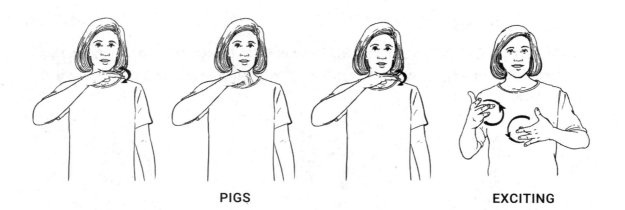

PIGS EXCITING

CAR RED THERE, ME WANT. (I want that red car.)

CAR RED

THERE ME WANT

Conditional Sentences

1. SUPPOSE ME SIGN FORGET, you-HELP-me PLEASE. (Please help me if I forget a sign.)
2. YOUR CAR BREAK-DOWN, YOU LATE WILL YOU. (If your car breaks down, you will be late.)

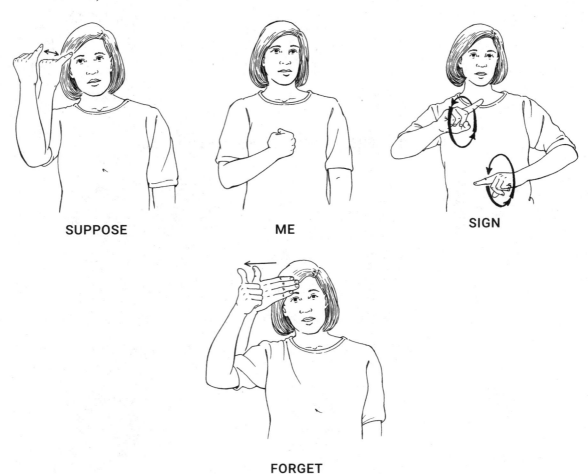

SUPPOSE ME SIGN

FORGET

you-HELP-me   PLEASE

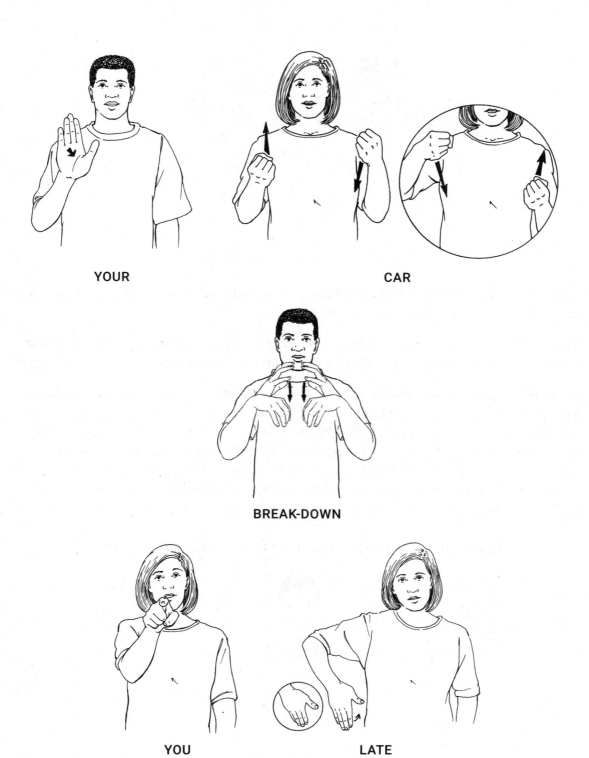

YOUR

CAR

BREAK-DOWN

YOU

LATE

WILL   YOU

Conditional sentences require nonmanual signals to alert the addressee to the stated condition. The nonmanual signs are:

(1) *the eyebrows raised*, (2) *the head tilted slightly to one side*, (3) *the last sign of the conditional clause held slightly longer than the other signs*, and (4) in some cases, *the body inclined forward.*

The head is usually tilted forward, but it may be tilted slightly backward depending upon the style of the signer and the context of the sentence. If the intent of the sentence "If you go to the store, I am taking your credit cards away" is humor, then it might be signed with the head tilted slightly backward. The sign SUPPOSE in the first sentence is an obvious indication of a conditional sentence. In the second sentence, the signer must rely on nonmanual signals to inform the addressee of the condition, "If your car breaks down." The conditional clauses requiring a nonmanual signal are underlined in the following sentences:

<u>YOU LOSE</u>, ME HAPPY STILL. (If you lose, I will still be happy.)

YOU   LOSE (TO LOSE A GAME)   ME

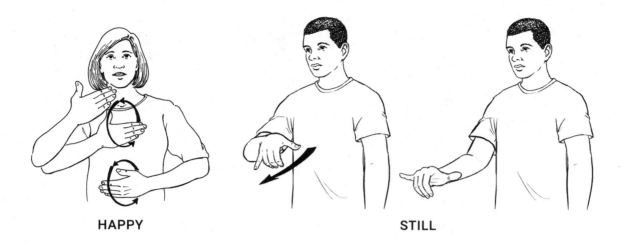

HAPPY   STILL

<u>SUPPOSE MY AUNT SHOW-UP</u>, ME GO HOME.
(If my aunt shows up, I'm going home.)

SUPPOSE   MY   AUNT

SHOW-UP   ME

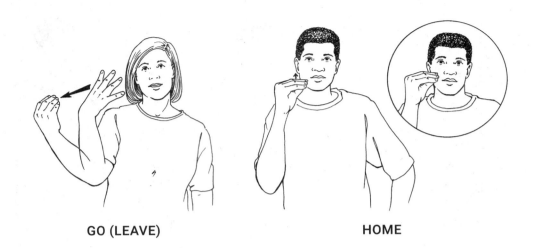

GO (LEAVE) HOME

TOMORROW RAIN, GAME CANCEL.
(If it rains tomorrow, the game will be canceled.)

TOMORROW RAIN

GAME CANCEL

<u>SUPPOSE HE HUNGRY</u>, you-GIVE-him APPLE.
(If he's hungry, give him an apple.)

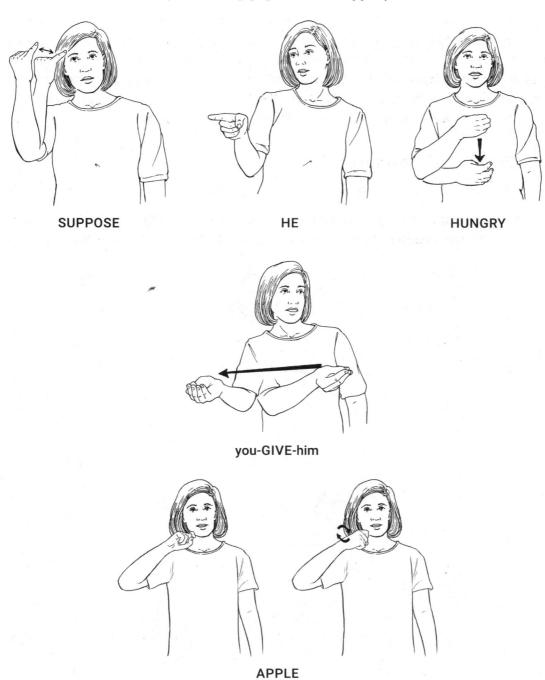

SUPPOSE   HE   HUNGRY

you-GIVE-him

APPLE

As with all signed sentences, if there is no grammatical reason for looking away, the signer should maintain eye contact with the addressee.

The Ten Rules of ASL Grammar

Your journey to become a fluent ASL signer will come into clearer focus when you cease to think entirely of language as being organized temporally. Oral languages are temporal; only one thought or word can be expressed at a time. Sign languages are spatial; not only can more than one thought be expressed simultaneously, but thoughts and events are also shaped in space or on the signer's body. Learning the ten basic rules of ASL grammar is an important step toward understanding how ASL is entwined in space.

Rule 1: Topic/Comment

In a simple topic/comment sentence, the topic is described first, followed by the comment.

HE WON THREE MILLION DOLLARS, HE HAPPY. (He won three million dollars and he is happy. Or: He's happy that he won three million dollars.)

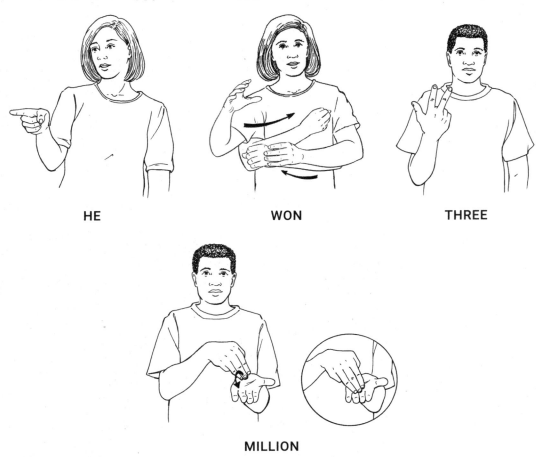

HE   WON   THREE

MILLION

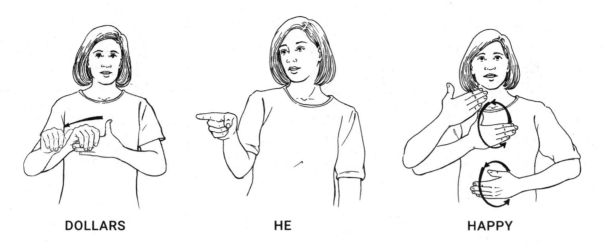

DOLLARS   HE   HAPPY

Many sentences are built on the simple concept of a topic and a comment. We can add to this concept the observation that ASL tends to structure sentences in the order that events occur. There must be a topic before there can be a comment about the topic; we have the rule for the common topic/comment structure in ASL.

From the preceding sentence, the topic and comment follow:

topic: HE WON THREE MILLION DOLLARS,

comment: HE HAPPY.

Here are more examples of topic/comment sentences with the topic underlined:

<u>ASL TEST</u>, EASY. (The ASL test is easy.)

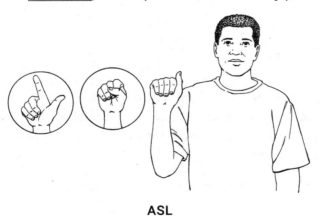

ASL

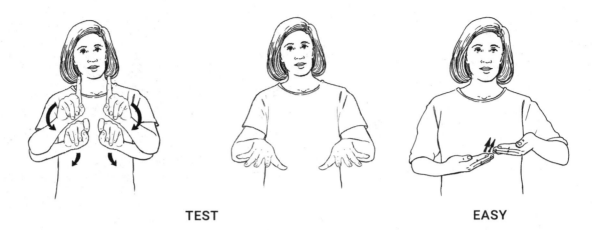

TEST   EASY

<u>DOG GOOD</u>, you-GIVE-it COOKIE. (The dog is good; give it a cookie.)

DOG

ASL TIP

DOG

The sign for DOG can be signed a few different ways. It is signed by fingerspelling D-O-G quickly with a twist in the wrist, by patting your thigh motioning calling a dog over, or signed with a snapping motion as shown in the video quiz for this chapter.

GOOD

you-GIVE-it

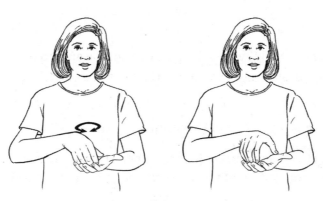

COOKIE

HER MONEY LOST, SHE UPSET. (She's upset that she lost her money.)

HER	MONEY	LOST

SHE	UPSET

The topic can vary according to what it is that the signer wants to emphasize. It is also important to note that if there is a time indicated, that goes first. Let's look at the following sentence:

Two years ago, I had a wonderful vacation.

With just this sentence to consider, we might suppose that *vacation* is the topic and *wonderful* is the comment. This could be represented in signs as follows:

topic:	TWO-YEARS-AGO <u>ME VACATION</u>
comment:	WONDERFUL

TWO-YEARS-AGO   ME   VACATION

WONDERFUL

What if the point of the discussion was the last time a signer had a great vacation? Then the topic changes, as the following order of the ASL sentence demonstrates:

topic:	<u>ME WONDERFUL VACATION</u>
comment:	TWO-YEARS-AGO

In English, the same sentence structure can be used to represent either of these two topics because a speaker would highlight the topic using the tone of voice.

Nonmanual Signals

The following nonmanual signals play a role in identifying the topic in a topic/comment sentence structure. The signer:

- *maintains eye contact with the person being addressed,*
- *raises the eyebrows and tilts the head slightly forward when signing the topic,*
- *holds the last sign of the comment a little longer than the other sign,* and
- *pauses slightly between signing the topic and the comment.*

When signing the comment, the signer uses facial expressions that convey the emotion of what is being signed. If the comment is SHE UPSET, then the signer should project a face associated with being upset. But the face does not always correspond with the emotions projected by the signs. For example, if the signer is being sarcastic, humorous, silly, or serious, then she or he might wish to convey these feelings rather than the feelings associated with the comment itself. If a signer is in fact being funny, then she or he might have a hint of a smile while signing SHE UPSET. Similarly, if a signer is serious about something, the lips might be pursed and the eyebrows squeezed together while signing a comment.

Rule 2: Tense with Time Adverbs

The time adverb is a *word that describes when or how long*, and it is *placed at the beginning or near the beginning of a sentence*. Using time adverbs is the most common means of indicating tense. Unlike in English, verb signs never undergo changes to indicate tense. Because there are no changes to a verb sign, the time that an action occurred must come before the verb sign.

1. LAST NIGHT, SUNSET BEAUTIFUL. (The sunset was beautiful last night.)

LAST   NIGHT   SUNSET

BEAUTIFUL

2. FOUR-DAYS, YOU GO-to WORK, WILL. (You go to work in four days.)

FOUR-DAYS   YOU

GO-to   WORK   WILL

3. ME YESTERDAY, STAY HOME. (I stayed home yesterday.)

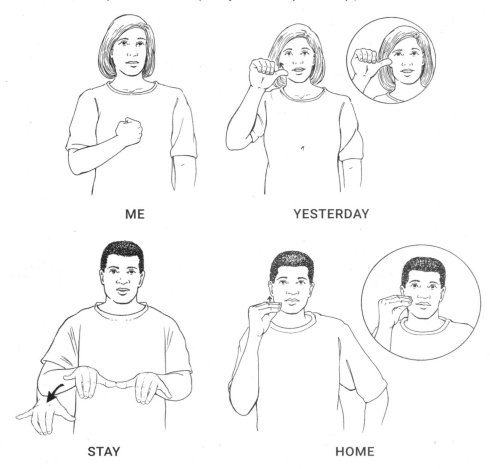

ME   YESTERDAY

STAY   HOME

Sentences 1 and 2 start off with a time adverb, whereas sentence 3 has the time adverb near the beginning of the sentence. Placing a time adverb at or near the beginning of a sentence marks the tense of the sentence.

After a time adverb has indicated tense in a sentence, all sentences after this sentence will have the *same* tense. There is no need to repeat the time adverb with each sentence. For example, sentence 1 indicated the time adverb as "last night." From this point forward in the conversation, we know the discussion is referring to "last night." Tense can be changed only by signing a different time adverb, changing the topic of discussion, or using a sign that is not a time adverb but tells about time.

FINISH, WILL, and NOT-YET

The signs FINISH, WILL, and NOT-YET are signs that tell about time that affect tense. The placement of each of these signs in a sentence varies. The sign FINISH is often used to indicate that an action has been completed. It is either placed before or after the verb, as in the following sentences:

Before the verb: HE MOVIE FINISH SEE. (He saw the movie.)

HE

MOVIE

FINISH

SEE

After the verb: ME WORK FINISH. (I have finished working.)

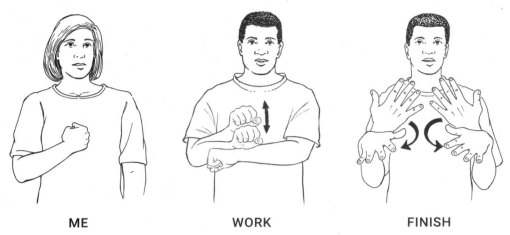

ME   WORK   FINISH

The sign WILL is often used in its emphatic sense to stress that an action is indeed going to take place in the future. It can be placed before or after a verb or at the end of a sentence. Three examples of how the sign WILL is used follow:

Before the verb: ME WILL SEND-you EMAIL. (I will send you an email.)

ME   WILL

SEND-you   EMAIL

After the verb: me-MEET-you WILL, TOMORROW PROMISE.
(I promise I will meet you tomorrow.)

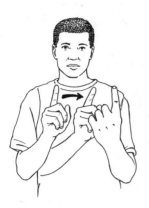

me-MEET-you   WILL   TOMORROW

PROMISE

End of a sentence: PHONE HOME TWICE WEEK, WILL.
(I will phone home twice a week.)

PHONE

HOME

TWICE

WEEK

WILL

The sign NOT-YET is used to show that an action has not yet occurred. It is often placed at the end of a sentence as in the first sentence A, which follows, or it can be used by itself in response to a question as demonstrated in sentence B.

ME HOMEWORK FINISH, NOT-YET. (I haven't done my homework yet.)

ME   HOMEWORK

FINISH   NOT-YET

Signer A: YOU EAT FINISH YOU? (Have you finished eating?)

Signer B: NOT-YET. (Not yet.)

YOU   EAT   FINISH   YOU

77

NOT-YET

Rule 3: Simple Yes/No Questions

In short sentences that ask a yes/no question, the order of the signs can vary as noted below. Nonmanual signals are imperative for conveying the meaning and indicating it as a question.

YOU   EXERCISE   WANT

1. YOU EXERCISE WANT?
2. YOU WANT EXERCISE?
3. WANT EXERCISE YOU?
4. EXERCISE YOU WANT?

In short questions such as those in sentences 1–4, the signer is asking a simple yes/no question, and the correct English translation for all of them is "Do you want to exercise?" However, the signs alone do not ask the question. The signer must use the correct nonmanual signals.

Nonmanual Signals

The following nonmanual signals play a role in identifying simple yes/no question sentence structure. The signer:

- *maintains eye contact with the person being addressed,*
- *raises the eyebrows,* and
- *tilts the head slightly forward.*

ASL TIP

Reminder

With short questions, nonmanual signals can be made throughout the question, like a head nod, raised eyebrows, and other nonmanual signals.

Rule 4: Long Yes/No Questions

Long yes/no questions use a topic/question format.

In longer yes/no questions, you first describe the topic and then place the sign that is asking the question at or near the end of the sentence.

1. CAT BLACK TREE CLIMB, YOUR? (Is that black cat climbing the tree yours?)

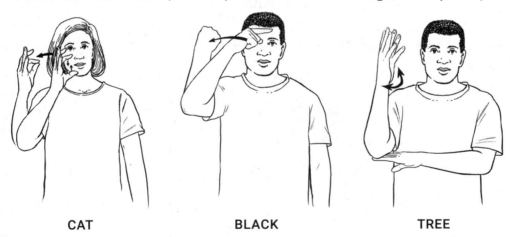

CAT   BLACK   TREE

CLIMB

YOUR

2. CLEAN DISHES WASH CLOTHES, HE? (Will he clean the dishes and wash the clothes?)

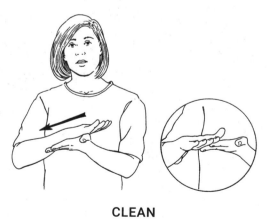

CLEAN

DISHES

WASH

CLOTHES

HE

3. GO-to STORE BUY FOOD MILK, READY YOU? (Are you ready to go to the store and buy food and milk?)

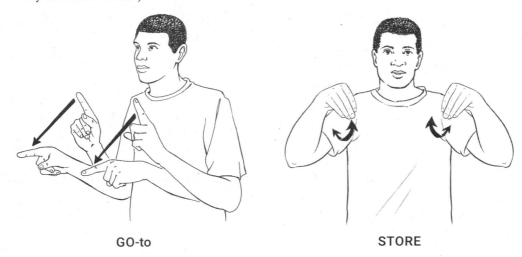

GO-to

STORE

BUY   **FOOD**

MILK

READY   **YOU**

You may recognize that questions 1–3 follow a variation of the topic/comment sentence structure. For convenience, we will refer to this structure as a topic/question structure to help you recall it more easily.

Nonmanual Signals

The following nonmanual signals play a role in identifying long yes/no question sentence structure. The signer:

- *maintains eye contact with the person being addressed,*
- *raises the eyebrows,* and
- *tilts the head slightly forward.*

The nonmanual signals in long questions usually fall on the last sign or phrase. In the preceding long questions, the nonmanual signals will accompany the signs YOUR?, HE?, and READY YOU?

Rule 5: Information-seeking Questions

Simple questions that ask for information have variable sentence structures and rely on nonmanual signals to distinguish them from declarative sentences.

1. AGE YOU? (How old are you?)
2. TIME? (What time is it?)
3. BOOK TITLE? (What is the title of the book?)

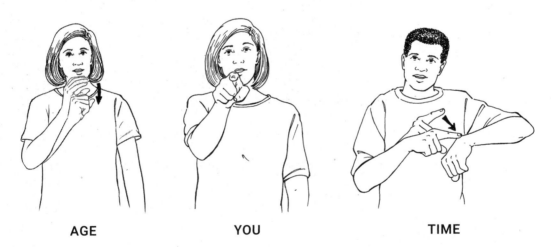

AGE   YOU   TIME

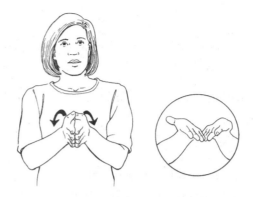

BOOK

TITLE

Questions 1–3 are simple and are distinguished from simple declarative statements by the nonmanual signals that would accompany them.

Nonmanual Signals

The following nonmanual signals play a role in information-seeking question sentence structure. The signer:

- *squeezes the eyebrows* and
- *tilts the head slightly forward.*

Wh-questions also seek information. Although the wh-question sign can come at the beginning of a sentence, most wh-questions follow a topic/question format and place the wh-question sign at or near the end of the question.

4. SHE WORK HERE, HOW LONG? (How long has she worked here?)
5. CITY DESTROY BUILDING, WHY? (Why did the city destroy the building?)

SHE   WORK   HERE

HOW   LONG

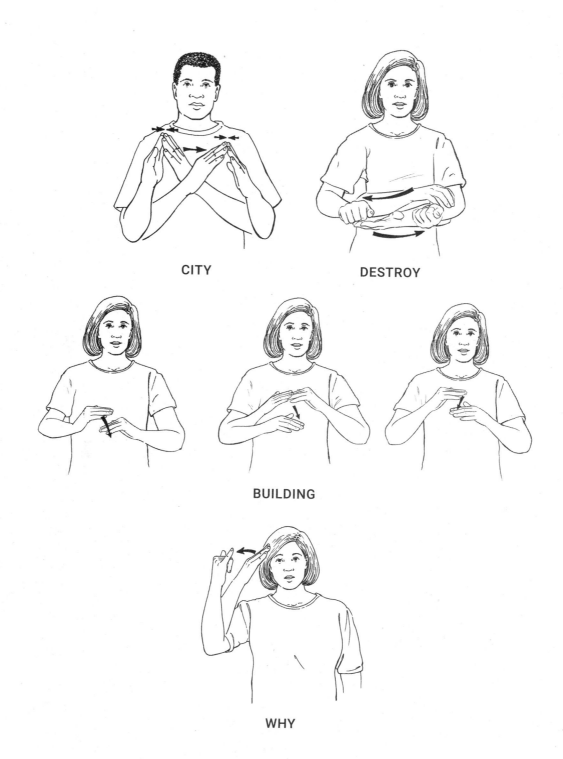

CITY

DESTROY

BUILDING

WHY

ASL TIP

WHY

WHY is also signed in the same position but by holding your hand still and wiggling your middle finger down, as pictured below.

WHY

In sentences 4 and 5, the wh-question sign or phrase comes at the end of the question. It follows a topic/question format because a topic is described followed by a question about it. It would still be correct to turn the questions around.

6. HOW LONG SHE WORK HERE?

7. WHY CITY DESTROY BUILDING?

Questions 6 and 7 are similar in structure to English. Many beginning signers find it difficult to ask a wh-question using the topic/question format as shown in sentences 4 and 5. Yet this format is very common in ASL, and for this reason it will be emphasized throughout this book.

It is also common practice to include the pronoun at the end or near the end of a wh-question. This is shown in the following examples:

PICNIC FOOD BRING, WHAT YOU? (What food are you bringing to the picnic?)

PICNIC FOOD BRING

WHAT YOU

BOY BORN, WHEN HE? (When was the boy born?)

BOY   BORN   WHEN

HE

YESTERDAY FIX FENCE, HOW YOU? (How did you fix the fence yesterday?)

YESTERDAY

FIX

FENCE

HOW

YOU

you-PICK-ON-me, WHY YOU? (Why are you picking on me?)

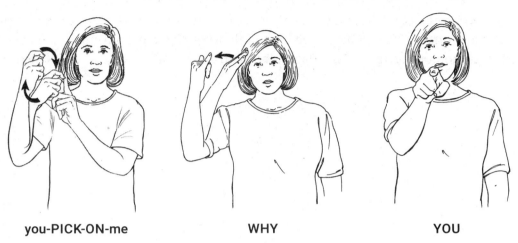

| you-PICK-ON-me | WHY | YOU |

Rule 6: Pronominalization

Pronouns are indicated by pointing to either (a) a person or thing that is present or (b) a place in the signing space that is used as a referent point, which is a point used to find or describe the location of something, for a person or thing. Pointing is mostly done with the index finger, but eye gazing and other handshapes are sometimes used.

To understand how pointing is used to indicate pronouns, you must first understand the dimensions and techniques for using the signing space. The *signing space* is the space in which a signer signs. The following diagram shows the typical dimensions of the signing space for a signer.

The signing space is roughly defined as the space from the waist to just above the head and to the left and right side of the body. This space is also the comfort zone of signing—the signer can move the hands about without stretching them to the point of discomfort.

Pronouns in the Presence of a Person or an Object

If a person or an object is present, then the signer merely points to them and the pointing becomes the pronoun. This is illustrated in the following diagram. Pointing to the person yields the pronoun SHE/HER or HE/HIM. Pointing to an animal or object is translated as IT.

Similarly, whomever or whatever the signer points to will be understood as the pronoun of the person or object indicated. For example, if several people are present, the signer sweeps the index finger past all of them to show the pronoun THEY or THEM. The pronoun ME is made by pointing to oneself, and the pronoun YOU is made by pointing to the addressee. Note that the pronouns WE/US cannot be established in the signing space because they include the signer who is always present. To sign WE/US, the signer moves the index finger in an arc from one shoulder to the other shoulder.

Pronouns in the Absence of a Person or an Object

The principle of identifying pronouns in the absence of a real person or object is similar to the principle of identifying pronouns when the referent is present. The signer uses the signing space to insert reference points that will represent a specific person or object. For example, the following diagrams illustrate the common reference points in the signing space for pronouns.

The phrases "point-right" or "point-left" are used in ASL sentences to show in which side of the signing space the signer is placing the reference point for HE/HIM, SHE/HER, or IT. The phrases "sweep-right" and "sweep-left" are used when showing in which side of the signing space the signer is placing THEY or THEM. You will note in the signing dialogues that these phrases are used to help you learn about placing people and places in the signing space. While signing your own conversations, outside of this book, determining the location is left for you to decide.

Before the signing space can be used to sign pronouns, the signer must first establish a referent in the space. The procedure for doing this is to name the person or object and then point to a spot in the signing space. This spot becomes the location for the pronoun associated with the referent. How this works can be shown with the following sentence:

My brother is deaf, and he is visiting me.

MY

BROTHER

DEAF

POINT RIGHT   HE

VISIT   ME

To establish the pronoun *he*, the signer must place the person called *brother* in the signing space. From an earlier diagram, we saw that the pronoun HE is typically set up either to the right or left side of the signer. If the signer chooses the right side, we would then get the following ASL sentence:

ASL TIP

Two Ways to Sign BROTHER and SISTER

BROTHER can be signed as seen in the illustration with two L handshapes or can be signed with the movement of the sign "BOY to an L handshape." The same can be done with SISTER. "GIRL to an L handshape" or two L handshapes can be used.

MY BROTHER point-right, HE VISIT ME.

MY   BROTHER

POINT RIGHT   HE

VISIT   ME

After the signer has signed "MY BROTHER point-right," a place has been identified in the signing space that is the reference point for "brother." Pointing to this place will always mean the sign HE until the signer either no longer talks about the brother or changes the location of brother in the signing space.

Another example of how pronouns are established in the signing space is seen in the following sentence:

The teachers showed up for class yesterday, but the students did not.

The tense of the sentence is first established. Then, the signer sets up the location for teachers and students in the signing space. Following this, the signer can point to these locations and tell what the teachers and students did yesterday. This is done in the following ASL sentence:

YESTERDAY, TEACHERS (sweep-left) STUDENTS (sweep-right)
THEY sweep-left SHOW-UP, THEY sweep-right DIDN'T (not).

This sentence can be broken down to show its various components.

YESTERDAY	establishes the tense of the sentence
TEACHERS sweep-left	establishes the location of "teachers" in the signing space
STUDENTS sweep-right	establishes the location of "students" in the signing space
THEY sweep-left SHOW-UP	sweep-left to refer to the teachers
THEY sweep-right DIDN'T.	sweep-right to refer to the students

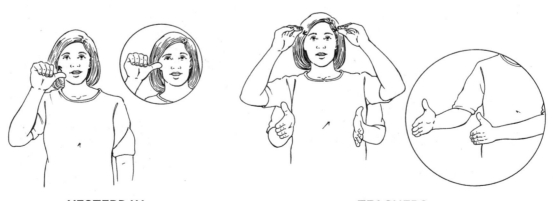

YESTERDAY   TEACHERS

sweep-left

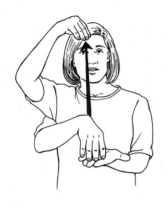

STUDENTS

sweep-right   **THEY-sweep-left**

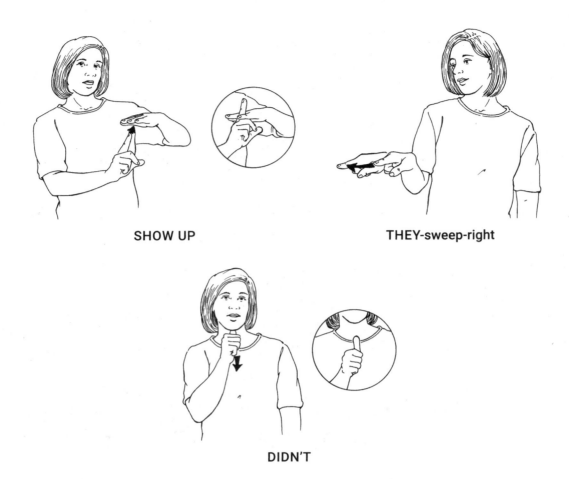

SHOW UP

THEY-sweep-right

DIDN'T

Note that in the above illustrations, the hands move to the side for TEACHERS and STUDENTS. This movement indicates the plural form of TEACHER.

Multiple reference points can be established in the signing space, as long as the signer and the addressee can recall what each place in the signing space represents. Because of the need to memorize the meaning of each location, you should not attempt to have more than three or four reference points in the signing space at any one time.

Subjective versus Objective Pronoun Forms

Both the subjective and objective forms of the pronoun make the same movement.

- The subjective forms of the pronoun are SHE, HER, HE, HIM, YOU, ME, THEY, THEM, WE, US, and IT. The handshape for signing them is the **index finger pointing out**.
- The objective forms of the pronoun are HER, HERS, HIS, YOUR, YOURS, MINE, THEIR, OUR, OURS, and ITS. The handshape for signing them is an open hand with the **palm facing outward**.

Rule 7: Rhetorical Questions

In a rhetorical question, the signer asks a question and then answers it.

1. ME KNOW ASL? YES. (I know ASL.)
2. ME LOST WHY? PAY-ATTENTION STREET NAME NOT. (I didn't pay attention to the name of the street and got lost.)

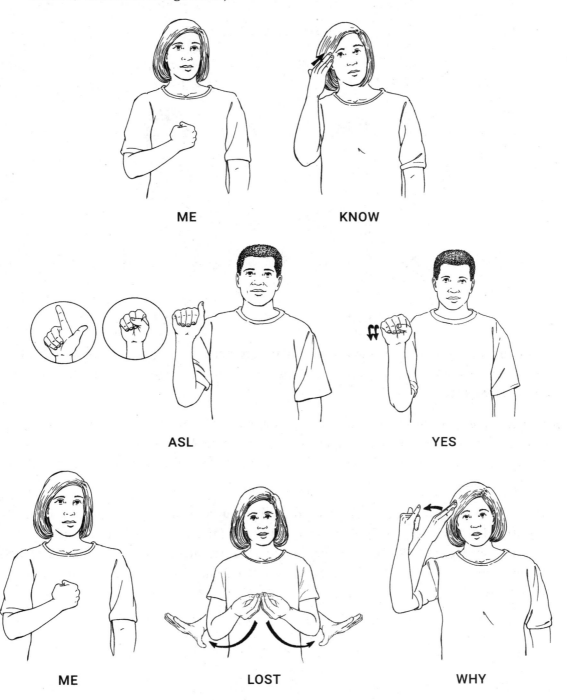

ME   KNOW

ASL   YES

ME   LOST   WHY

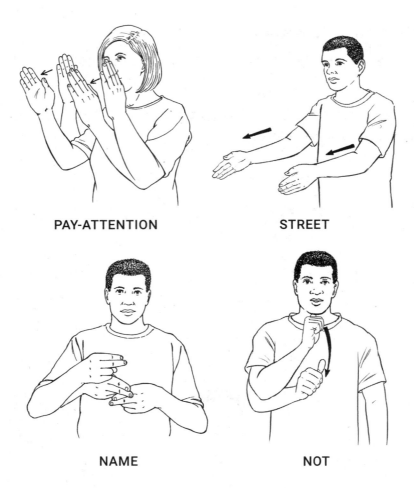

PAY-ATTENTION

STREET

NAME

NOT

The rhetorical question is a common grammatical structure in ASL. As shown in sentences 1 and 2, the signer asks a question and then answers it. There is no expectation that someone else will answer the question.

Rhetorical questions often make use of signs for wh-questions, such as WHY and HOW. However, a proper translation to English will seldom include a direct reference to these signs. For example, when WHY is used, the proper translation will often include the conjunction *because*.

Notice the liberty taken in omitting the word *yes* in the translation of sentence 1. A good translation is *not* a matter of finding a word for each of the signs made. An English translation attempts to capture the signer's intended meaning including the nonmanual signals and the manner of signing. Nevertheless, sentence 1 could also be correctly translated as "Yes, I know ASL."

Nonmanual Signals

The following nonmanual signals play a role in rhetorical sentence structure. The signer:

- *maintains eye contact with the person being addressed,*
- *raises the eyebrows,*
- *tilts the head slightly forward,* and
- *holds the last sign of the rhetorical question slightly longer than the other signs.*

Recall that the correct nonmanual signal for rhetorical wh-questions is signed during the question and is *not* the same as that for other wh-questions. Also, it is important to hold (slight pause) the last sign of the rhetorical question before answering the question.

Rule 8: Ordering of Simple Sentences

In simple sentences, the verb can be placed before or after the object of the sentence.

1. ME PLAY GAME.
2. ME GAME PLAY.

ME   PLAY

GAME

Sentences 1 and 2 translate to "I play a game." The difference between them is that sentence 1 has a subject-verb-object (SVO) word ordering. SVO is a basic sentence structure in English. Sentence 2 has a subject-object-verb (SOV) word order. SOV is not a sentence structure in English, but it is basic in ASL. For this reason, beginning signers will tend to use SVO word ordering more frequently than SOV word ordering.

Not all simple sentences can have an SOV word order. The phrase

TY KATE KISS.

yields the translation "Ty and Kate kiss." Whereas, the phrase

TY KISS KATE.

means "Ty kisses Kate." It is possible to sign a variation of TY KATE KISS so that *it appears* that the verb comes after the object. You can do this by using the pronominalization rule. For example, you first fingerspell TY (or use a name sign for Ty) and then point to the right. You do the same for KATE but point to the left. At this stage, you have established reference points in the signing space for Ty and Kate. You then make the sign KISS moving from the right side to the reference point for Kate, which is on the left side. The movement of the verb shows who kisses whom. But is this an example of SOV word ordering? Let's look at this sentence:

TY point-right KATE point-left he-KISS-her.

In this sentence, the verb sign KISS has the subject and the object incorporated into its movement.

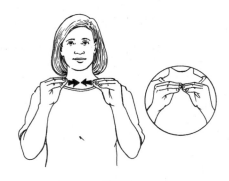

KISS

Rule 9: Conditional Sentences

In a conditional sentence, first the condition is described, then the outcome of this condition is described.

In all types of conditional sentences, nonmanual signals are critical.

SUPPOSE

The condition can be clearly marked with the use of the sign SUPPOSE as shown in the following sentences:

1. SUPPOSE HE SHOW-UP, DO-what YOU? (If he shows up, what are you going to do about it?)
2. SUPPOSE SHE SEE ME, ME HAVE-TO LEAVE. (I will have to leave if she sees me.)
3. SUPPOSE TONIGHT SNOW, TOMORROW YOU CANCEL SCHOOL. (If it snows tonight, then you will cancel school tomorrow.)

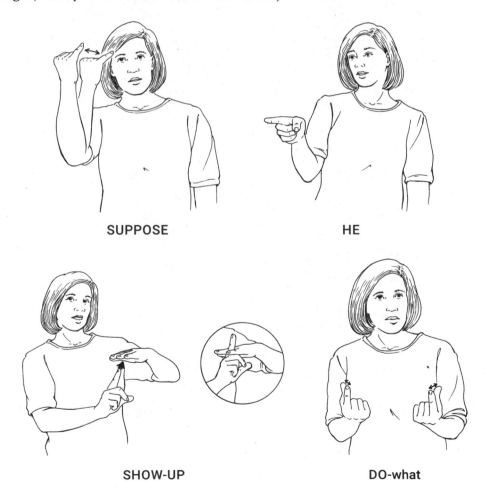

SUPPOSE   HE

SHOW-UP   DO-what

YOU

SUPPOSE

SHE

SEE

ME

ME   HAVE-TO   LEAVE

SUPPOSE   TONIGHT

SNOW   TOMORROW   YOU

CANCEL   SCHOOL

The conditional clause is always at the beginning of the sentence, and it must clearly describe the condition.

The outcome of the condition is described in the second part of the sentence. The preceding sentences show three different types of outcomes. In sentence 1, the outcome is a question; in sentence 2, it is a statement; and in sentence 3, it is a command.

Notice that the three English translations do not all have the condition stated at the beginning of the sentence. In sentence 2, the condition is at the end of the sentence. Another suitable translation for sentence 2 is "If she sees me, I will have to leave." Even though there is flexibility in the ordering of conditional clauses in English, ASL always states the condition first, followed by the outcome.

IF

The fingerspelling of I-F is also used to construct a conditional clause. Although I-F can be used interchangeably with the sign SUPPOSE, it is often used to give greater emphasis to a condition. I-F is fingerspelled with the upright fingers of the F handshape, often wiggling depending on the type of emphasis a signer is trying to give. It is also common for a signer to hold the letter F for a short time to increase the emphasis given to the condition. Some uses of I-F as a condition follow:

1. I-F SHE CAN'T COME, YOU LOSE CONTRACT. (If she can't come, you lose the contract.)
2. I-F YOU WIN GAME, YOUR TEAM CHAMPION. (If you win the game, your team will be the champions.)

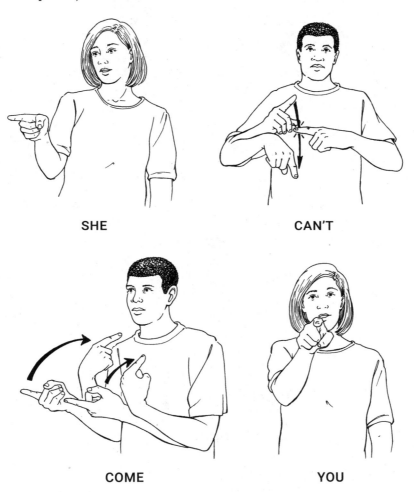

SHE   CAN'T

COME   YOU

LOSE/LOST

CONTRACT

YOU

WIN

GAME

YOUR

TEAM   CHAMPION

In sentences 1 and 2, the signer uses I-F to emphasize the consequences of the condition. In sentence 1, the signer might be warning someone and in essence is saying "She must come or you are going to lose the contract." In sentence 2, the signer might be pleading "You had better win this game so your team can be champions."

Nonmanual Signals

The following nonmanual signals play a role in conditional sentence structure. The signer:

- *raises the eyebrows,*
- *tilts the head slightly to one side,*
- *holds the last sign of the conditional clause slightly longer than the other signs,* and in some cases,
- *in some cases, inclines the body forward.*

All conditional sentences must be accompanied by nonmanual signals. There are some conditional sentences where the nonmanual signal is the only indicator that a condition is being stated. If we take out the sign I-F in sentence 1, we have

SHE CAN'T COME, YOU LOSE CONTRACT.

In the absence of nonmanual signals, this sentence translates to "She can't come, so you lose the contract." If the nonmanual signals for conditional sentences are added to the phrase SHE CAN'T COME, then the translation will be the same as if the signs I-F or SUPPOSE were used.

Rule 10: Negation

You can negate a thought by placing a negative sign before the verb or by first describing a topic and then signing the appropriate negative sign or by giving a negative head shake.

1. ME NOT WATCH FOOTBALL GAME. (I'm not watching the football game.)
2. ME CHEAT, NEVER. (I never cheat.)
3. ME GO HOME NOW? NEG-headshake. (No, I am not going home now.)

ME   NOT   WATCH

FOOTBALL   GAME

ME   CHEAT

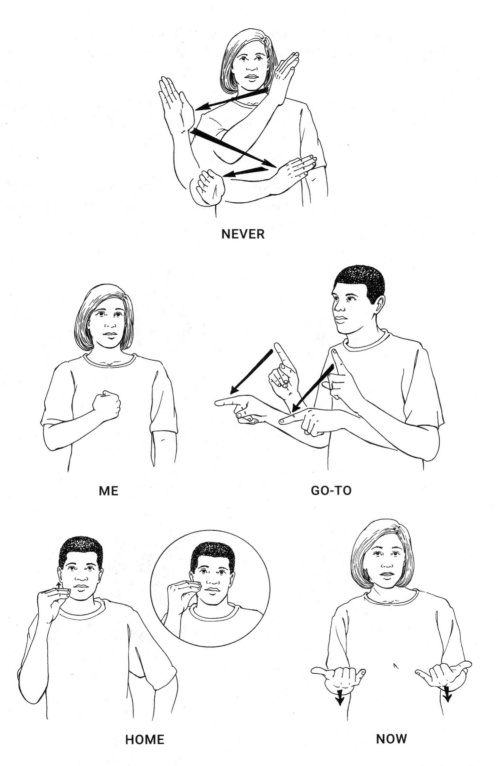

NEVER

ME   GO-TO

HOME   NOW

Sentence 1 is an example of negating a thought by placing a negative sign before the verb. The sign NOT negates the action sign WATCH.

Sentence 2 is an example of a topic/comment sentence. The topic is about cheating. The signer uses the negative sign NEVER to make a comment about cheating, which is that it never happens.

Sentence 3 does not have a negative sign. To respond negatively to the rhetorical question ME GO HOME NOW?, the signer uses the nonmanual signal of shaking the head to say "no."

Nonmanual Signals

Shaking the head to say "no" can accompany any negative sign. It can also accompany the topic that is being negated. Although it is good practice to use this nonmanual signal when expressing a negative thought, it is not always necessary to do so.

ME MONEY HAVE? NONE!

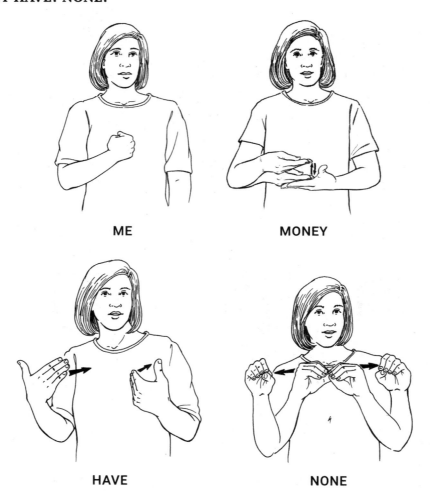

ME   MONEY

HAVE   NONE

In this sentence, the signer is adamantly denying having any money.

Some negative signs call up different nonmanual signals. An example of this occurs in the preceding *rhetorical statement*:

- *eyebrows raised,*
- *tightly closed lips,*
- *head tilted forward,* and
- *body inclined forward.*

The eyebrows raised and the head tilted together would be proper if the signer is surprised at the question and is denying having any money. The eyebrows might be squeezed together, the head tilted forward, and lips tightly closed if the signer is angry at an accusation that she or he has money.

Most negative signs can be used as adjectives or adverbs such as NO, NOT, NONE, NOTHING, NEVER, NOT-YET, DON'T-WANT, NOT-POSSIBLE, NO-GOOD, ILLEGAL, NOT-FAIR, and NOT-WORTHWHILE. A few negative signs are verbs including DENY, DECLINE, CAN'T, WON'T, REFUSE, DON'T, DON'T-BELIEVE, DON'T-KNOW, DON'T-LIKE, and FORBID.

ASL TIP

Eye Contact

As with all signed sentences, if there is no grammatical reason for looking away, the signer should maintain eye contact with the addressee.

Chapter Review

Answer these questions with a partner. When you have answered them, practice signing them in ASL.

State the name of the rule associated with each of the following explanations.

1. In a wh-question, the sign for the wh-word is usually placed at or near the end of the question.

2. First the topic is described and then the sign that is asking a yes/no question about the topic is placed at or near the end of the sentence.

3. The sign NOT can be placed before the verb or at the end of the sentence.

4. The topic of a sentence is first described, followed by a comment about the topic.

5. A signer points to a place in the signing space to establish a reference point for a person or thing.

6. A sign such as LAST-YEAR can be used to establish the tense of a sentence.

7. Nonmanual signals can be used in place of the signs IF and SUPPOSE.

8. In some sentences, the verb can follow the object.

9. A question is asked and then the signer answers it.

10. The order of signs in this type of question is variable.

11. Sign all of the ASL sentences in this chapter while using proper facial grammar. Take your time and practice being overly expressive. It is not natural for a hearing person to use bold facial expressions on a regular basis. This will be a challenge for you, but it is the first step and is necessary to sign proper ASL.

12. Eye contact is important in ASL; however, eye contact can be broken to make proper ASL sentences. This chapter gives you five examples of when this can happen: 1. Ask a particular type of question. 2. Draw attention to a particular place in the signing space in which a person or thing has been established. 3. Highlight key information in a sentence. 4. Reinforce the direction in which certain signs might be moving. 5. Reveal emotions about a topic. Create an ASL sentence for each example, and practice breaking the eye contact rule.

13. Describe the nonmanual signals that accompany yes/no questions, question-seeking information, rhetorical questions, topic/comment sentence structure, and conditional sentences.

14. In ASL, it is important to say with your face what you are signing with your hands. Many people do this most of the time when speaking. Many beginning signers, on the other hand, find themselves concentrating so hard on the formation of a sign that they often just have neutral expressions on their faces. With a partner or while standing in front of a mirror, practice making facial expressions to suit each of the following actions. Beside each action, make notes about what happens to your eyebrows, head, shoulders, and hands.

    - You are looking for someone in an auditorium.
    - The ice cream you were given is not the one you ordered.
    - Your car has two flat tires.
    - You are thanking someone for finding your wallet.
    - You find out that the money in your returned wallet is missing.
    - You are telling the stranger at your door to go away.
    - You just spilled a can of soda pop on your computer keyboard.
    - You have just tasted something that is very sour.
    - You are telling a friend that you have just won a new car in a raffle.

15. Create a short story using only facial expressions and minimal signs. Write it down, practice it, then act it out with a partner. Ask your partner if she or he followed your story. Be expressive! Try to limit your story to five ASL signs.

 Video Quiz Visit online.barronsbooks.com for scored practice on ASL grammar.

CHAPTER 4

Fingerspelling

> **Learning Objectives**
>
> In this chapter, you will learn:
>
> o How and when to fingerspell properly in ASL with an illustrated guide to the ASL alphabet
>
> o How to stretch and warm up your hands, wrists, and arms for finger-spelling (this applies to signing numbers as well)
>
> o Tips and tricks and simple introductions to fingerspelling

When to Fingerspell

When a signer does not know the sign for a word or if there is no sign for the word, such as a name, the signer will often spell out the word letter by letter. This is called fingerspelling. To begin fingerspelling, you must first learn the handshapes of the manual alphabet. Additionally, most proper nouns do not have signs and are typically fingerspelled, such as Walt Disney, Atlantic Ocean, and Queen Elizabeth.

How to Fingerspell

Follow the below steps to fingerspell properly in ASL:

- Raise your hand in a comfortable position by bending your elbow.
- Face your palm out from your body at a 45-degree angle.
- Right-handed signers fingerspell with the right hand, their dominant hand. Left-handed signers fingerspell with the left hand, their dominant hand.
- For those of you who are ambidextrous, pick the hand you use most, and only fingerspell with that hand.

- Your arm moves slightly away from your body when fingerspelling, and each hand-shape is clearly formed.
- Pause slightly between words.
- In words containing double letters, move your hand slightly to the outside for the repeated letter or tap the letter twice with your fingers.

Tips and Tricks

- Fast fingerspelling does not mean better fingerspelling.
- Do not "erase the air" with your hand if you make a mistake; instead, pause slightly and start again.
- Mouth the word you are fingerspelling, not each letter.
- If you are missing what is being fingerspelled to you, do not be afraid to ask the signer to repeat in a slower manner.
- Your wrist may start to hurt. When this happens, stretch your hands, wrists, and arms and take a short break. Over time, your wrists will get stronger.

ASL TIP

Missing What's Being Fingerspelled?
Sound out the spelling in your head, much like a child does as they are learning to read phonetically. Learn to see the fingerspelling as a word, not letter by letter.

ASL Alphabet

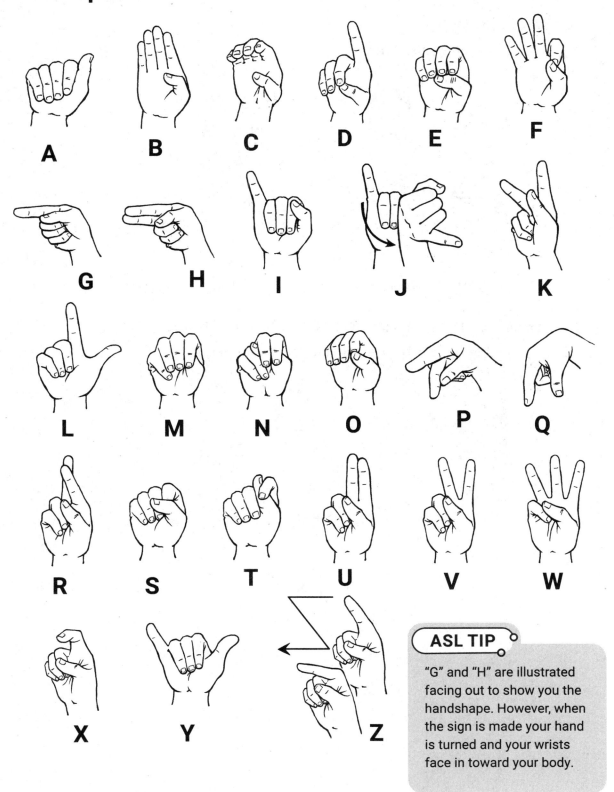

ASL TIP

"G" and "H" are illustrated facing out to show you the handshape. However, when the sign is made your hand is turned and your wrists face in toward your body.

Signing Dialogue

1. Kacey: NAME YOU?

   What is your name?

NAME   YOU

2. Markie: MY NAME M-A-R-K-I-E. NAME YOU WHAT PLEASE?

   My name is Markie. What is your name, please?

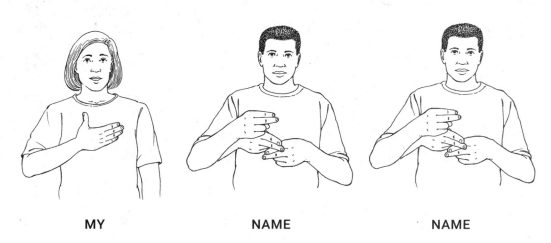

MY   NAME   NAME

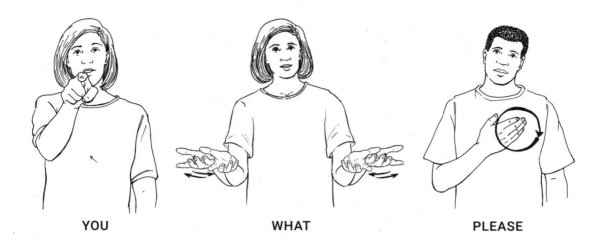

YOU WHAT PLEASE

3. Kacey: MY NAME K-A-C-E-Y.

My name is Kacey.

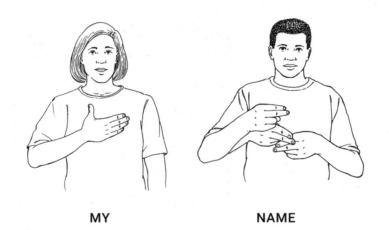

MY NAME

4. Markie: STATE CITY YOU LIVE WHERE?

What city and state do you live in

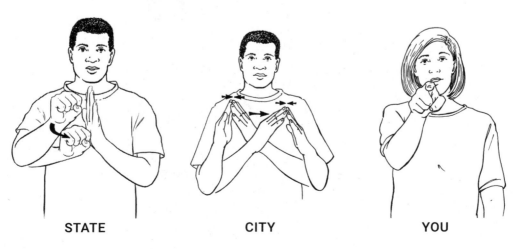

STATE CITY YOU

LIVE   WHERE

5.   Kacey: I LIVE WHERE? O-H-I-O CITY NAME D-A-Y-T-O-N. YOU?

I live in Dayton, Ohio. What about you?

I   LIVE   WHERE

CITY   NAME

6.   Markie: I LIVE WHERE? M-I-C-H-I-G-A-N, CITY NAME L-A-N-S-I-N-G.

I live in Lansing, Michigan.

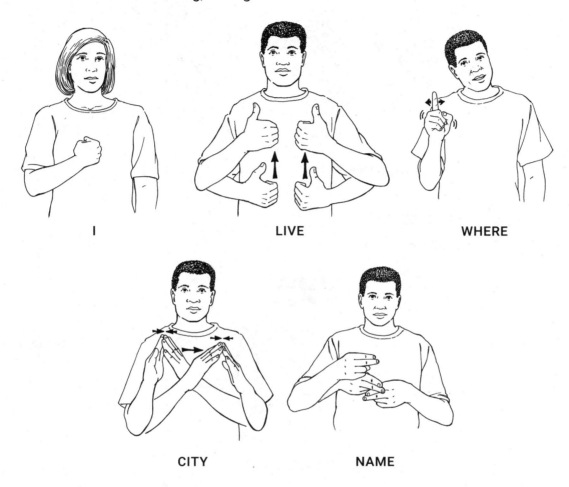

| I | LIVE | WHERE |

| CITY | NAME |

7.   Kacey: COOL NICE WEATHER HAVE?

Cool, do you have nice weather there?

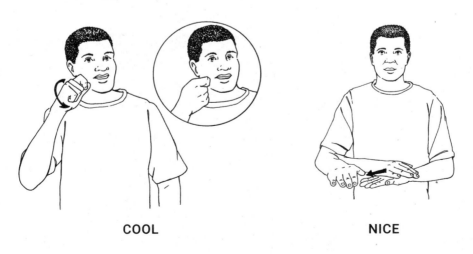

| COOL | NICE |

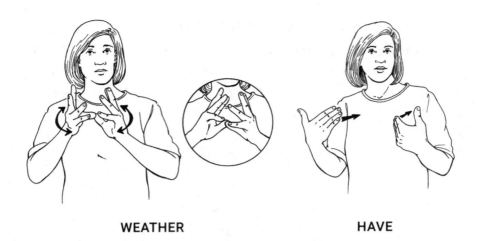

WEATHER   HAVE

8. Markie: SOMETIMES.

Sometimes.

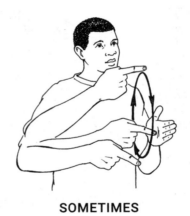

SOMETIMES

Chapter Review

NOTE: Stretch your hands, wrists, and arms first to help avoid injury or pain.

1. Slowly fingerspell the alphabet twice through. **NOTE:** Do not fingerspell the alphabet more than twice. After you have completed this, practice by fingerspelling words only.

2. Ideally, with a partner, practice the Signing Dialogue on pages 116–120.

3. With a partner, look around the room you are in and fingerspell the names of what you see. Make sure you are signing slowly and clearly so your partner can tell you what you are spelling. Example: Fingerspell D-E-S-K and your partner should be able to guess DESK!

4. Fingerspell the following two-, three-, and four-letter short words. Some will have double letters: *at, am, are, art, arm, arch, be, been, bear, bit, bite, cat, claw, cool, car, clue, dad, did, dim, did, doll, dear, eat, elm, elf, eek, each, fly, fit, frog, fire, flee, go, get, gone, glow, good, hi, hey, hip, hit, hype, if, is, ill, ice, iced, jip, jump, june, joke, jagg, kit, kot, knot, kept, kiss, lap, lit, like, loot, loop, lets, mom, met, mate, moon, mite, no, non, nil, nope, nook, oz, owl, open, oil, ouch, pi, pop, pep, pool, pour, qu, qui, que, quad, quit, rip, rug, rest, rule, rock, si, set, sock, sour, seek, tie, two, true, time, tick, tune, un, uni, unit, udon, ugly, vet, van, vair, vine, vail, we, wet, word, when, woot, xi, xit, xen, xeme, xemo, yes, yet, your, year, yack, zed, zags, zany, zeal, zati.*

5. Find a partner and fingerspell the following proper nouns. Practice copy-signing what your partner is fingerspelling. When you have completed the list, think of five of your own proper nouns and fingerspell them. Write down what your partner is spelling. *United States, Hockeytown, Subaru, Golden Retriever, ABC Cinema, the White House, Central Park, President Lincoln, Mount Everest, MacBook, Doctor Dolittle, Waterloo Station, Trafalgar Square, Pacific Ocean, Mississippi, Ellen DeGeneres, the Himalayas, Royal Theater, Sunday Post, Statue of Liberty, Prime Minister, Ritz Hotel, United Nations, President Washington.*

6. Although the following sentences are written in English form and mostly have ASL signed words, practice signing the entire sentences by *only using fingerspelling*.

- Hi, my name is (insert name), and I am learning American Sign Language.
- What are you signing? Can you please repeat yourself?
- My goal is to fingerspell slowly and clearly.
- My hand is starting to hurt; my wrists are not used to this.
- The more I practice my fingerspelling, the more comfortable I will become.

 Video Quiz Visit online.barronsbooks.com for scored practice on fingerspelling.

CHAPTER 5

Numbering

Learning Objectives

In this chapter, you will learn:

- How to sign numbers properly in ASL
- The "palm rule" and when you can break it
- How to sign phone numbers and addresses

The Basics

Counting in ASL is not limited to the sum of the fingers, nor is it encumbered by the numbers that the fingers can literally draw in the air. This chapter shows you how numbers are made in ASL—not just one number but millions of them.

Numbers 1–19

The following illustrations show the signs for numbers 1–19. Note that the palm faces the body for numbers 1–5 and it faces away from the body for numbers 6–9. The palm faces the body again for numbers 11–15, and then it faces away from the body for numbers 16–19.

ONE	TWO	THREE
FOUR	FIVE	SIX
SEVEN	EIGHT	NINE

TEN   ELEVEN

TWELVE   THIRTEEN   FOURTEEN

FIFTEEN   SIXTEEN   SEVENTEEN

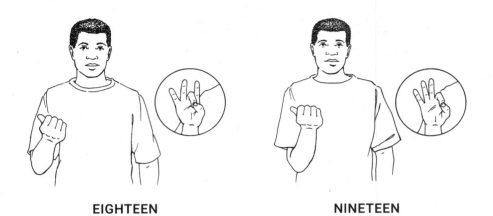

EIGHTEEN   **NINETEEN**

Numbers 20–29

In ASL, there are multiple ways to sign numbers. The L handshape is used to sign numbers 20–29 in this book. It is a very common handshape, and many people find it easier to manipulate than using the 2 handshape to represent the concept of twenty. In the following illustrations, note that numbers 20–22 are made in a different manner from numbers 23–29.

> **ASL TIP**
>
> **Numbers 23 and 25**
>
> Numbers 23 and 25 can also be signed differently. For 23, you can hold the handshape 3 with your palm facing out and wiggle your middle finger down. For 25, you can do the same but with a 5 handshape.

TWENTY   **TWENTY-ONE**

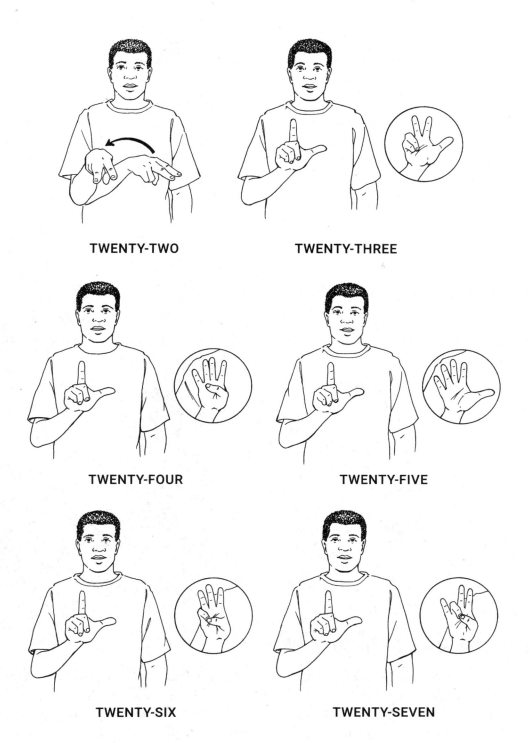

TWENTY-TWO

TWENTY-THREE

TWENTY-FOUR

TWENTY-FIVE

TWENTY-SIX

TWENTY-SEVEN

TWENTY-EIGHT   TWENTY-NINE

Numbers 22, 33, 44 . . . 99

For double-digit numbers in which both of the digits are the same, the hand bounces once toward the side of the body with the palm facing slightly down. In other words, one number is repeated.

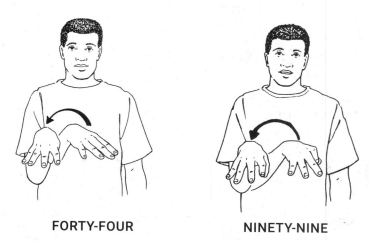

FORTY-FOUR   NINETY-NINE

Other Numbers from 30 to 98

All other numbers from 30 to 98 are made by signing the first digit and then the second digit of the number. For these numbers, the palm of the hand always faces away from the signer. For numbers 67–69, 76–79, 86–89, and 96–98, the hand twists upward when the second digit is higher than the first digit (78) and twists downward when the first digit is higher than the second digit (96).

Addresses and Phone Numbers

You sign numbers in addresses and phone numbers in the same manner that you say them in English.

When to Break the 1–5 Palm-Facing Rule

When signing phone numbers, addresses, or anything more than a single number of 1–5, your palm faces away from you for the numbers 1–5.

Keep the rule; palm faces body. Example sentence:

BOOK, THREE HAVE

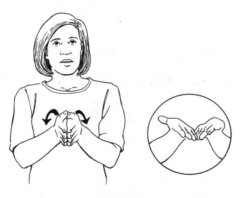

BOOK

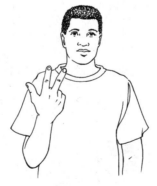

THREE

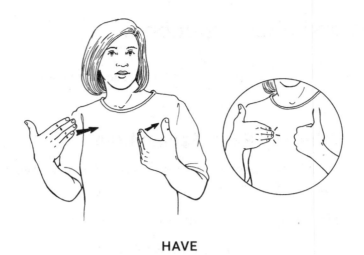

HAVE

I have three books.

Break the rule; palm faces out. Example sentence:

PHONE NUMBER WHAT? 555-383-6071

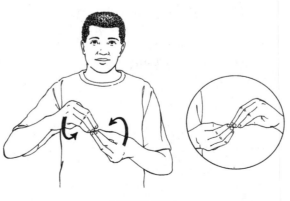

PHONE

NUMBER

WHAT

Now sign the provided phone number, palm facing out.

The phone number is 555-383-6071.

Hundreds, Thousands, Millions, and Beyond

The following illustrations show the general signs for HUNDRED, THOUSAND, and MILLION.

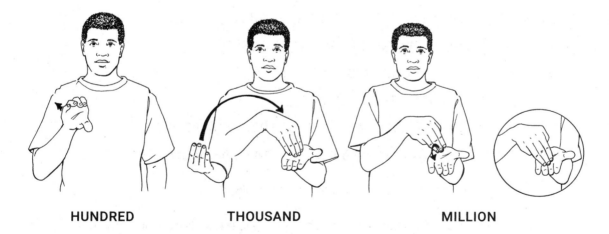

HUNDRED   **THOUSAND**   **MILLION**

You might have noticed that the sign HUNDRED is made with a C handshape, which is the Latin letter for *hundred*. Note that the sign MILLION is simply repeating the sign THOUSAND once, which represents the concept of 1,000 × 1,000, which equals 1,000,000. It is also acceptable to fingerspell M-I -L-L-I -O-N.

Would you believe that the sign BILLION is made by repeating the sign THOUSAND twice to get 1,000 × 1,000 × 1,000, which is 1,000,000,000? It is. But this is the end of using the sign THOUSAND to represent numbers. To sign larger numbers that are beyond billions, you must fingerspell the name for the larger number. For example, 3,000,000,000,000 is signed by first signing the number 3 and then fingerspelling T-R-I-L-L-I-O-N. It is also acceptable to fingerspell B-I-L-L-I-O-N.

All numbers signed from 100 and up are mostly made with your palm facing outward (with the exception of numbers 11–15).

ASL TIP

Large Number Trick
Large numbers are signed in the same way that you say them in English. As you practice signing the numbers in the practice activity, say them out loud in English first, then sign them while quietly saying them in English in your head. For example, 34,589 is signed as 34 THOUSAND 5 HUNDRED 89.

 Chapter Review

1. Sign the following numbers.

   2; 3; 6; 13; 19; 11; 5; 14; 15; 9; 12; 8; 10; 1; 17; 18

   16; 48; 21; 33; 79; 88; 92; 65; 54; 97; 67; 83; 4; 20; 80

   382; 973; 147; 583; 990; 481; 609; 355; 111; 225

   9,940; 28,408; 777,594; 17,003; 458,762

   3,000,857; 574,389,338; 66,999,515; 478,000,000; 987,488,223

   2,385; 13; 74,908; 20,747; 91; 54,893,894; 309,475; 88; 160; 57,081

2. Give two examples of when the palm rule is broken.

3. Describe the "trick" for making sure you sign large numbers correctly, then practice this out loud with large numbers.

4. Practice signing the following phone numbers:

   555-328-2348

   800-934-1092

   888-342-6501

   1-800-234-0025

   1-888-361-2647

5. Fingerspell these addresses:

   4619 East Woodward Avenue, Elora, Ontario N8K 3D8

   3140 Brookside Lane, Suite J-8, El Paso, Texas 98927

   218 North Lexington Street, Redondo Beach, California 49283

 Video Quiz Visit online.barronsbooks.com for scored practice on numbers, phone numbers, and addresses.

CHAPTER 6

Everyday ASL

Learning Objectives

In this chapter, you will learn:

○ How to apply the following grammar rules to create sentences: topic/comment, information-seeking questions, simple yes/no questions, rhetorical questions, long yes/no questions, ordering of simple sentences, tense with time adverbs

○ How to use new signs in everyday conversations and to describe feelings

○ How to use new signs relating to major and minor courses of study in schools, colleges, or universities

○ The correct usage of nonmanual signals in sentences that correspond to grammar rules

○ The directional verb sign me-MEET-you

○ How to respond affirmatively to a yes/no question

○ How to use correct procedures for indicating the time

LESSON 1: GETTING STARTED

Signing Dialogue

1. **Celia:** **EXCUSE-me, ME NAME C-E-L-I -A. NAME YOU?**

   Excuse me, I'm Celia, what's your name?

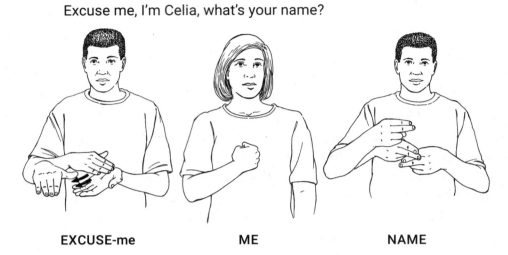

EXCUSE-me   ME   NAME

NAME   YOU

2. **Liz:** **ME L-I-Z. NICE me-MEET-you.**

I'm Liz. It is nice to meet you.

ME   NICE   me-MEET-you

3. **Celia:** **NICE me-MEET-you. YOU TAKE-UP A-S-L?**

It's nice to meet you. Are you taking ASL?

NICE   me-MEET-you   YOU

TAKE-UP   ASL

4. **Liz:** **YES, ME TAKE-UP ASL. YOU?**

Yes, I am taking ASL. How about you?

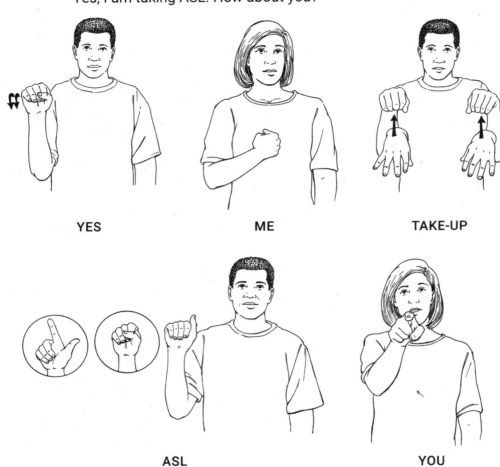

YES · ME · TAKE-UP

ASL · YOU

5. **Celia:** **SAME-HERE (me-SAME-you). ME TAKE-UP ASL.**

Same as you, I'm taking ASL, too.

SAME-HERE (me-SAME-you) · ME · TAKE-UP

ASL

Breaking Down the Dialogue

Topic/Comment and Information-seeking Questions

EXCUSE-me, ME NAME C-E-L-I -A. NAME YOU?

There are three parts to this sentence.

The first part is a form of common courtesy, used when attempting to get someone's attention:

EXCUSE-me

The signer does not sign the object of the sentence, which is *me*. The object is implied from the context of the sentence. The English translation of the phrase is simply "Excuse me." If the signer wishes to refer to an object other than herself or himself, then the object must be signed.

The second part of the sentence:

ME NAME C-E-L-I -A

is an example of a simple topic/comment sentence structure.

topic:	ME NAME
comment:	C-E-L-I -A.
translation:	My name is Celia.

The use of the sign ME when introducing oneself may be confusing to English speakers who are accustomed to using *my*, the possessive form of *me*, when referring to things that belong to them. It is still correct ASL to sign MY NAME. You are introduced to the phrase ME NAME in the dialogue because it is commonly used in the Deaf community. Learn and practice this phrase to help you begin to think in ASL.

The third part of the sentence is a demonstration of a question that seeks information:

NAME YOU?

This translates as "What is your name?" The pronoun can also be placed at the beginning of the phrase, YOU NAME? What is most important about this sentence is the nonmanual signals or the facial grammar that accompanies the sentence.

Simple Yes/No Questions

An example of a simple yes/no question is shown in the following sentence:

YOU TAKE-UP ASL?

When this sentence is signed with the appropriate nonmanual signal, its English translation is "Are you taking ASL?"

The sign YOU is used in the dialogue to ask a simple yes/no question in the following sentence:

YES, ME TAKE-UP ASL. YOU?

The signer is saying that she or he is taking ASL. The topic of the sentence then becomes "taking ASL." The sign YOU asks a question about the topic. The sign YOU? can be translated into "How about you?" or, more specifically, "Are you taking ASL?"

Introductions

In the dialogue, Liz signs

ME L-I-Z. NICE me-MEET-you.

The first part of this sentence:

ME L-I-Z

is a response to the question NAME YOU? The signer simply fingerspells her first name. If the last name is also fingerspelled, then the signer should pause slightly after fingerspelling the first name.

The second part of this sentence:

NICE me-MEET-you

is a common form of courtesy that a person uses when introduced to someone. Using the lowercase for the pronouns *me* and *you* in the sign me-MEET-you means that they are not signed directly. Rather, they are implied in the direction in which the sign is moved. The sign MEET is called a *directional verb sign*.

Responding Affirmatively to a Yes/No Question

To respond affirmatively to a yes/no question, the signer can sign YES directly, as in the sentence

YES, ME TAKE-UP ASL.

In this sentence, the signer also repeats the topic of the question—ME TAKE-UP ASL. The signer could also nod when signing YES or simply nod and not sign YES.

Facial Grammar/Nonmanual Signals

See "Facial Grammar" in Chapter 3 to review the appropriate nonmanual signals to use with the following sentence structures:

1. Topic/comment
2. Yes/no questions
3. Information-seeking questions

What's the Sign?

EXCUSE-me

A common error made by beginning signers is to sign ME when making the sign EXCUSE-me. The sign ME should *not* be signed. The illustration for the sign EXCUSE-me shows one hand brushing across the other hand twice. This is the general manner in which this sign is made. However, it is common practice to brush the hand several times and in some cases to continue making the sign until a desired result is achieved. The repeated brushing of the hand is used, for example, when a person must pass between two or more people carrying on a conversation in signs.

ASL

ASL is the abbreviated form for American Sign Language. The arm should not move when forming the handshapes A, S, and L.

me-MEET-you

The general sign for MEET has the two hands moving from the side of the signing space to the center where they meet. For the sign me-MEET-you, also called a *directional sign*, one hand is held away and to the front of your body while the other hand is held in front of your body. The hand by the body then moves out to meet the other hand, which is held stationary. The following illustrations show the difference between MEET and MEET-you:

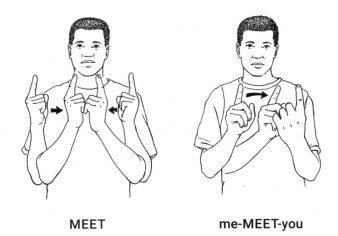

MEET   me-MEET-you

What would the meaning of the sign be if the hand that is held away from the body moved to meet the hand that is held stationary by the body? The answer is you-MEET-me. The direction in which the sign moves indicates the subject and the object of the sentence. We can show this relationship by writing:

subject-VERB-object

a. me-MEET-you

b. you-MEET-me

SAME-HERE

When making the sign SAME-HERE, your thumb should be pointed toward your chest and your little finger should be pointed toward the person with whom you are indicating agreement. Do not flip your wrist back and forth like the "hang loose" universal sign used in Hawaii; rather, move your arm back and forth with a stiff wrist.

ASL Synonyms

Some signs can be used to mean other things.

Sign	Also used for
ASL	AMERICAN-SIGN-LANGUAGE
EXCUSE-me	FORGIVE
NICE	CLEAN
SAME-HERE	ME-TOO, SAME-as-you, me-SAME-as-you
TAKE-UP	ADOPT

Practice Activities

1. PRACTICE TOPIC/COMMENT AND INFORMATION-SEEKING QUESTIONS

   NOTE: Always practice correct facial grammar.

Practice Signing with a Partner

Signer A:	ME NAME (fingerspells name). NAME YOU?
Signer B:	ME NAME (fingerspells name).
Signer A:	NICE me-MEET-you.
Signer B:	NICE me-MEET-you.

2. Practice this SIMPLE YES/NO QUESTION

Practice

Signer A:	YOU TAKE-UP A-S-L?
Signer B:	YES, ME TAKE-UP A-S-L. YOU?
Signer A:	SAME-HERE. ME TAKE-UP A-S-L.

3. When you feel comfortable signing these phrases, practice signing the entire dialogue shown at the beginning of the lesson. Practice the dialogue until you can sign the part of each character smoothly while using the appropriate facial grammar. Change the names to people you know for more fingerspelling practice.

4. Practice asking people their names using the following sentence:

   EXCUSE-ME, ME NAME (spell your name), NAME YOU?

   (Spell the other person's name), NICE me-MEET-you.

LESSON 2: LEARNING ASL

Signing Dialogue

1. **Elsie:** **YOU TAKE-UP ASL WHY?**

   Why are you taking ASL?

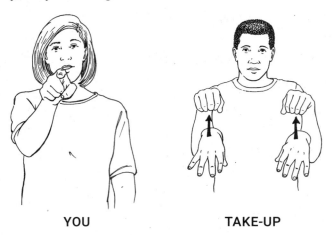

YOU   TAKE-UP

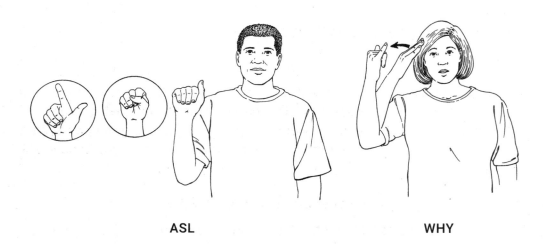

ASL   WHY

2. **Diane:** **ME TAKE-UP ASL WHY? ME ENJOY.**

I am taking ASL because I enjoy it.

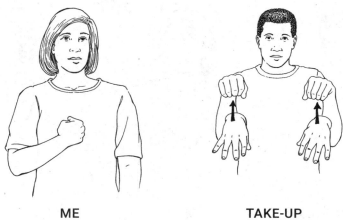

ME   TAKE-UP

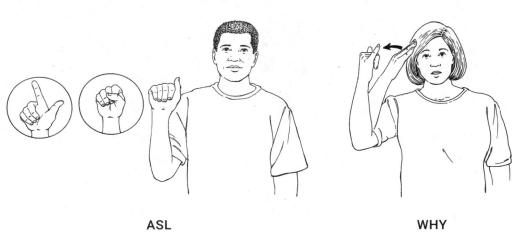

ASL   WHY

ME   ENJOY

3. **Elsie:**   **SAME. ME SIGN, ME FEEL GOOD.**

The same with me, I feel good when I sign.

SAME (me-SAME-you)   ME   SIGN

ME   FEEL   GOOD

4. **Diane:**   **YOU MORE ASL LEARN, READY YOU?**

Are you ready to learn more ASL?

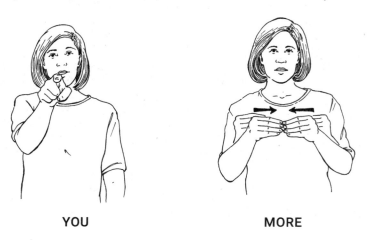

YOU   MORE

ASL   LEARN

READY   YOU

5. **Elsie:**   **YES, ME READY. YOU?**

Yes, I'm ready. How about you?

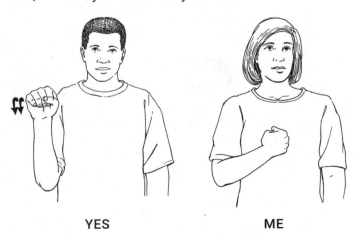

YES   ME

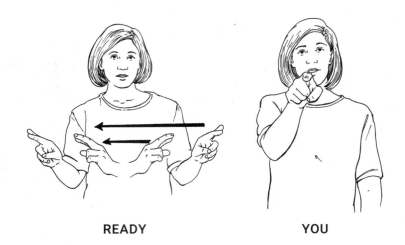

READY · YOU

6. **Diane:** **LEARN MORE ASL, ME READY ALWAYS.**

I am always ready to learn more ASL.

LEARN · MORE

ASL · ME

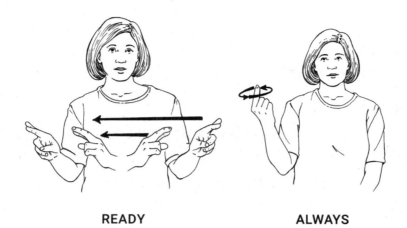

READY ALWAYS

7. **Elsie:** **ME AGREE.**

I agree with that.

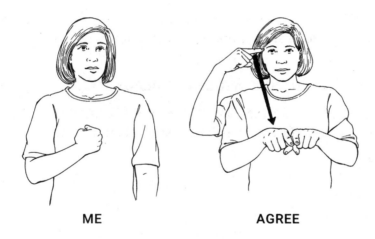

ME AGREE

Breaking Down the Dialogue

Information-seeking Questions

When asking a wh-question, the wh-sign is commonly placed at the end of the sentence.

YOU TAKE-UP ASL WHY?

First, the signer describes the topic and then adds the wh-sign at the end of the sentence.

topic:	YOU TAKE UP ASL
question:	WHY?

Nonmanual signals:

1. *the squeezed eyebrows*
2. *the head tilted forward slightly*

Rhetorical Questions

In the dialogue, Tina responds to the question YOU TAKE-UP ASL WHY? with the following rhetorical question and answer:

ME TAKE-UP ASL WHY? ME ENJOY.

Nonmanual signals:

1. *tilts the head forward*
2. *raises the eyebrows*

Long Yes/No Questions

The sign READY can be used to ask a simple question that was demonstrated in the dialogue:

YOU MORE ASL LEARN, READY YOU?

The question has two parts. In the first part, YOU MORE ASL LEARN, the signer describes the topic. In the second part, the signer asks a question about the topic, READY YOU?

Nonmanual signals:

1. *tilts the head forward*
2. *raises the eyebrows*

Topic/Comment

The topic/comment sentence structure was used twice in the dialogue:

ME SIGN, ME FEEL GOOD.

LEARN MORE ASL, ME READY ALWAYS.

Breaking them down we get

Topic	Comment	Translation
ME SIGN,	ME FEEL GOOD.	I feel good when I sign.
LEARN MORE ASL,	ME READY ALWAYS.	I am always ready to learn more ASL.

The facial grammar accompanying the sentence helps the addressee clearly identify the topic of the sentence.

Nonmanual signals:

1. *maintain eye contact with the person being addressed*
2. *raise the eyebrows and tilt the head slightly forward when signing the topic*
3. *hold the last sign of the topic a little longer than the other signs*
4. *pause slightly between signing the topic and the comment*

What's the Sign?

ALWAYS

The sign ALWAYS is often placed at the end of a sentence because it is usually making a comment about a topic. By placing it at the end of the sentence, its importance to the meaning of the sentence is emphasized.

GOOD

Signs that indicate feelings or emotions, such as GOOD and ENJOY, are often accompanied by nonmanual signals that reinforce the feelings being expressed. For example, if you are feeling good, then this should easily be detected from your facial expression.

FEEL

The sign FEEL is made either with a single movement up the chest or a double movement. Some signers will use a single movement when stating how they feel ("I feel dizzy") and a double movement when inquiring how someone else feels ("How do you feel?").

ASL Synonyms

Some signs can be used to mean other things.

Sign	Also used for
ENJOY	PLEASURE, PLEASANT
GOOD	WELL
LEARN	ACQUIRE

 Practice Activities

1. MODEL FOR INFORMATION-SEEKING QUESTIONS AND RHETORICAL QUESTIONS

Signer A: 1.   Describe the topic;
            2.   use a wh-sign to ask a question about the topic.

   Topic: YOU TAKE-UP ASL
   Question: WHY?

Signer B: 1.   Repeat the wh-question to form a rhetorical wh-question;
            2.   answer the question.

   Rhetorical question: ME TAKE-UP ASL WHY?
   Answer: ME ENJOY.

Signer A: 1.   Acknowledge the answer with a remark.

   Remark: SAME

Practice Short Conversations

Signer A: YOU TAKE-UP ASL WHY?

Signer B: ME TAKE-UP ASL WHY? ME ENJOY.

Signer A: SAME.

2. MODEL FOR SIMPLE YES/NO QUESTIONS

Signer A: 1. Describe the topic;

           2. ask a yes/no question about the topic using READY.

           Topic: YOU MORE ASL LEARN,

           Question: READY YOU?

Signer B: 1. Answer the question affirmatively.

           Answer: YES, ME READY.

Practice Short Conversations

Signer A: YOU MORE ASL LEARN, READY YOU?

Signer B: YES, ME READY.

3. MODEL TOPIC/COMMENT

Signer: 1. Describe the topic while using nonmanual signals to highlight the topic;

           2. sign the comment related to the topic.

           Topic: ME SIGN,

           Comment: ME FEEL GOOD.

Practice

Signer: ME SIGN, ME FEEL GOOD.

Signer A: 1. Describe the topic using nonmanual signals to highlight the topic;

           2. sign the comment related to the topic.

           Topic: LEARN MORE ASL,

           Comment: ME READY ALWAYS.

Signer B: 1. Make a remark about the comment.

           Remark: ME AGREE.

Practice

Signer A:	LEARN MORE ASL, ME READY ALWAYS.
Signer B:	ME AGREE.

4. MASTERY LEARNING

When you feel comfortable signing these phrases, practice signing the entire dialogue shown at the beginning of this lesson. Be sure to include the appropriate nonmanual signals. Practice the dialogue until you can sign each character smoothly. Practice alone or with a partner.

5. FURTHER PRACTICE

Create three of your own dialogues using the signs you have learned so far. Keep the sentences and dialogue short, and then practice signing them. Write the approximate English translation for your dialogue, then practice signing alone or with a partner. For example:

Signer A:	ME FEEL GOOD. YOU?
	I feel good. How about you?
Signer B:	SAME. NAME YOU?
	The same with me. What's your name?
Signer A:	ME NAME D-O-N-T-E. YOU?
	My name is Donté. What's your name?
Signer B:	K-E-L-L-I -E. NICE me-MEET-you.
	Kellie. It is nice to meet you.

LESSON 3: COURTESY PHRASES

Signing Dialogue

1. **Carlee:** **HOW YOU?**

   How are you?

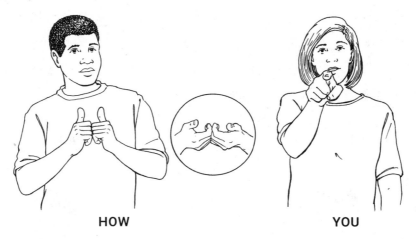

HOW   YOU

2. **Tucker:** **FINE. YOU?**

   I am fine. How about you?

FINE   YOU

3. **Carlee:** **FINE. ASL CLASS WHERE?**

I am fine. Where is the ASL class?

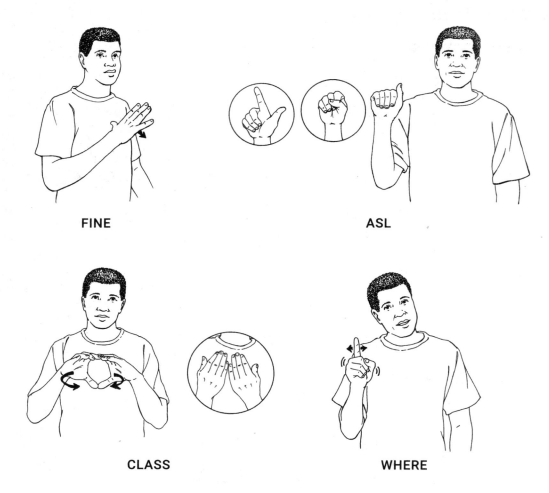

4. **Tucker:** **ASL CLASS WHERE? ROOM NUMBER 4.**

The ASL class is in room number 4.

WHERE   ROOM

NUMBER   FOUR

5.   **Carlee: ROOM 5?**

Room 5?

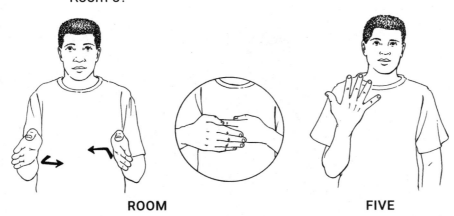

ROOM   FIVE

6. **Tucker:**   **NO. ROOM 4.**

    No. Room 4.

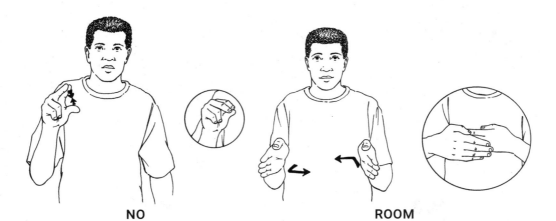

NO   ROOM

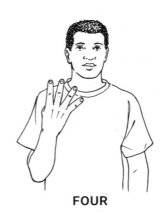

FOUR

7. **Carlee:**   **THANK-YOU.**

    Thank you.

THANK-YOU

8.   **Tucker:**   **WELCOME (or THANK-YOU). SEE-YOU-LATER.**

You're welcome. See you later.

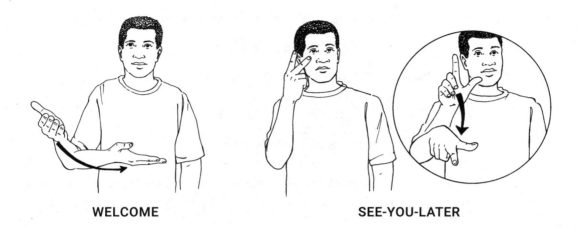

WELCOME   SEE-YOU-LATER

ASL TIP

WELCOME

The sign WELCOME is used for "you're welcome" in a formal setting. It is also acceptable to sign for THANK-YOU, FINE, and SURE in response to THANK-YOU.

Breaking Down the Dialogue

Information-seeking Questions

The dialogue introduces the use of the sign WHERE in the following wh-question:

ASL CLASS WHERE?

The signer describes the topic and asks a question about it.

topic:	ASL CLASS
question:	WHERE?

The nonmanual signals for a wh-question are applied here. The dialogue also introduces the common courtesy question "How are you?" which is signed as HOW YOU? and the common response, FINE.

Rhetorical Questions

In a rhetorical question, the signer asks a question and then answers it as in the following:

ASL CLASS WHERE? ROOM NUMBER 4.

Although the sign WHERE is in the ASL sentence, it does not appear in the English translation. To translate to English, a person must first observe the entire expression and then translate the sense of the ASL meaning into English. In this sentence, the sense relates to the room in which the ASL class is. Therefore, a proper English translation directly points this out, "The ASL class is in room number 4." Recall that the correct nonmanual signals for rhetorical questions with wh-signs are different than the nonmanual signals used for wh-questions and other information-seeking questions.

Simple Yes/No Questions

A simple question is asked simply by (1) *raising the eyebrows* and (2) *tilting the head forward* when signing.

ROOM 5?

What's the Sign?

THANK-YOU

A common error when signing THANK-YOU is to add the sign YOU. This is not only unnecessary but can be confusing. The meaning is vague in the following sentence:

THANK-YOU, YOU.

It reads like an incomplete sentence. Another signer would look at this and wonder what was supposed to come after the sign YOU.

WELCOME

The English translation of WELCOME is either "welcome" or "you're welcome" depending upon the context of the sentence. It is not necessary to add the sign YOU or YOU'RE before WELCOME because the pronoun *you* is already a part of the sign WELCOME.

SEE-YOU-LATER

This sign is a modification of three signs—SEE, YOU, and LATER. The sign YOU is dropped as you develop fluency in signing this phrase.

Numbers 1–5

For counting, the numbers 1–5 are typically formed with the palm of the hand facing toward the signer's body. However, when signing a phone number, the numbers are all signed with the palm facing out.

ASL Synonyms

Some signs can be used to mean other things.

Sign	Also used for
CLASS	CATEGORY
ROOM	BOX
THANK-YOU	THANK, THANKS
WELCOME	YOU'RE-WELCOME

Practice Activities

1. MODEL FOR USING COURTESY PHRASES

Signer A:	1.	Use a courtesy question to ask how a person is.

Courtesy question: HOW YOU?

Signer B:	1.	Respond to the question with a common courtesy sign;
	2.	repeat the courtesy question by just signing YOU?

Response: FINE.
Courtesy question: YOU?

Signer A:	1.	Respond to the question with a common courtesy sign.

Response: FINE.

Practice

Signer A: HOW YOU?
Signer B: FINE. YOU?
Signer A: FINE.

2. MODEL FOR INFORMATION-SEEKING QUESTIONS AND RHETORICAL QUESTIONS

Signer A:	1.	Describe the topic you want to ask a question about;
	2.	sign the wh-sign WHERE.

Topic: ASL CLASS
Question: WHERE?

Signer A:	1.	Repeat the wh-question to form a rhetorical wh-question;
	2.	answer the question.

Rhetorical question: ASL CLASS WHERE?
Answer: ROOM NUMBER 4.

Practice

Signer A: ASL CLASS WHERE?
Signer B: ASL CLASS WHERE? ROOM NUMBER 4.

3. MODEL FOR SIMPLE YES/NO QUESTIONS

Signer A:	1.	Ask a yes/no question about the room number.

Question: ROOM 5?

Signer B:	1.	Respond negatively to the question;
	2.	state the room number.

Negative: NO.
Statement: ROOM 4.

Signer A:	1.	Acknowledge the answer with a courtesy remark.

Remark: THANK-YOU.

Signer B:	1.	Acknowledge the courtesy remark with another one;
	2.	sign a remark commonly used when departing company.

Remark: THANK-YOU.
Remark: SEE-YOU-LATER.

Practice

Signer A:	ROOM 5?
Signer B:	NO. ROOM 4.
Signer A:	THANK-YOU.
Signer B:	SEE-YOU-LATER.

Repeat practice: Repeat this exercise replacing the number 4 with the numbers 1, 2, 3, and 5.

4. MASTERY LEARNING

When you feel comfortable signing these phrases, practice signing the entire dialogue shown at the beginning of this lesson. Practice the dialogue until you can sign the part of each character smoothly. Pay particular attention to the nonmanual signals you use to accompany each phrase you sign. It is better to exaggerate your facial expressions slightly than to project none at all or to project one that is inappropriate for the sentence being signed.

5. FURTHER PRACTICE

Create your own dialogue using the signs you have learned in previous lessons. Keep the sentences short and write an English translation for your dialogue. Practice signing your dialogue with a partner.

LESSON 4: DESCRIPTIVE SIGNS

Signing Dialogue

1. **Milly:**   **FEEL+ YOU?**

    How are you feeling?

FEEL   YOU

2. **Charly: ME FEEL SATISFIED. FEEL+ YOU?**

I'm feeling satisfied. How do you feel?

ME   FEEL

SATISFIED   FEEL   YOU

3. **Milly:**   **HUNGRY.**

      I'm hungry.

HUNGRY

Plus the following thirty adjectives or signs for feelings:

Sign:	**Also used for:**
ANGRY	ANGER, FURY, RAGE, WRATH

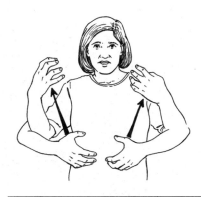

ASHAMED	SHAME

BAD	NAUGHTY

Sign: **Also used for:**

BORED/BORING

COLD   WINTER, CHILLY

COMFORTABLE   CONVENIENT

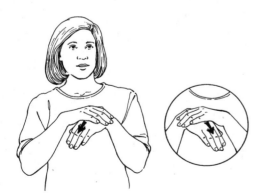

Sign:

Also used for:

CRAZY

DAFT, LUNATIC

DEPRESSED

DEVASTATED,
DESPONDENT, DOWNCAST

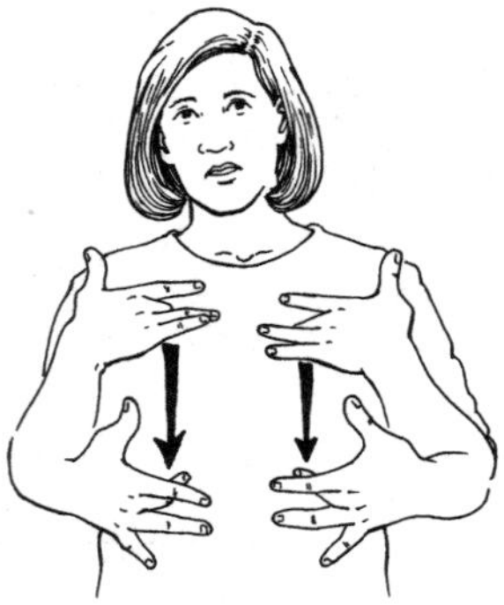

DUMB

DOLT, IDIOT, MORON, OAF,
STUPID

Sign:	**Also used for:**

EMBARRASSED

FLUSTERED, HUMILIATED

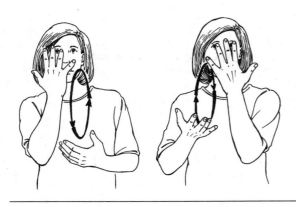

ENTHUSIASTIC

EAGER, ZEAL, MOTIVATED

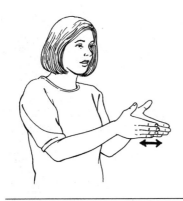

EXCITED

AGITATED, ECSTATIC, EXCITING, THRILLED

Sign:	**Also used for:**

FRUSTRATED

FRUSTRATE, FRUSTRATION

(repeating small movement, up to the mouth)

FUNNY

HUMOR

(slightly brush fingers down tip of nose)

HAPPY

GLAD, JOY

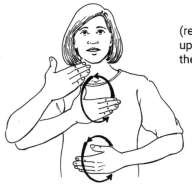

(repeating movement, upward and outward on the chest)

Sign: **Also used for:**

HOT

HUMBLE   MEEK, MODEST, UNASSUMING

JEALOUS   ENVIOUS

Sign: **Also used for:**

LAZY

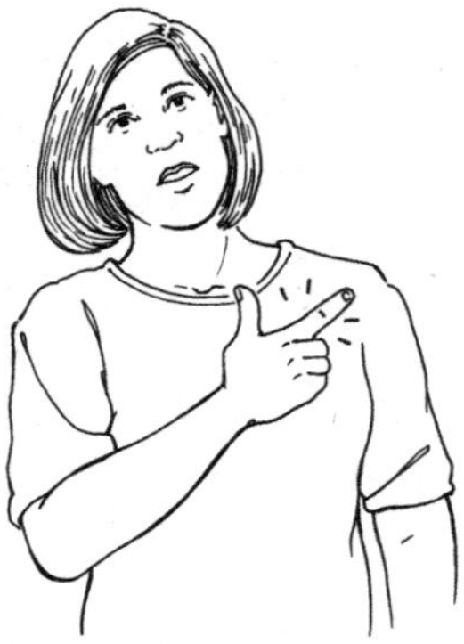

LONELY   LONESOME

LOUSY

Sign:

Also used for:

LUCKY

FORTUITOUS, FORTUNATE

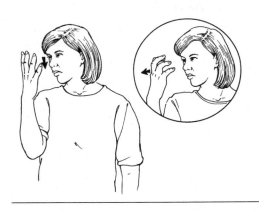

MAD

ANGRY, CROSS, GROUCHY

SAD

DISMAL, DREARY, GLOOMY, MOROSE, SORROWFUL, UNFORTUNATE

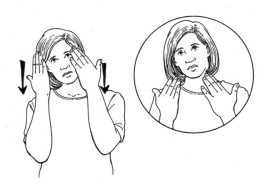

Sign:  **Also used for:**

SCARED   AFRAID, FRIGHTENED

SHOCKED   ASTOUNDED, HORRIFIED, STARTLED

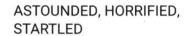

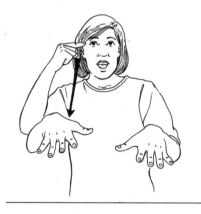

SHY   BASHFUL, RETICENT, TIMID

Sign:

Also used for:

SLEEPY

SO-SO

FAIR

Sign:	**Also used for:**
STRANGE	BIZARRE, ODD, PECULIAR, UNUSUAL

TERRIBLE	APPALLING, AWFUL, DREADFUL, FRIGHTFUL, HORRIBLE

TERRIFIC	EXCELLENT, FABULOUS, FANTASTIC, GREAT, MARVELOUS, SUPER, WONDERFUL

ASL TIP

Sign Production Variations

Sign production variations exist due to numerous factors, such as age, gender, socioeconomic status, and more. The sign illustration above for TERRIBLE may sign TERRIBLE lower and with one hand, versus two.

THIRSTY THIRST

TIRED   EXHAUSTED, FATIGUED

WARM   TEPID

Nonmanual Signs for TIRED
The nonmanual signals that accompany the sign TIRED are puffed cheeks and shoulders that slouch. Other nonmanual signals for these "feeling signs" include natural body movements and facial expressions. Example: For EXCITED, look excited!

Breaking Down the Dialogue

Information-seeking Questions

A simple question asking about how a person is feeling can be formed using the sign FEEL, as shown in the following:

FEEL+ YOU?

The plus sign (+) after the sign FEEL means to repeat the sign. To express the appropriate nonmanual signals (1) *the head tilts forward* and (2) *the eyebrows squeeze together*.

Ordering of Simple Sentences

In response to the question FEEL+ YOU? a simple sentence following a subject-verb-adverb structure can be used to get the following:

ME FEEL SATISFIED.

It is not necessary to sign the subject and the verb in response to a question about how you feel. Because the question is directed at you, you can simply respond by stating how you feel as Milly did in the dialogue:

HUNGRY.

What's the Sign?

FEEL

The sign for FEEL is made with one movement of the middle finger moving up the middle of the chest.

FUNNY

The sign for FUNNY can also use a repeated motion. When the sign is made with a slow, single motion, it means STRANGE as in "I feel strange" or "That's strange."

Practice Activity

In the dialogue, substitute adjectives from the signs introduced in this lesson. You should match your facial expression with the feelings that the adjective indicates. Practice signing each adjective in a dialogue until you feel comfortable that you can match the sign with the appropriate facial expression.

Signer A:	FEEL+ YOU?
Signer B:	ME FEEL **SATISFIED**. FEEL+ YOU?
Signer A:	**HUNGRY**.

LESSON 5: TAKING CLASSES

Signing Dialogue

1. **Eboni:** **HELLO. WHAT'S-UP?**

   Hello, what's up?

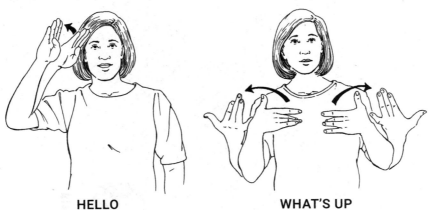

HELLO   WHAT'S UP

183

2. **Amal:** **HI. NOW ME CLASS GO-to.**

Hi. I am going to my class now.

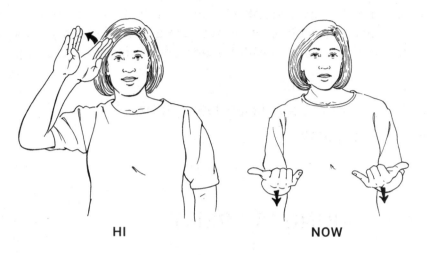

HI   NOW

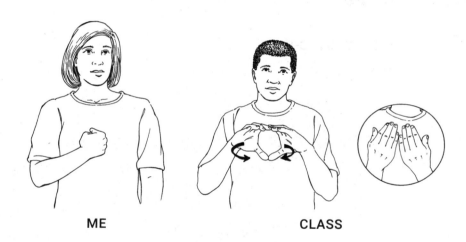

ME   CLASS

GO-TO

3. **Eboni:** **REALLY? YOU MORNING CLASS NAME?**

Is that so? What is the name of your morning class?

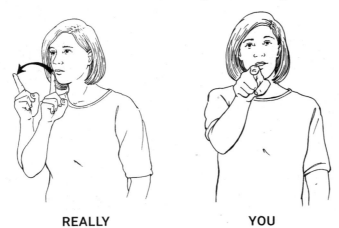

REALLY   YOU

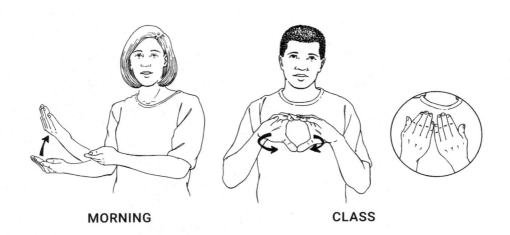

MORNING   CLASS

NAME

4. **Amal:** **MY MORNING CLASS NAME? SCIENCE.**

The name of my morning class is Science.

MY

MORNING

CLASS

NAME

SCIENCE

5. **Eboni:** **YOU TAKE-UP SCIENCE, ME SURPRISED.**

I am surprised that you are taking science.

YOU

TAKE-UP

SCIENCE

ME

SURPRISED

6. **Amal:** **YOU SURPRISED, WHY?**

Why are you surprised?

YOU   SURPRISED

WHY

7. **Eboni:** **ME TAKE-UP SCIENCE, me-SAME-as-you.**

I am taking science, too.

ME   TAKE-UP

SCIENCE   SAME-HERE (me-SAME-you)

8. **Amal:** **REALLY? TWO-of-us TAKE-UP SCIENCE, WONDERFUL.**

Is that so? That's wonderful that the two of us are taking science.

REALLY

TWO-of-us

TAKE-UP

SCIENCE

WONDERFUL

Breaking Down the Dialogue

Initiating a Conversation

The sign WHAT'S-UP is commonly used to initiate a conversation or to inquire about what's happening. It is typically signed all by itself

WHAT'S-UP?

and is translated as "What's up?" or "What's happening?"

Ordering of Simple Sentences

Some simple sentences can have a subject-object-verb (SOV) or a subject-verb-object (SVO) word order as in the following sentence:

a. ME CLASS GO-to.

b. ME GO-to CLASS.

The meaning of both phrases is "I am going to class." The meaning usually does not change with the placement of the GO-to sign. A signer might place a key sign at the end of the sentence if she or he wishes to emphasize that concept. If a signer wishes to emphasize the action verb GO-to, then sentence a should be used. Likewise, if CLASS is being emphasized, then sentence b would be appropriate.

Information-seeking Questions

A signer creates a wh-question by setting up the topic and then using a wh-sign to ask a question about the topic. This is seen in the questions YOU MORNING CLASS NAME? and YOU SURPRISED, WHY?

topic:	YOU MORNING CLASS
question:	NAME?

The nonmanual signals are the same as for information-seeking questions—(1) *the eyebrows are squeezed* and (2) *the head is tilted forward.*

Tense with Time Adverbs

In the sentence

NOW ME CLASS GO-to.

the time frame is established by placing the time adverb NOW at the beginning of the sentence. A proper translation of this sentence is "I am going to class now."

Rhetorical Questions

In the dialogue, Amal asks a question and then responds to it:

MY MORNING CLASS NAME? SCIENCE.

Topic/Comment

With the following sentence structure

YOU TAKE-UP SCIENCE, ME SURPRISED.

the signer describes the topic and then makes a comment about it, as shown in the following sentence:

topic:	YOU TAKE-UP SCIENCE,
comment:	ME SURPRISED.
translation:	I am surprised that you are taking science.

In ASL, events are typically laid out in the order that they occur. In the preceding sentence, Eboni was surprised only after she had found out that someone was taking science. Therefore, the comment ME SURPRISED comes at the end of the sentence. Two more examples of the topic/comment structure are in the following dialogue:

Topic	Comment	Translation
ME TAKE-UP SCIENCE,	me-SAME-as-you.	I am taking science, too.
TWO-of-us TAKE-UP SCIENCE,	WONDERFUL.	That's wonderful that the two of us are taking science.

What's the Sign?

GO-to

Which direction should the hands move when signing GO-to? The sign GO-to is typically moved forward to the right or left side of the body. Where it is moved will establish the location of the object of the sentence. In the sentence

ME CLASS GO-to.

you might sign GO-to to the left side of the body. This action places the object of the sentence, CLASS, to the left of the body. Future references to CLASS will always be to the left of the body until you change the location of CLASS. ASL grammar is dependent upon where signs are made in the signing space. Thus, how the hands are moved for the sign GO-to can be important in telling the meaning of a sentence.

REALLY

The translation of the sign REALLY depends upon the dialogue. The same sign is used for the signs REAL, TRUE, SURE, and CERTAIN, among others. In the dialogue, the sign REALLY could have been translated as "Is that a fact?" which has the same meaning in English as "Is that so?"

TWO-of-us

The sign for TWO-of-us is an example of Rule #6, pronominalization. To make this sign, the 2 handshape is moved between the signer and one other person. This other person might be present physically as she is in the dialogue, or the person might just exist in the signing space. The movement of the 2 handshape is not random. The hand is usually twisted so that the middle finger points toward the signer and the index finger points toward the other person. Depending on the context, this sign can be translated to mean "both of us," "you and I," and "we."

me-TOO

This sign is made in the same way as the sign SAME-HERE.

ASL Synonyms

Some signs can be used to mean other things.

Sign	Also used for
MY	MINE
NOW	PRESENTLY, TODAY
REALLY	CERTAIN, CERTAINLY, REAL, SURE, SURELY, TRUE, TRULY, VERY
SURPRISED	AMAZED, SHOCKED
WHAT'S-UP?	WHAT'S-HAPPENING?
WONDERFUL	AMAZING, EXCELLENT, FABULOUS, FANTASTIC, GREAT, MARVELOUS, SUPER, TERRIFIC

Practice Activities

1. MODEL FOR INITIATING A CONVERSATION AND TENSE WITH TIME ADVERBS

Signer A: 1.   Sign a greeting;

                 2.   use the sign WHAT'S-UP to ask a question.

Greeting:	HELLO.
Question:	WHAT'S-UP?

Signer B: 1.   Sign a greeting;

                 2.   establish the tense of the sentence with a time adverb;

                 3.   describe an action.

Greeting:	HI.
Tense:	NOW
Action:	ME CLASS GO-to.

Practice

Signer A:	HELLO. WHAT'S-UP?
Signer B:	HI. NOW ME CLASS GO-to.

2. MODEL FOR TENSE WITH TIME ADVERBS, INFORMATION-SEEKING QUESTIONS, AND RHETORICAL QUESTIONS

Signer A: 1.   Describe the topic you want to ask a question about;

                 2.   make the sign asking the question.

Topic:	YOU MORNING CLASS
Question:	NAME?

Signer B: Ask a rhetorical question by repeating the question;

                  answer the question.

Rhetorical question:	MY MORNING CLASS NAME?
Answer:	SCIENCE.

Practice

Signer A:	YOU MORNING CLASS NAME?
Signer B:	MY MORNING CLASS NAME? SCIENCE.

3. MODEL FOR TOPIC/COMMENT AND INFORMATION-SEEKING QUESTIONS

Signer A: 1. Describe the topic;
            2. make a comment about it.

            Topic: YOU TAKE-UP SCIENCE,

            Comment: ME SURPRISED.

Signer B: 1. Respond to the comment with a wh-question using WHY.

            Response: YOU SURPRISED, WHY?

Signer A: 1. Describe the topic;
            2. make a comment about it.

            Topic: ME TAKE-UP SCIENCE,

            Comment: me-SAME-as-you.

Signer B: 1. Describe the topic;
            2. make a comment about it.

            Topic: TWO-of-us TAKE-UP SCIENCE,

            Comment: WONDERFUL.

Practice

Signer A: YOU TAKE-UP SCIENCE, ME SURPRISED.

Signer B: YOU SURPRISED, WHY?

Signer A: ME TAKE-UP SCIENCE, me-SAME-as-you.

Signer B: TWO-of-us TAKE-UP SCIENCE, WONDERFUL.

4. MASTERY LEARNING

Review the notes on facial grammar and nonmanual signals prior to practicing the sentences. When you feel comfortable signing these phrases, practice signing the entire dialogue shown at the beginning of this lesson. Practice the dialogue until you can sign the part of each character smoothly.

5. FURTHER PRACTICE

Create your own dialogue using the signs you have learned in previous lessons. Keep the sentences short and write an English translation for them. Practice signing the dialogue with a partner.

LESSON 6: CLASS TIME

Signing Dialogue

1. **Luna:** **YOUR ASL CLASS START WHEN?**

   When does your ASL class start?

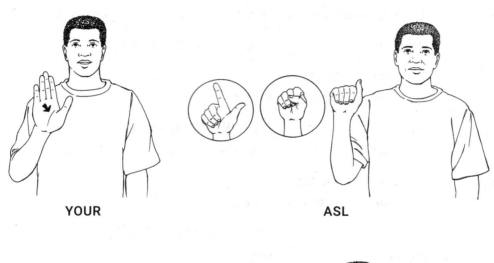

YOUR · ASL

CLASS · START

WHEN

2.   **Jackson: MY ASL CLASS START, TIME 7.**

My ASL class starts at seven o'clock.

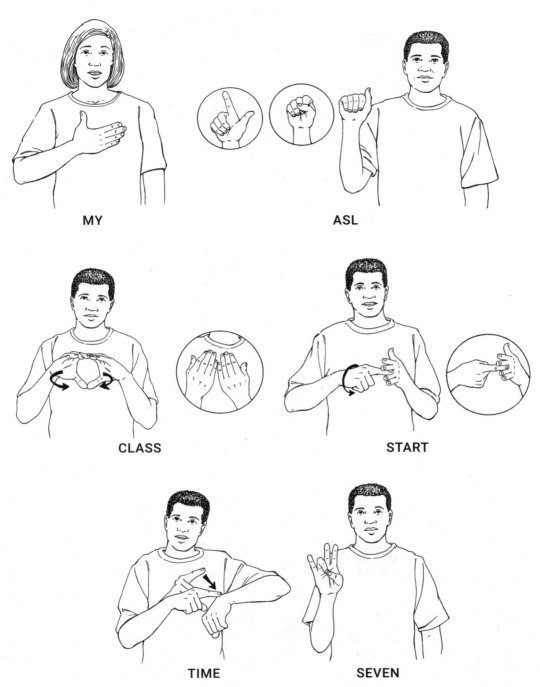

MY   ASL

CLASS   START

TIME   SEVEN

3. **Luna:**   **TIME AGAIN PLEASE?**

Say the time again, please?

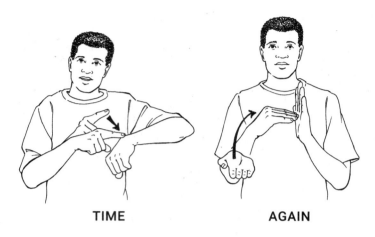

TIME   AGAIN

PLEASE

4. **Jackson:**   **TIME 7.**

Seven o'clock.

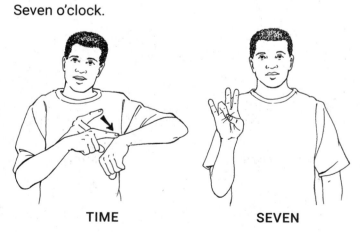

TIME   SEVEN

5. **Luna:** **YOUR ASL CLASS END WHEN?**

When does your ASL class end?

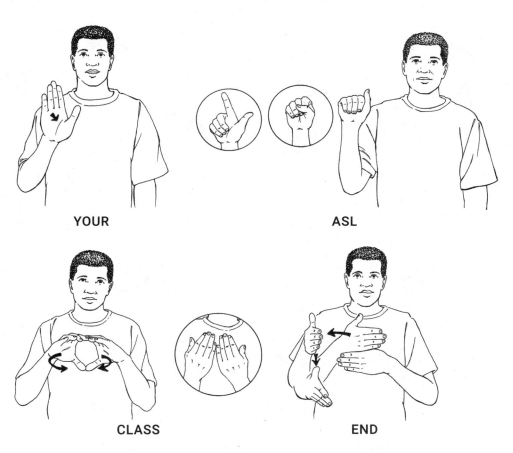

YOUR ASL

CLASS END

WHEN

6. **Jackson:** **MY ASL CLASS END, TIME 8.**

My ASL class ends at eight o'clock.

MY   ASL

CLASS   END

TIME   EIGHT

7. **Luna:** **O-K. me-MEET-you, TIME 8.**

Okay. I will meet you at eight o'clock.

O-K   me-MEET-you

TIME   EIGHT

8. **Jackson:** **you-MEET-me WHERE?**

Where will you meet me?

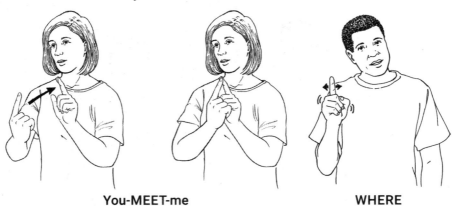

You-MEET-me WHERE

9. **Luna:** **me-MEET-you HERE.**

I will meet you here.

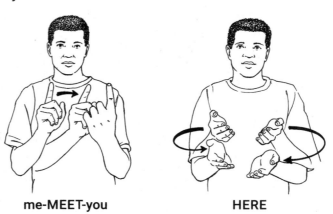

me-MEET-you HERE

10. **Jackson:** **FINE.**

That's fine.

FINE

Breaking Down the Dialogue

Information-seeking Questions

The dialogue uses the signs WHEN and WHERE to ask questions. In these questions, the topic is first described followed by a question sign:

Topic	Question
YOUR ASL CLASS START	WHEN?
YOUR ASL CLASS END	WHEN?
you-MEET-me	WHERE?

What is the appropriate nonmanual signal for information-seeking questions?

Topic/Comment

In the dialogue, a topic/comment format is used to respond to the questions described previously.

Topic	Comment
MY ASL CLASS START,	TIME 7.
MY ASL CLASS END,	TIME 8.
me-MEET-you	HERE.

Another sentence using the topic/comment format is:

me-MEET-you,	TIME 8.

Indicating the Time

When telling the time that something starts or ends, it is common practice to place the time at the end of the sentence. The following sentences have time at the end of them:

MY ASL CLASS START, TIME 7.

MY ASL CLASS END, TIME 8.

me-MEET-you, TIME 8.

The formula for indicating the time is TIME + #, which yields TIME 7 and TIME 8 in the foregoing sentences. In the translation, a person uses the common English means for saying the time, which could be "My class starts at seven" or "My class starts at seven o'clock."

Ordering of Simple Sentences

The following is an example of a simple sentence requesting information:

TIME AGAIN PLEASE.

What's the Sign?

FINE

The sign for FINE is a frequently used sign in ASL. It is most often used alone. Its meaning is often translated in English to "That's fine," "It was fine," "That's okay," "That's all right," and so forth. It is not used to mean the superior quality of material as in "They used a fine cloth to make a cover," nor is it used to mean exceptionally small as in "Read the fine print."

MY

The signs ME and MY are distinguished by the index finger pointing for the sign ME and the hand being opened for the sign MY. The open hand is used to indicate the possessive form of all pronouns.

YOUR

The sign for YOUR is another example of the open hand being used to indicate the possessive form of a pronoun.

me-MEET-you, you-MEET-me

Recall that MEET is a directional verb (see Chapter 8 for information about directional verbs); therefore, the subject and object of the sentence are incorporated into the movement of the sign MEET. For you-MEET-me, the hand that is away from the body moves toward the hand that is held stationary by the chest. See Lesson 1 for an illustration of this sign.

ASL Synonyms

Some signs can be used to mean other things.

Sign	Also used for
AGAIN	REPEAT
END	CONCLUDE, CONCLUSION, FINISH, TERMINATE
MY	MINE
START	BEGIN, INITIATE, ORIGINAL, ORIGINATE

Practice Activities

1. MODEL FOR TOPIC/COMMENT AND INFORMATION-SEEKING QUESTIONS, AND FOR INDICATING THE TIME

Signer A:	1. Describe the topic;	
	2. ask a question using WHEN.	
	Topic:	YOUR ASL CLASS START
	Question:	WHEN?
	Topic:	YOUR ASL CLASS END
	Question:	WHEN?
Signer B:	1. Describe the topic;	
	2. tell the time.	
	Topic:	MY ASL CLASS START,
	Time:	TIME 7.
	Topic:	MY ASL CLASS END,
	Time:	TIME 8.

Practice

Signer A:	YOUR ASL CLASS START WHEN?
Signer B:	MY ASL CLASS START, TIME 7.
Signer A:	YOUR ASL CLASS END WHEN?
Signer B:	MY ASL CLASS END, TIME 8.

More practice: Repeat this exercise using the numbers 6, 9, 10, 11, and 12 for the numbers 7 and 8 in the following phrases:

MY ASL CLASS START, TIME 7.

MY ASL CLASS END, TIME 8.

2. MODEL FOR ORDERING OF SIMPLE SENTENCES

Signer A: 1. Make a request;
              2. add the courtesy sign PLEASE.

              Request: TIME AGAIN
              Courtesy sign: PLEASE.

Signer B: 1. Respond to the request.

              Response: TIME 7.

Practice

Signer A: TIME AGAIN PLEASE.

Signer B: TIME 7.

3. MODEL FOR INFORMATION-SEEKING QUESTIONS

Signer A: 1. Describe the topic;
              2. ask a question using the sign WHERE.

              Topic: you-MEET-me
              Question: WHERE?

Signer B: 1. Repeat the topic;
              2. answer the question.

              Topic: me-MEET-you
              Answer: HERE.

Practice

Signer A: you-MEET-me, WHERE?

Signer B: me-MEET-you, HERE.

4. MASTERY LEARNING

When you feel comfortable signing these phrases, practice signing the entire dialogue shown at the beginning of this lesson. Practice the dialogue using appropriate facial grammar until you can sign the part of each character smoothly.

5. FURTHER PRACTICE

Write four sentences stating what time your ASL class starts and ends, what room it is in, and where you will meet someone. Figure out how you will sign each of these sentences, then write the English gloss for your signing. Sign these sentences to a partner, who will write down an English translation of what you have signed.

LESSON 7: COURSES

Signing Dialogue

1. **Jerome:** **YOU SCHOOL MAJOR WHAT?**

   What is your major?

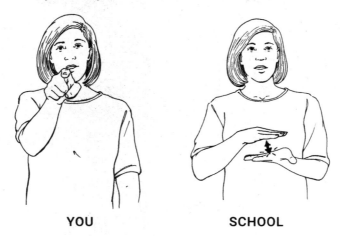

YOU   SCHOOL

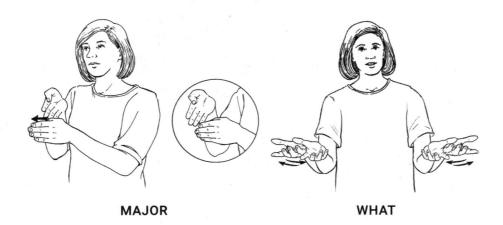

MAJOR   WHAT

2. **Paula:** **ME MAJOR, BUSINESS.**

My major is business.

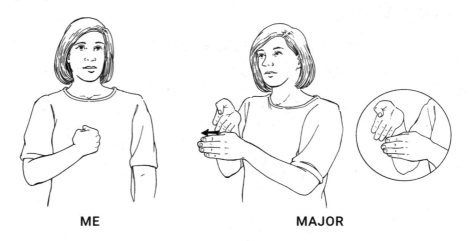

ME   MAJOR

BUSINESS

3.   **Jerome:**   **YOU MINOR WHAT?**

What is your minor?

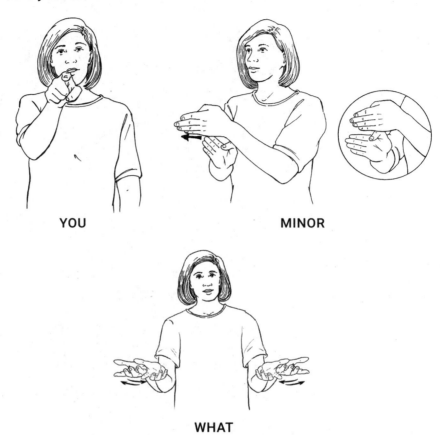

YOU   MINOR

WHAT

4. **Paula:** **ME MINOR, ART.**

My minor is art.

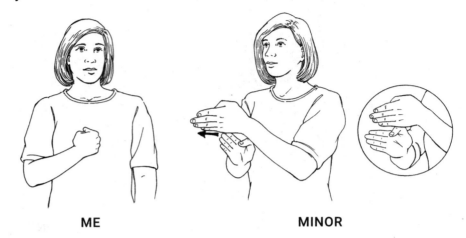

ME   MINOR

ART

Course-related Signs

ACCOUNTING

ALGEBRA

BIOLOGY

CHEMISTRY

COMPUTER

DRAMA

ECONOMICS

ENGINEERING

ENGLISH

GEOGRAPHY

HISTORY

LANGUAGE

MUSIC

LAW

MATH

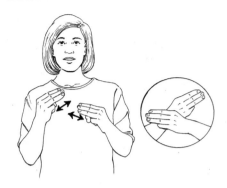

NURSING

PHYSICS

PSYCHOLOGY

Breaking Down the Dialogue

Information-seeking Questions

The dialogue is centered on asking two simple questions:

YOU MAJOR WHAT?

YOU MINOR WHAT?

In both questions the wh-sign comes at the end.

Topic/Comment

The signer responds to both questions describing the topic and then making a comment about it:

ME MAJOR, BUSINESS.

ME MINOR, ART.

What's the Sign?

Computer/Laptop

Some signs have many variations. Some of these variations are regional. For example, the state of Michigan has a sign for STORE that is not used in any other state or province. There are a number of ways to make the sign COMPUTER. In fact, it is not uncommon to find two or more variations of the sign COMPUTER used in a single city. The sign COMPUTER selected for this book is a common one, but it is wise to compare the signs you learn in this book with the ones used in your local Deaf community. Now, you will see the sign for LAPTOP being used as well.

Initialization

Some signs are made in the same manner except for their handshapes. The handshape used in these signs is based on the first letter of the sign. This strategy for creating a sign is called *initialization*. ALGEBRA and MATH are signed in the same manner except ALGEBRA is signed with the A handshape and MATH is signed with the M handshape. The same is true for BIOLOGY and CHEMISTRY. Oftentimes, there is a root sign (or base sign) from which the other signs are derived. For BIOLOGY and CHEMISTRY, the root sign is SCIENCE, which is not initialized. The root sign for ECONOMICS is the sign MONEY.

ASL Synonyms

Some signs can be used to mean other things.

Sign	Also used for
ART	DRAW
ACCOUNTING	COUNTING
DRAMA	ACT, ACTING, THEATER
ENGINEERING	MEASURE, DRAFT
GEOGRAPHY	EARTH
LAW	LEGAL
MAJOR	PROFESSION, CAREER, FIELD (of study)
MUSIC	SING, SONG
SCHOOL	ACADEMIC

☞ Practice Activities

1. MODEL FOR TOPIC/COMMENT AND INFORMATION-SEEKING QUESTIONS

    Signer A: 1. Describe the topic;
              2. ask a question about the topic.

Topic:	YOU MAJOR	or	YOU MINOR
Question:	WHAT?	or	WHAT?

    Signer B: 1. Describe the topic;
              2. make a comment about the topic.

Topic:	ME MAJOR	or	ME MINOR
Comment:	ALGEBRA	or	ART

Practice

Signer A:	YOU MAJOR WHAT?
Signer B:	ME MAJOR, ALGEBRA.
Signer A:	YOU MINOR WHAT?
Signer B:	ME MINOR, ART.

2. MASTERY LEARNING

Practice signing the dialogue until you become familiar with the formation of the signs ALGEBRA and ART, and then substitute these signs with other signs from the lesson. Repeat the process until you have mastered all the signs for school subject matter.

ASL TIP

You Major/Minor

If the major or minor of your choice is not listed in this lesson, search the Internet to see if there is a sign. If not, fingerspell.

---

3. FURTHER PRACTICE

Create a dialogue using the format for discussing course work from chapter lessons. Write an English translation for each sentence. Then practice signing your dialogue with a partner. When you and your partner feel comfortable signing the dialogue, sign it to a third person and see if that person can interpret it correctly. For example:

Signer A:	YOU CLASS, DRAMA? Is your class drama?
Signer B:	NO. MY CLASS, HISTORY. No. My class is history.
Signer A:	YOU MAJOR, HISTORY? Are you majoring in history?
Signer B:	NO. ME MINOR, HISTORY. No. My minor is in history.
Signer A:	CLASS START, TIME? What time does class start?
Signer B:	CLASS START, TIME 9. Class starts at nine o'clock.

 Video Quiz Visit online.barronsbooks.com for scored practice on everyday ASL expressions.

Grammar Practice

For each of the following sentences, translate it to ASL, sign it, and then write the English gloss of the signs you used in your translation.

Note that there may be other ways of translating these sentences than the ones shown here.

1. Are you taking geography?

2. The computer class starts at six o'clock.

3. Are you discouraged?

4. How do you feel?

5. When did you learn ASL?

6. I feel lucky, how about you?

7. I am learning ASL numbers now.

8. You're always tired.

9. You go to the business class in the morning.

10. Where is the drama room?

CHAPTER 7

Conversational ASL

Learning Objectives

In this chapter, you will learn:

o How to apply the following grammar rules to create sentences: simple yes/no questions, information-seeking questions, topic/comment, tense with time adverbs, ordering of simple sentences

o New signs for common phrases in general conversations

o How to use the sign FINISH to indicate that an action has been completed

o Proper procedures for indicating the time

o How to organize thoughts in the correct order to create ASL sentences

LESSON 8: COMMON PHRASES

Signing Dialogue

You will create your own dialogue for this lesson. Check out the Practice Activities for directions and examples.

Sign: **Also used for:**

GOOD-MORNING

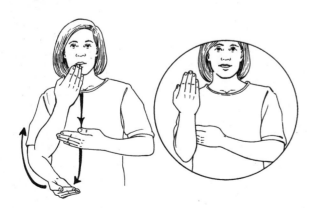

Sign:	**Also used for:**
GOOD-BYE	BYE, BYE-BYE

SEE-YOU-LATER

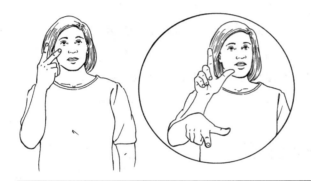

SORRY	APOLOGY, APOLOGIZE, REGRET, REGRETS

Sign: **Also used for:**

OH-I-see

GOOD-LUCK   THAT'S-GOOD

BE-CAREFUL   TAKE-CARE

Sign: **Also used for:**

I-LOVE-YOU

DOUBT-it

DOESN'T-MATTER   ANYHOW, ANYWAY, DESPITE,
                                                                        HOWEVER, EVEN-THOUGH,
                                                                        NEVERTHELESS, WHATEVER

Sign: **Also used for:**

POOR-thing   PITY, MERCY, SYMPATHIZE

KNOW   AWARE

DON'T-KNOW/DIDN'T-KNOW/DOESN'T-KNOW

Sign: **Also used for:**

DIDN'T-KNOW-THAT

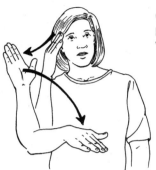

(hand can land in a "Y"
palm down position as
well)

DON'T-CARE   WHO-CARES?

(fingertips of the closed
right hand rest on the
nose and then are
thrown away)

TIME+ (WHAT-TIME?)

Sign:	**Also used for:**

LET'S-SEE

WINTER

COLD, CHILLY

SPRING

GROW, PLANT

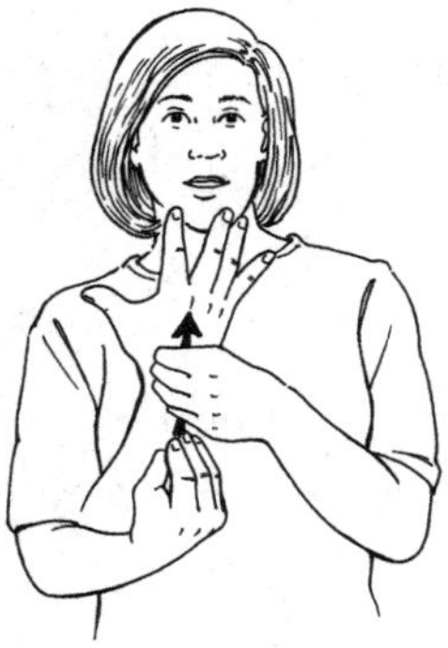

Sign: **Also used for:**

SUMMER

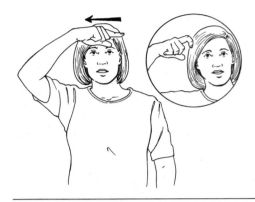

AUTUMN (FALL)   SEPTEMBER

WEATHER

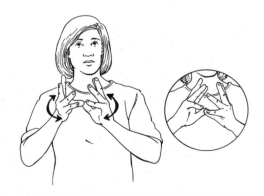

Sign: **Also used for:**

RAIN

SNOW

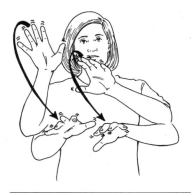

SUN   SUNSHINE, SUNNY

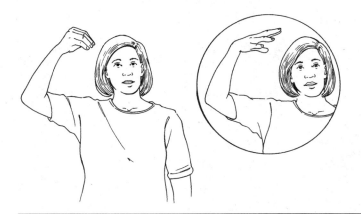

Sign: **Also used for:**

MOON

STARS

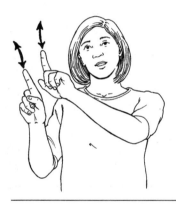

FROST   FREEZE, FROZEN

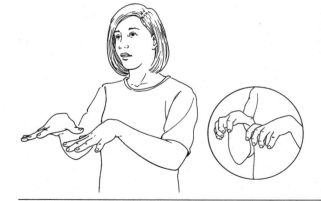

Sign:

CLOUDS

CLOUDY

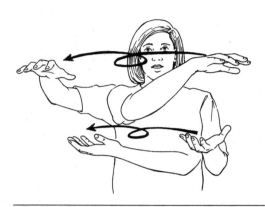

WIND

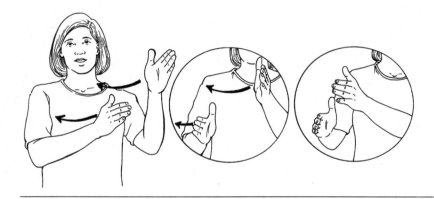

RAINBOW

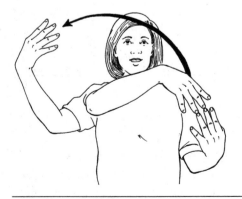

Sign: **Also used for:**

THUNDER

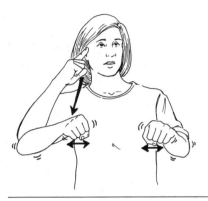

LIGHTNING

What's the Sign?

GOOD-MORNING

Although the sign for GOOD-MORNING is a compound derived from the signs GOOD and MORNING, it is made with a single fluid motion.

I-LOVE-YOU

The sign for I-LOVE-YOU is typically used as a gesture of goodwill. It can be used when saying good-bye to someone you are fond of or when waving to a crowd of people to show your appreciation. It can also be used in its intimate sense to mean "I love you very much."

TIME+

Repeating the sign TIME and adding the appropriate nonmanual signals for asking an information-seeking question produces "What time is it?"

OH-I-see

The sign for OH-I-see is used by itself to indicate that a person understands something. Its translations include "Oh, I see," "Oh, I get it," and "I understand now."

POOR-thing

This is a directional verb and therefore the middle finger of the hand should be pointing toward the person to whom it is referring.

KNOW-that

This sign is used in an emphatic sense to mean "I know that."

 ## Practice Activities

1. Create dialogues using the signs that you have learned in previous lessons in combination with signs introduced in this unit. Use rules for simple yes/no questions, information-seeking questions, and ordering of simple sentences to guide you. Keep your sentences short and pay attention to your facial expressions when signing them.

2. Notice how all of the dialogues in this book have different names. This is to help you practice fingerspelling. Use unique names or names of people you know to create this dialogue.

3. Write the number of the rule beside each sentence (See "The Ten Rules of ASL Grammar" in Chapter 3). An example of a dialogue follows:

Signer A: GOOD-MORNING. TIME+? (Rule #5)

Good morning. What time is it?

Signer B: ME DON'T-KNOW. (Rule #8)

I don't know.

Signer A: FEEL+ YOU? (Rule #5)

How are you feeling?

Signer B: ME FEEL DEPRESSED. (Rule #8)

I'm feeling depressed.

Signer A: YOU FEEL DEPRESSED WHY? (Rule #5)

Why do you feel depressed?

Signer B: ME ALGEBRA TAKE-UP. (Rule #8)

I'm taking up algebra.

Signer A: OH-I-see. POOR-thing. (Rule #8)

Oh, I see. You poor thing.

Signer B: THANKS. YOU ALGEBRA TAKE-UP? (Rule #3)

Thanks. Are you taking algebra?

Signer A: NO.

No.

Signer B: YOU LUCKY. (Rule #8)

You're lucky.

LESSON 9: KEEP ON PRACTICING

Signing Dialogue

1. **Juan:** **GOOD-MORNING. YOU BIOLOGY STUDY FINISH YOU?**

   Good morning. Have you finished studying biology?

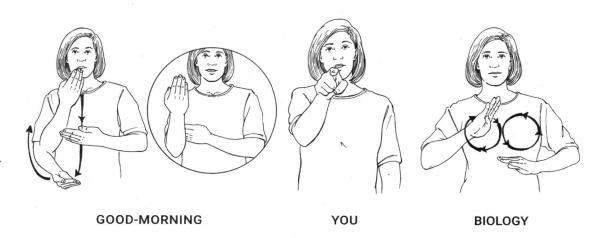

GOOD-MORNING   YOU   BIOLOGY

STUDY   FINISH   YOU

2. **Benji:** **YES, YESTERDAY ME BIOLOGY STUDY FINISH.**

Yes, I finished studying biology yesterday.

YES   YESTERDAY   ME

BIOLOGY   STUDY   FINISH

3. **Juan:** **YOU ASL STUDY FINISH YOU?**

Have you finished studying ASL?

YOU   ASL

STUDY   FINISH   YOU

4.   **Benji:**   **NO, ME PLAN STUDY ASL TODAY.**

No, I plan to study ASL today.

NO   ME

PLAN   STUDY

ASL   TODAY

5. **Juan:** **REALLY? ME STUDY WITH YOU, DON'T-MIND YOU?**

Is that so? Do you mind if I study with you?

REALLY   ME   STUDY

WITH   YOU   DONT-MIND

YOU

6. **Benji:** **ME DON'T-MIND. ME ASL PRACTICE MUST.**

I don't mind. I must practice ASL.

ME   DONT-MIND   ME

ASL   PRACTICE

MUST

7.   **Juan:**   **ME AGREE. ME PRACTICE MORE, NEED ME.**

I agree. I need to practice more.

ME   AGREE   ME

PRACTICE   MORE   NEED

ME

8. **Benji:** **START PRACTICE ASL, READY YOU?**

Are you ready to start practicing ASL?

START

PRACTICE

ASL

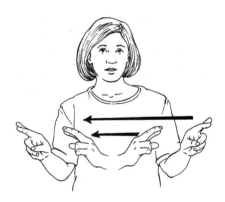

READY

YOU

9. **Juan:** **READY!**

I'm ready!

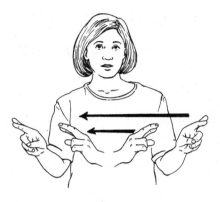

READY

Breaking Down the Dialogue

Simple Yes/No Questions

The sign FINISH is often used to ask if an action is completed:

YOU BIOLOGY STUDY FINISH YOU?

Another way of signing this question is to place the FINISH sign before the action sign or verb:

Question	Translation
FINISH STUDY YOU?	Have you finished studying?
YOU BIOLOGY FINISH STUDY YOU?	Have you finished studying biology?

Another yes/no question in the dialogue was

YOU ASL STUDY FINISH YOU?

Notice that the sign YOU is placed at the beginning and end of the question. Although it is not necessary to sign YOU twice in the sentence, it is a common practice to do so.

Using FINISH to Show that an Action Is Completed

The FINISH sign is placed before or after a verb to show that an action is completed.

Before the verb:	ME FINISH STUDY ME.
After the verb:	ME STUDY FINISH ME.

Both phrases mean "I have finished studying."

To add information about what was studied to the above phrases, you place the information before each phrase:

ME BIOLOGY STUDY FINISH. or ME BIOLOGY FINISH STUDY.

A proper translation of both phrases is "I have finished studying biology."

Tense with Time Adverbs

You place the sign for time at the beginning of a FINISH phrase:

YESTERDAY ME BIOLOGY STUDY FINISH ME.

Placing the sign for time at the beginning of a sentence establishes the tense. Notice that if a signer wishes to emphasize the point that the studying was finished yesterday, then he or she might place the sign YESTERDAY at the end of the phrase to get ME BIOLOGY STUDY FINISH ME, YESTERDAY. This new sentence is an example of a topic/comment sentence structure.

Topic/Comment

The signer describes the topic and then makes a comment about it. The following examples are taken from the dialogue:

Topic	Comment
ME PLAN STUDY ASL	TODAY.
ME ASL PRACTICE	MUST.
ME PRACTICE MORE,	NEED ME.

Simple Yes/No Questions with the Signs DON'T-MIND and READY

Use the signs DON'T-MIND and READY with the formula for creating a yes/no question:

Topic	Question
ME STUDY WITH YOU,	DON'T-MIND YOU?
START PRACTICE ASL,	READY YOU?

What's the Sign?

DON'T-MIND

The translation of the sign DON'T MIND depends upon the context in which it is used. By itself or in a sentence, it usually means "I don't mind." As a question, it is commonly translated to "Do you mind?"

TODAY/YESTERDAY

The body and the signing space combine to indicate time in ASL. The body itself represents the present time or present tense. That's why the signs TODAY and NOW move in a vertical plane close to the body. To indicate the future, signs move to the front of the body (e.g., TOMORROW). To indicate the past tense, signs move toward the back of the body, and YESTERDAY is an example of this.

ASL Synonyms

Some signs can be used to mean other things.

Sign	Also used for
FINISH	ALREADY, STOP
MUST	HAVE-TO
NEED	NECESSARY, SHOULD
PLAN	ARRANGE, ORDER, PREPARE
PRACTICE	TRAIN, REHEARSE, WORK-ON

Practice Activities

1. MODEL FOR TOPIC/COMMENT, TENSE WITH TIME ADVERBS, SIMPLE YES/NO QUESTIONS

Signer A:	1. Make a greeting;
	2. describe the action;
	3. ask a question with the FINISH sign.

Greeting:	GOOD-MORNING.
Action:	YOU BIOLOGY STUDY
Question:	FINISH YOU?

Signer B:	1. Answer the question with the sign YES;
	2. establish the time frame of the sentence by using the time adverb YESTERDAY;
	3. make a comment.

Response:	YES,
Tense:	YESTERDAY
Comment:	ME BIOLOGY STUDY FINISH.

| Signer A: | 1. Describe the action; |
| | 2. ask a question with the FINISH sign. |

| Action: | YOU ASL STUDY |
| Question: | FINISH YOU? |

Signer B:	1. Answer the question with the sign NO;
	2. describe a topic;
	3. make a comment about the topic.

Answer:	NO,
Topic:	ME PLAN STUDY ASL
Comment:	TODAY.

Practice

Signer A: GOOD-MORNING. YOU BIOLOGY STUDY FINISH YOU?

Signer B: YES, YESTERDAY ME BIOLOGY STUDY FINISH.

Signer A: YOU ASL STUDY FINISH YOU?

Signer B: NO, ME PLAN STUDY ASL TODAY.

2. MODEL FOR TOPIC/COMMENT AND SIMPLE YES/NO QUESTIONS WITH DON'T-MIND AND READY

Signer A: DON'T-MIND.

1. Describe the topic for the question;
2. ask the question about the topic using the DON'T-MIND sign.

Topic: ME STUDY WITH YOU,

Question: DON'T-MIND YOU?

Signer B:

1. Answer the question with the DON'T-MIND sign;
2. describe a topic;
3. make a comment about the topic.

Answer: ME DON'T-MIND.

Topic: ME ASL PRACTICE

Comment: MUST.

Signer A:

1. Make a remark acknowledging what was just said;
2. describe the topic;
3. make a comment about the topic.

Remark: ME AGREE.

Topic: ME PRACTICE MORE,

Comment: NEED ME.

Signer A: READY.

    1. Describe the topic for the question;
    2. ask the question about the topic using the READY sign.

    Topic: START PRACTICE ASL,

    Question: READY YOU?

Signer B: 1. Answer the question with the READY sign.

    Answer: ME READY!

Practice

Signer A: ME STUDY WITH YOU, DON'T-MIND YOU?

Signer B: ME DON'T-MIND. ME ASL PRACTICE MUST.

Signer A: ME AGREE. ME PRACTICE MORE, NEED ME.

Signer A: START PRACTICE ASL, READY YOU?

Signer B: ME READY!

3. MASTERY LEARNING

When you feel comfortable signing these phrases, practice signing the entire dialogue shown at the beginning of this lesson. Practice the dialogue until you can sign the part of each character smoothly using the appropriate facial grammar.

4. FURTHER PRACTICE

Write a short story about taking a class at school, and include the following information: the name of the class, the time it starts and ends, your feelings about the class (e.g., ENTHUSIASTIC, BORED), and which room it is in. Translate the story and write it down in English gloss. Sign the story to someone who will then write down what she or he thinks you signed. Compare this story with your original one. You should not only use the signs that you learned in your lessons but also their synonyms. For example, the sign DRAMA is also used for ACT, ACTING, and THEATER (see Lesson 7).

LESSON 10: DISCUSSING TIME

Signing Dialogue

1. **Joy:**   **TWO-of-us PRACTICE WHEN?**

      When will the two of us practice?

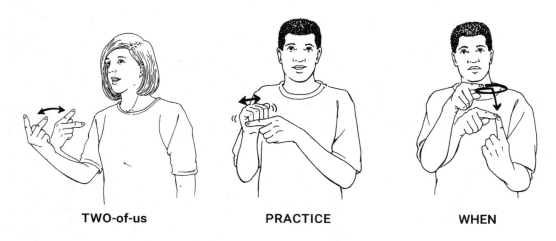

TWO-of-us   PRACTICE   WHEN

2. **Jay:**   **TOMORROW AFTERNOON, TIME 3.**

      Tomorrow afternoon at three o'clock.

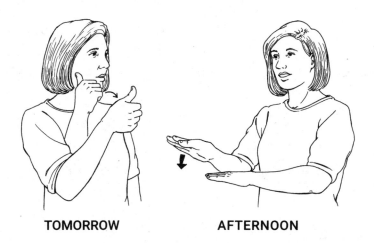

TOMORROW   AFTERNOON

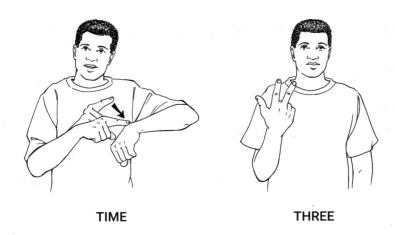

TIME THREE

3. **Joy:** **SUPPOSE ME LATE, DO-what YOU?**

What will you do if I am late?

SUPPOSE ME LATE

DO-what YOU

4. **Jay:** **ME WAIT, ASL PRACTICE MYSELF.**

I'll wait and practice ASL by myself.

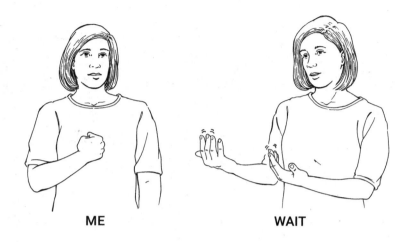

ME   WAIT

ASL

PRACTICE   MYSELF

5. **Joy:**   **SUPPOSE ME FORGET, DO-what YOU?**

What will you do if I forget?

SUPPOSE   ME   FORGET

DO-what   YOU

6. **Jay:**   **ME ASL PRACTICE MYSELF.**

I'll practice ASL by myself.

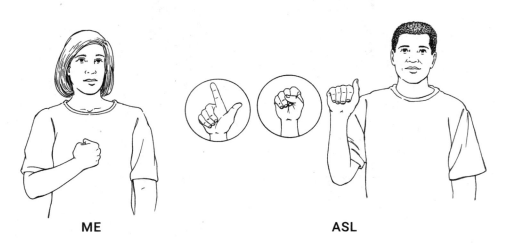

ME   ASL

PRACTICE   MYSELF

7. **Joy:**   **TOMORROW AFTERNOON, TIME 3 me-MEET-you HERE.**

I will meet you here tomorrow afternoon at three o'clock.

TOMORROW   AFTERNOON   TIME

THREE   me-MEET-you   HERE

8. **Jay:** **ALL-RIGHT. BYE.**

All right. Bye.

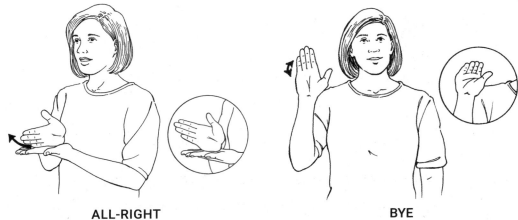

ALL-RIGHT   BYE

Breaking Down the Dialogue

Information-seeking Questions

The rule for creating a wh-question is demonstrated in the dialogue with the sign WHEN. The signer sets up the topic and then asks a wh-question:

topic:	Two-of-us PRACTICE
wh-question:	WHEN?

The question is asking for information, and the proper nonmanual signals are for the signer to (1) *tilt the head forward* and (2) *squeeze the eyebrows together*.

Conditional Sentences

A conditional sentence with the sign SUPPOSE can be formed by stating the conditional clause first and then the question:

conditional clause:	SUPPOSE ME LATE,
question:	DO-what YOU?

Another example of this type of conditional sentence follows:

conditional clause:	SUPPOSE ME FORGET,
question:	DO-what YOU?

The proper nonmanual signals for signing the conditional clause are to (1) *raise the eyebrows* and (2) *tilt the head forward slightly*. The proper nonmanual signals for the question consist of (1) *tilting the head forward* and (2) *squeezing the eyebrows together*.

Depending upon the context of the sentence, the sign DO-what has several meanings including the following:

Phrase	Translations
DO-what YOU?	What are you going to do?
	What will you do?
	What do you want to do?
DO-what ME?	What am I going to do?
	What will I do?
	What do I want to do?

In a question, DO-what is placed at the end of the sentence:

SUPPOSE ME LATE, DO-what YOU?

SUPPOSE ME FORGET, DO-what YOU?

Indicating Time

The time phrase, TIME + #, is typically placed after other signs for time:

TOMORROW AFTERNOON, TIME 3.

This translates to "Tomorrow afternoon at three o'clock" or "Three o'clock tomorrow afternoon."

What's the Sign?

AFTERNOON

The formation of the sign for AFTERNOON shows the horizon (represented by the horizontal arm) and the sun midway between the zenith and the horizon (represented by the other hand). Lowering the hand that represents the sun will indicate that the time is later in the afternoon.

DO-what

The sign for DO-what is often used by itself to mean "What are you going to do about it?" or "What do you want to do about it?" The signer should maintain eye contact with the person to whom she or he is signing.

SUPPOSE

The sign for SUPPOSE essentially means "if." It is used to establish a conditional clause. It *does not* have the English meaning "imagine" or "think" as in the sentence "I suppose you would like to walk."

TOMORROW

The body and the signing space combine to indicate time in ASL. The body represents the present time or present tense. The signs TODAY and NOW move in a vertical plane close to the body. To indicate the future tense, the sign TOMORROW moves to the front of the body. To indicate the past tense, signs move toward the back of the body (e.g., YESTERDAY).

ASL Synonyms

Some signs can be used to mean other things.

Sign	Also used for
ALL-RIGHT	OKAY
LATE	NOT-YET
MYSELF	SELF
SUPPOSE	IF

Practice Activities

1. MODEL FOR INFORMATION-SEEKING QUESTIONS AND FOR INDICATING THE TIME

   Signer A: 1. Describe the topic;

   2. ask a question about the topic using the sign WHEN.

   Topic: TWO-of-us PRACTICE

   Question: WHEN?

   Signer B: 1. Respond to the question indicating the time.

   Response: TOMORROW AFTERNOON, TIME 3.

Practice

   Signer A: TWO-of-us PRACTICE WHEN?

   Signer B: TOMORROW AFTERNOON, TIME 3.

2. MODEL FOR CONDITIONAL SENTENCES

   Signer A: 1. Describe the conditional clause;

   2. ask a question using DO-what.

   Conditional clause: SUPPOSE ME LATE,

   Question: DO-what YOU?

   Signer B: 1. Respond to the question.

   Response: ME WAIT, ASL PRACTICE MYSELF.

   Signer A: 1. Describe the conditional clause;

   2. ask a question using DO-what.

   Conditional clause: SUPPOSE ME FORGET,

   Question: DO-what YOU?

   Signer B: 1. Respond to the question.

   Response: ME ASL PRACTICE MYSELF.

Practice

Signer A:	SUPPOSE ME LATE, DO-what YOU?
Signer B:	ME WAIT, ASL PRACTICE MYSELF.
Signer A:	SUPPOSE ME FORGET, DO-what YOU?
Signer B:	ME ASL PRACTICE MYSELF.

3. MASTERY LEARNING

When you feel comfortable signing these phrases, practice signing the entire dialogue shown at the beginning of this lesson. Practice the dialogue until you can sign the part of each character smoothly using the appropriate facial grammar.

4. FURTHER PRACTICE

Write five to ten conditional sentences in English, translate them to ASL, and then write the English gloss of the ASL translation. Each conditional sentence should contain the sign SUPPOSE. Sign these to a partner and have your partner write in English a translation of your sentences. Also, have your partner respond to you in signs.

LESSON 11: LEISURE ACTIVITY

Signing Dialogue

1. **Stanley:**   **WHAT'S-UP? YOU ASL STUDY FINISH YOU?**

   What's happening? Have you finished studying ASL?

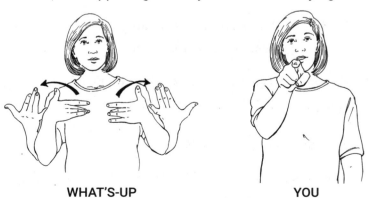

WHAT'S-UP	YOU

ASL STUDY

FINISH YOU

2. **Alexander:** **YES, ME STUDY FINISH, NOW HOME GO-to.**

Yes, I have finished studying and I am going home now.

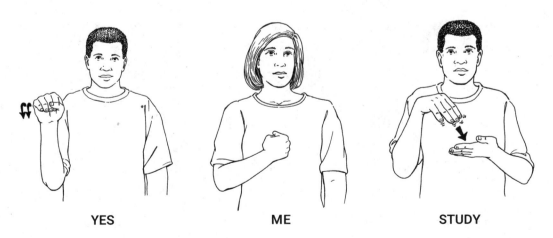

YES ME STUDY

FINISH

NOW

HOME

GO-to

3. **Stanley:** **TONIGHT, YOU DO-what?**

What are you doing tonight?

TONIGHT

YOU

DO-what

4. **Alexander:**   **TONIGHT, ME VIDEO WATCH.**

I am watching a video tonight.

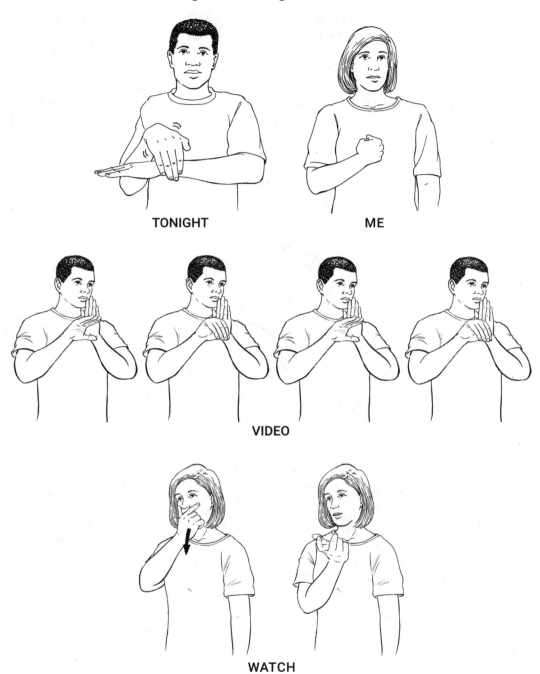

TONIGHT   ME

VIDEO

WATCH

5. **Stanley:**   **VIDEO CALLED?**

                    What is the video called?

VIDEO

CALLED

6. **Alexander:**   **VIDEO CALLED, TITLE "S-T-U-D-Y A-S-L."**

                    The video's called "Study ASL."

VIDEO

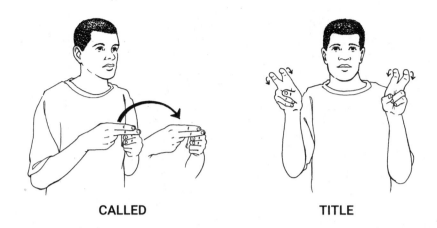

CALLED   TITLE

7. **Stanley:**   **HA-HA. HUMOR WORK-ON NEED YOU.**

Ha-ha. You need to work on your humor.

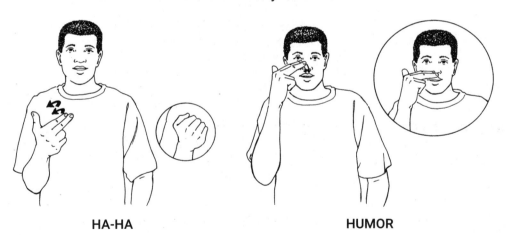

HA-HA   HUMOR

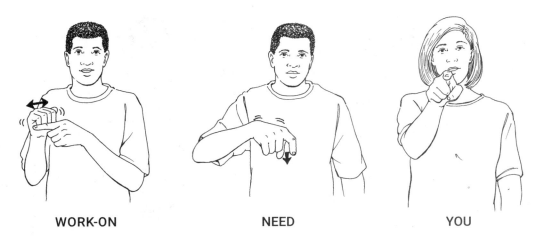

WORK-ON NEED YOU

8. **Alexander: ME KNOW.**

   I know.

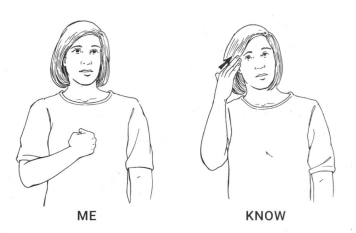

ME KNOW

Breaking Down the Dialogue

Simple Yes/No Questions

The question

YOU ASL STUDY FINISH YOU?

sets up the topic of the question and then uses the FINISH sign to ask a yes/no question.

Sequencing Thoughts

Sentences can be organized by signing about events and thoughts in the order they occur. In the following sentence, two phrases are linked together in the order in which they occur:

first event:	ME STUDY FINISH,
second event:	NOW HOME GO-to.

In the translation, the thoughts are joined by the conjunction *and*:

I have finished studying and I am going home now. OR

I have finished studying and now I am going home. OR

I am done studying and I am going home now. OR

I am done studying and now I am going home.

Information-seeking Questions

In the previous lesson, you learned to place the subject pronoun YOU after the sign DO-what. In this lesson, the subject pronoun YOU is placed before the sign DO-what. Both placements are correct. When DO-what is not a sentence by itself, it is commonly placed at the end of the sentence as in

TONIGHT, YOU DO-what?

The English translation of this sentence is "What are you doing tonight?"

Ordering of Simple Sentences

In simple sentences, the verb can be placed before or after the object. That is, the sentence can be SOV (subject-object-verb) or SVO (subject-verb-object):

SOV:	ME VIDEO WATCH.
SVO:	ME WATCH VIDEO.

Both word orderings are correct, but the SOV ordering is not found in English.

Naming Things Using the Sign CALLED

The sign CALLED is used to name things or inquire about the names of things. When the name is the title of a video, movie, book, or conference, it is common practice to precede the title with the sign TITLE as in the following:

VIDEO CALLED, TITLE "S-T-U-D-Y A-S-L."

Topic/Comment

The signer describes the topic and then makes a comment about it, as in the following sentence from the dialogue:

topic:	YOU HUMOR WORK-ON
comment:	NEED YOU.

What's the Sign?

HA-HA

The sign for HA-HA is a variation of fingerspelling H-A several times. The fingerspelling of the letters H and A is not complete. Instead, the sign is made with the thumb up and the index and middle fingers flapping in and out quickly. It has several meanings depending upon the situation in which it is used. In the sentence

HA-HA. HUMOR WORK-ON NEED YOU.

the HA-HA sign is not meant to indicate that something was terrifically funny, and the signer is not laughing. It is used with a bit of sarcasm due to not believing your friend will continue to study. HA-HA is used in good humor to mean

You need to work on your humor.

TITLE

This sign TITLE is used to show that the signer is about to give the title of a book, movie, title, conference, or something else that has a proper title. It is signed before the title is given, and in a written English translation, it usually appears as quotation marks. It can be used to refer to a title as in the following:

CLASS TITLE (SUBJECT) WHAT?

Translation: What is the name of your class?

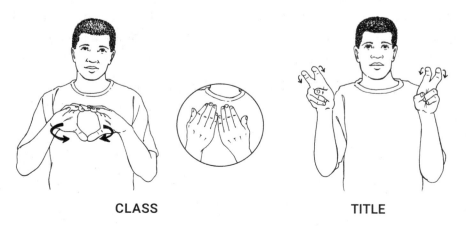

CLASS   TITLE

WHAT

CLASS TITLE (SUBJECT), COMPUTER SCIENCE.

Translation: My class is called Computer Science.

CLASS   **TITLE**

COMPUTER   **SCIENCE**

TONIGHT

You have learned that the body and the signing space combine to indicate time in ASL. The sign TONIGHT, like the signs TODAY and NOW, moves in a vertical plane close to the body to represent the present time.

WATCH

There are many signs to describe the many different ways of looking at something. Different signs are used to show that someone is staring, glaring, scanning, watching, seeing, and so forth. The handshape is typically the V handshape with the two fingers representing the eyes. In the sign WATCH, the V handshape is horizontal and is moved forward firmly once. There are also variations of the sign WATCH.

ASL Synonyms

Some signs can be used to mean other things.

Sign	Also used for
CALLED	NAMED
HUMOR	COMEDY, FUNNY
TITLE	QUOTE, QUOTATION
VIDEO	VIDEOTAPE, RECORD, FILM
WORK-ON	PRACTICE, REHEARSE

 ## Practice Activities

1. MODEL FOR SIMPLE YES/NO QUESTIONS

    Signer A: 1. Describe the topic;
                  2. ask a question using the FINISH sign.

    Action: YOU ASL STUDY
    Question: FINISH YOU?

    Signer B: 1. Answer the question affirmatively with the sign YES;
                  2. describe what action was finished;
                  3. add a follow-up comment.

    Affirmative answer: YES,
    Describe action finished: ME STUDY FINISH,
    Follow-up comment: NOW HOME GO-to.

Practice

Signer A:	YOU ASL STUDY FINISH YOU?
Signer B:	YES, ME STUDY FINISH, NOW HOME GO-to.

2. MODEL FOR INFORMATION-SEEKING QUESTIONS, TENSE WITH TIME ADVERBS, AND ORDERING OF SIMPLE SENTENCES

Signer A: 1. Describe the time relating to the DO-what question;
2. ask the question using the DO-what sign.

Time:	TONIGHT,
Question:	YOU DO-what?

Signer B: 1. Repeat the time;
2. describe the activity that responds to the DO-what question using an SOV sentence.

Time:	TONIGHT,
Response:	ME VIDEO WATCH.

Practice

Signer A:	TONIGHT, YOU DO-what?
Signer B:	TONIGHT, ME VIDEO WATCH.

3. MODEL FOR USING THE SIGN CALLED

Signer A: 1. Describe an object;
2. ask for its name using the sign CALLED.

Description:	VIDEO
Question:	CALLED?

Signer B: 1. Repeat the question;
2. state the title.

Question:	VIDEO CALLED,
Title:	TITLE "STUDY ASL WITH J-U-D-Y."

Practice

Signer A: VIDEO CALLED?

Signer B: VIDEO CALLED, TITLE "STUDY ASL WITH J-U-D-Y."

4. MODEL FOR TOPIC/COMMENT

Signer A: 1. Use the sign HA-HA to make a remark on someone's attempt at humor;

              2. describe the topic;

              3. make a comment about it.

              Remark: HA-HA.

              Topic: YOU HUMOR WORK-ON

              Comment: NEED YOU.

Signer B: 1. Respond to the comment.

              Response: ME KNOW.

Practice

Signer A: VIDEO CALLED?

Signer B: VIDEO CALLED, TITLE "S-T-U-D-Y A-S-L."

Signer A: HA-HA. YOU HUMOR WORK-ON NEED YOU.

Signer B: ME KNOW.

5. MASTERY LEARNING

When you feel comfortable signing these phrases, practice signing the entire dialogue shown at the beginning of this lesson. Practice the dialogue until you can sign the part of each character smoothly using appropriate facial grammar.

6. FURTHER PRACTICE

Write ten sentences that ask a yes/no question using the sign FINISH. The FINISH sign is typically used to indicate that an action is completed. Translate each sentence to ASL and then write the English gloss of the ASL translation. Sign these to a partner and have your partner write in English a translation of your sentences. Also, have your partner respond to you in signs.

 Video Quiz Visit online.barronsbooks.com for scored practice on conversational ASL.

Directional Verbs and Communicating

LESSON 12: DIRECTIONAL VERBS

Change the Meaning of Sentences in Space

In American Sign Language, certain verbs tell us who did what to whom, without any help from nouns or pronouns. In English, you rely on words to identify the who (subject) and the whom (object) of a sentence. In the sentence "He contacted her," three words are spoken, and there is no doubt as to who contacted whom. In ASL, only the sign CONTACT is made to give us the ASL sentence, he-CONTACT-her. Three ASL characteristics make this possible. The first is that nouns can be established in the signing space, and after they are established, these nouns can be used to refer to someone or something. The second characteristic is that certain verbs can move in different directions to tell us who did what to whom. The third characteristic is the orientation of the hand(s) during the signing. The orientation also tells us about the subject and the object of a sentence. Therefore, to understand what a verb is telling us, we must know what action the verb is describing, and we must also map its movement. This chapter describes the rules for using verbs in space.

J-O-E-Y point-right, C-H-A-R-L-O-T-T-E point-left

This phrase is an example of Rule #6 on pronominalization. The signer establishes two reference points in the signing space for two people. In the signing space, JOEY is placed to the right of the signer; Charlotte is placed to the left. After this is done, the signer merely points to the right to refer to Joey and points to the left when talking about Charlotte. In the following sentence, the signer is telling us which sports Joey and Charlotte play:

HE-point-right PLAY SOCCER, SHE-point-left PLAY BASEBALL.

HE-point-right   PLAY

SOCCER   SHE-point-left

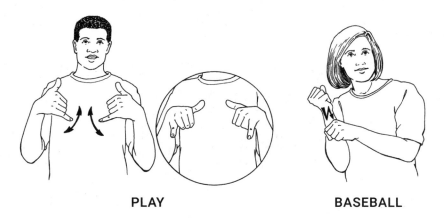

PLAY   BASEBALL

The signer points to the right for HE and to the left for SHE. This sentence translates to "He plays soccer and she plays baseball."

Let's keep the same positions in the signing space for Joey and Charlotte and look at the ASL translation of the sentence "She gives the book to him":

BOOK she-GIVE-him.

The sign she-GIVE-him is made by moving the sign GIVE from the left side of the signing space to the right side or from the position of SHE to the position of HIM. This is shown in the following diagram.

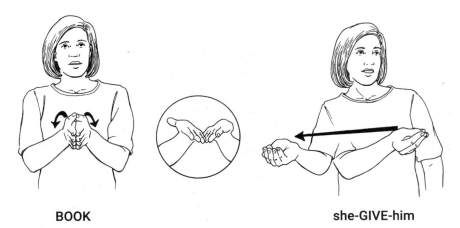

BOOK   she-GIVE-him

Notice that it is not necessary to sign the subject and object of the sentence because they are already incorporated into the movement of the sign. Although she-GIVE-him is just one sign, it shows Charlotte (who) doing something to Joey (whom). That is, Charlotte is giving the book to Joey. In the following diagram, the neutral sign for GIVE is shown.

In a neutral sign, the subject and object of a sentence are not indicated.

Verbs that can move about in space to indicate who is doing what to whom are called *directional verbs*. Not all verbs are directional verbs. This chapter provides a listing of many of the common directional verbs used in ASL.

The Four Aspects of Directional Verbs

1. she-GIVE-him
2. you-PICK-ON-me

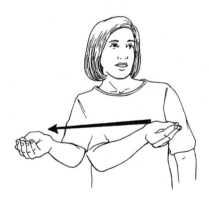

she-GIVE-him

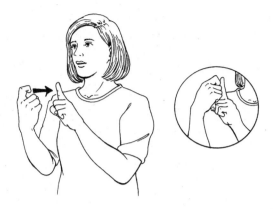

you-PICK-ON-me

Directional verbs can inflect for source, subject, object, or goal. The *source* is the beginning location of the verb. The *goal* is the end location of the verb. The *subject* is the doer of the action described by the verb. The *object* is the recipient of the action. Subject and source are typically in the same location, and object and goal are also usually in the same location.

In sentence 1, the source is the position in the signing space where the sign GIVE begins, which is where SHE has been established. The subject is the person represented by "she." The object is the person representing "him." The goal is the end position of the sign GIVE, which is the location in the signing space of the person represented by HIM.

In sentence 2, the source is the position in the signing space where the sign PICK-ON begins, which is where YOU is placed. The subject is the person represented by "you." The object is the signer who is represented by "me." The goal is the end position of the sign PICK-ON, which is the location in the signing space of the person represented by ME.

Using these four aspects, we can now further explore how verbs show the relationship between the subject and object of a sentence.

Verbs that Indicate the Subject and the Object

1. he-BLAME-me, ALWAYS. (He's always blaming me.)
2. NEXT-WEEK she-HELP-you. (She will help you next week.)
3. he-ASK-them, NAME. (He asked them their names.)

In each of these sentences, only one sign is used for the verb. The following illustrations show the direction of movement of each verb relative to the signer.

he-BLAME-me

ALWAYS

NEXT-WEEK

she-HELP-you

he-ASK-them

NAME

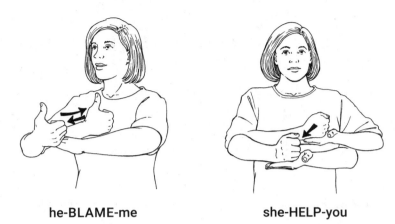

he-BLAME-me   she-HELP-you

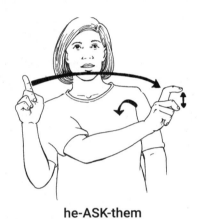

he-ASK-them

The source or starting position for all directional verbs indicates the subject of the sentence. The goal or ending position for these verbs is the object of the sentence. Before the verbs can be signed as they are in these illustrations, the signer must first establish a position for each person referred to by the pronouns. Only the pronouns ME and YOU do not have to be established because the persons they represent are present. Notice that the verb he-ASK-them is a sweeping movement. This is because the pronoun "them" is made by sweeping the index finger either on the right side or the left side of the signing space, depending on where the signer has placed the people who are represented by THEM.

List of Verbs that Indicate the Subject and Object

Following is a list of verbs whose movements indicate the subject and object of a sentence.

ADVISE-ME

ADVISE

APPROACH

ASK

BAWL-OUT (To yell at someone)

(for example: beat at a game, race, competition, etc.)

BEAT

BLAME

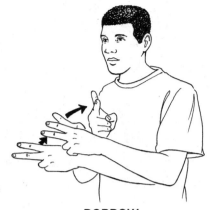

BORROW

FORCE

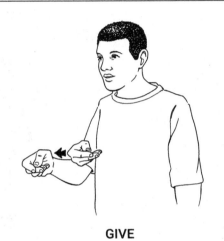

GIVE

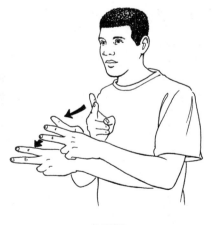

LEND

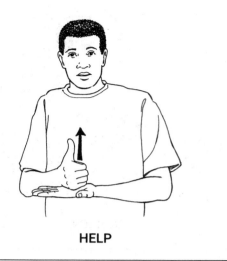

HELP

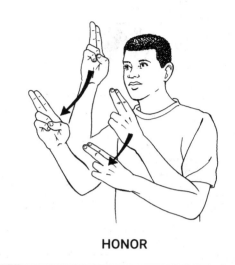

HONOR

FINGERSPELL

HATE

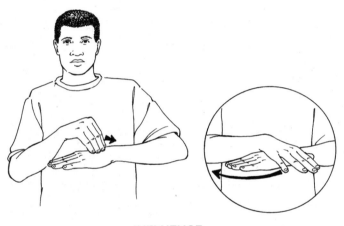

INFLUENCE

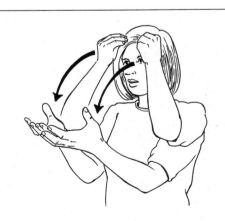

INFORM

INSULT

INTERROGATE

KICK

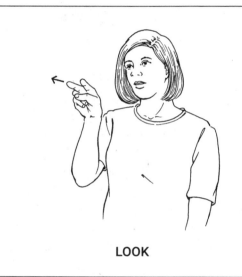

LOOK

ORDER/COMMAND

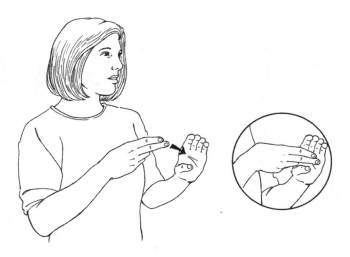

PARTICIPATE/JOIN

OVERCOME

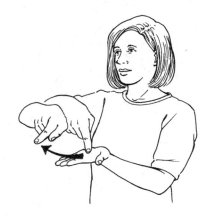

PAY

PAY-ATTENTION

PICK

PITY

PREACH

QUIT

RESPECT

RIDICULE

SCOLD

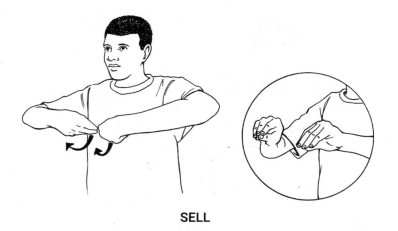

SELL

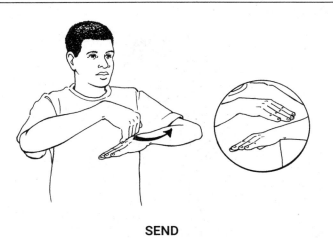

SEND

SHOW

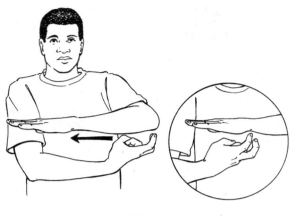

STEAL

TEACH

The Role of the Dominant Hand and Nondominant Hand in Verbs that Indicate the Subject and Object of a Sentence

There are more verbs that indicate the subject and the object of a sentence. The principle for using them is the same as for the verbs listed previously with one exception: The non-dominant hand is placed in front of the referent for the object of the sentence while the dominant hand moves toward it. Thus, placement of the hands is critical where one of the hands moves and the other one does not. The sentence

he-PICK-ON-me.

means "He is picking on me." The neutral sign for PICK-ON is shown in the following illustration.

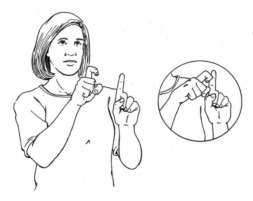

In this sign, the right hand moves while the left hand does not. We call the hand that moves the dominant hand and the hand that does not move the nondominant hand. Let's look at an illustration of the sign for you-PICK-ON-me.

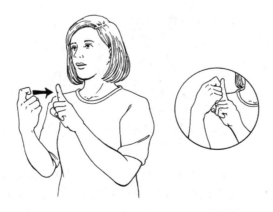

In this sign, the left hand is the nondominant hand, and it is held stationary in front of the signer's body. This hand indicates the object of the sentence. The right hand is the dominant hand, and it is moved toward the nondominant hand. This configuration of the hands shows "who is doing what to whom." The dominant hand moves from the subject or the position of YOU in the signing space toward the signer. The signer is represented by ME in the sentence.

Because of the presence of the nondominant hand in the position of the object of a sentence, it is difficult to sweep the hand to indicate pronouns for more than one person such as THEY, THEM, and the plural form of YOU. Thus, instead of a sweep, the signer simply repeats the sign while moving it to the side. This is shown in the following illustration of the sign me-CONTACT-them.

CONTACT

This example is typical of the relationship between the dominant hand and the nondominant hand in directional verbs. The orientation of the hands is also important. The drawings for the verbs listed in this chapter are for the neutral position of the verb. Yet, when signing, the orientation of the hands will change depending upon where the subject and object of the sentence are placed in the signing space. For this reason, beginning signers are advised to seek out a skilled signer or an ASL instructor to demonstrate both the orientation and the movement of the hands for directional verbs.

List of Directional Verbs that Use a Nondominant Hand to Indicate the Object of a Sentence

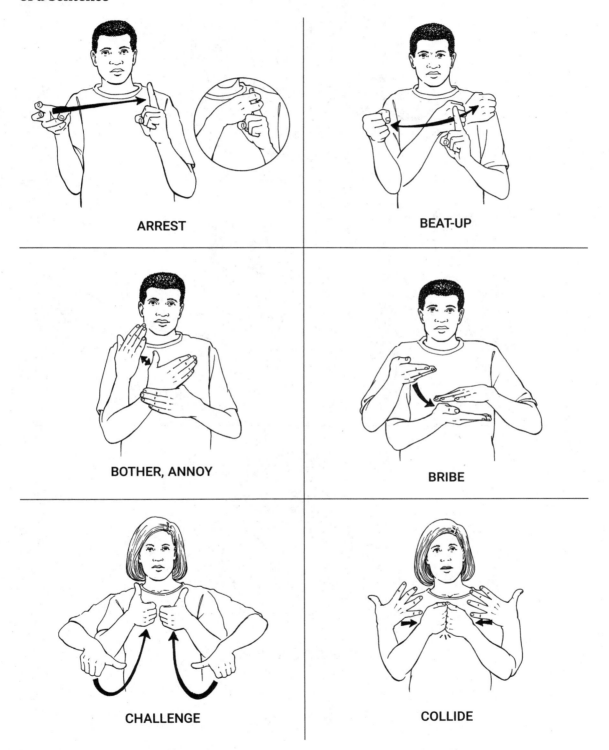

ARREST

BEAT-UP

BOTHER, ANNOY

BRIBE

CHALLENGE

COLLIDE

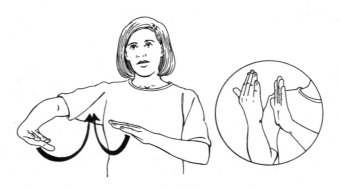

CONFRONT

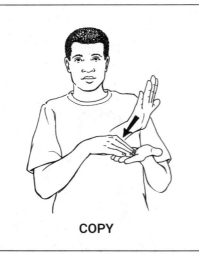

COPY

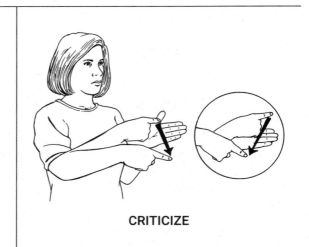

CRITICIZE

DECEIVE/FOOL/CON

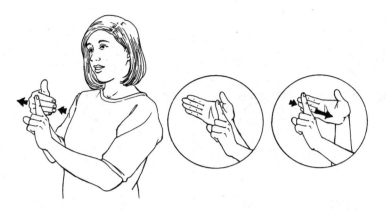

FLATTER

GET-EVEN-WITH

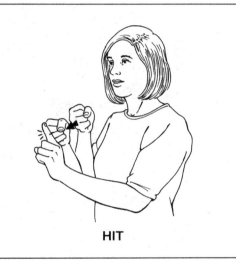

HIT

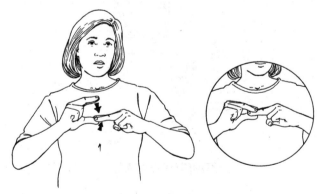

MOOCH-FROM

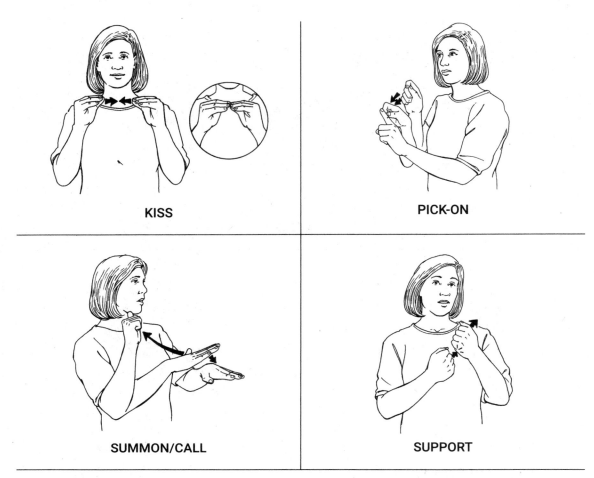

KISS

PICK-ON

SUMMON/CALL

SUPPORT

TOUCH/CONTACT

Verbs that Indicate the Movement from a Source to a Goal

1. me-FLY-to LOS-ANGELES (L-A). (I fly to Los Angeles.)
2. SANDWICHES she-BRING-here. (She brings the sandwiches here.)
3. YESTERDAY, HOME you-GO-to. (You went home yesterday.)

me-FLY-to

SANDWICHES

she-BRING-here

YESTERDAY

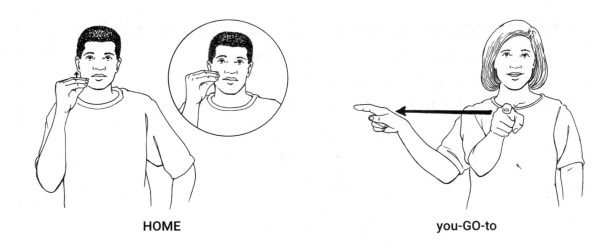

HOME   you-GO-to

The movement of some action verbs shows the movement associated with this verb. In sentence 1, the sign FLY-to begins where the subject ME is and then moves outward. In sentence 2, the sign she-BRING-here begins where the subject SHE has been placed in the signing space and then moves to a place in front of the signer to represent the concept "here." In sentence 3, the sign you-GO-to begins where the addressee (i.e., YOU) is and then moves away. Each of these signs is shown in the following illustrations.

Oftentimes, the action verb is moving to a place that has not yet been identified. In this instance, the signer moves the verb to a neutral position and then identifies the place. This principle is illustrated in sentences 1 and 2.

List of Verbs that Indicate the Movement from a Source to a Goal

ARRIVE

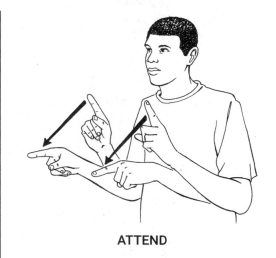

ATTEND

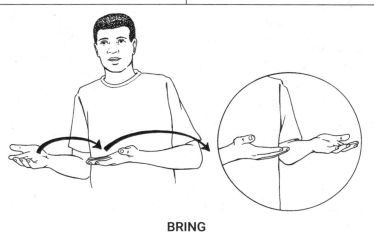

BRING

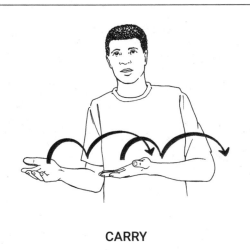

CARRY

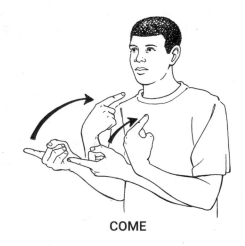

COME

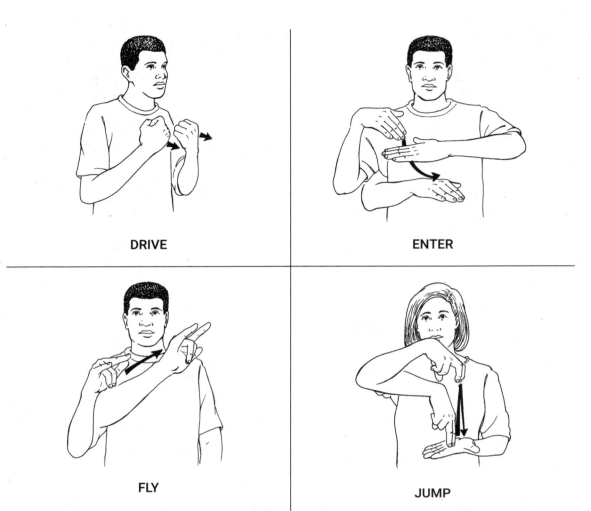

DRIVE

ENTER

FLY

JUMP

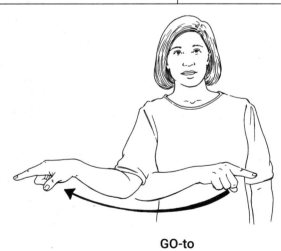

GO-to

MOVE

PATRONIZE, HUMILIATE,
TALK DOWN TO

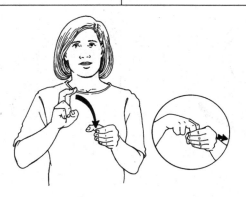

RIDE-IN

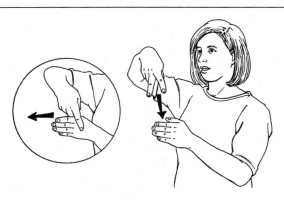

RIDE-ON

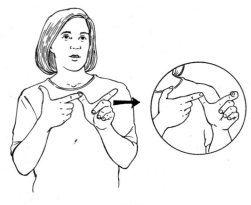

RUN

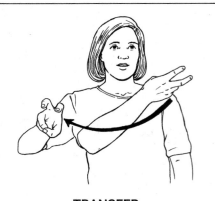

TRANSFER

WALK

Reciprocal Verbs

1. they-LOOK-each-other. (They looked at each other.)
2. TOMORROW, they-INFORM-each-other. (We will inform each other tomorrow.)
3. LAST-NIGHT they-PITY-each-other. (They pitied each other last night.)

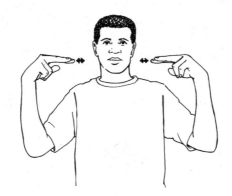

they-LOOK-each-other

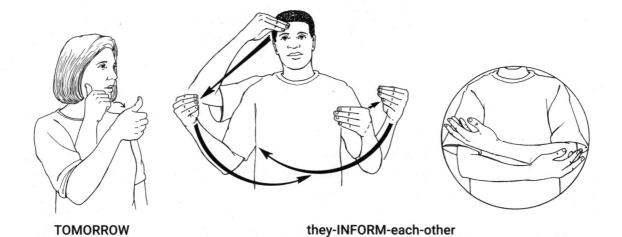

TOMORROW   they-INFORM-each-other

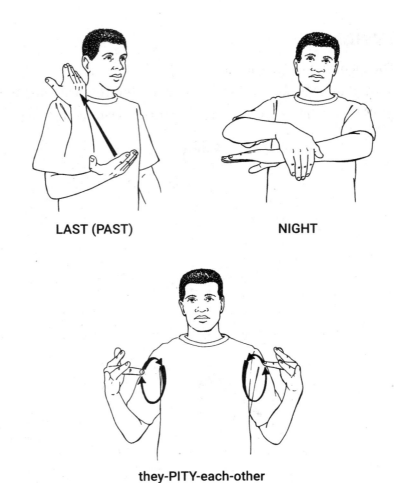

LAST (PAST)   NIGHT

they-PITY-each-other

Some verbs can be modified to indicate that two people, two things, or two groups are performing a particular action to one another. These verbs are called *reciprocal verbs*. Their movements are linked to the location in the signing space of the two people, two things, or two groups. Reciprocal verbs are signed differently than the verbs when signed in a neutral manner. The illustrations for the neutral sign for the verbs LOOK, INFORM, and PITY were shown earlier.

List of Reciprocal Verbs

AGREE

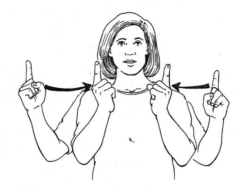

APPROACH

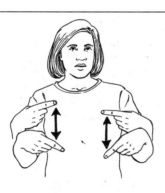

ARGUE

CHALLENGE

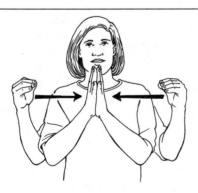

CLASH

COLLIDE

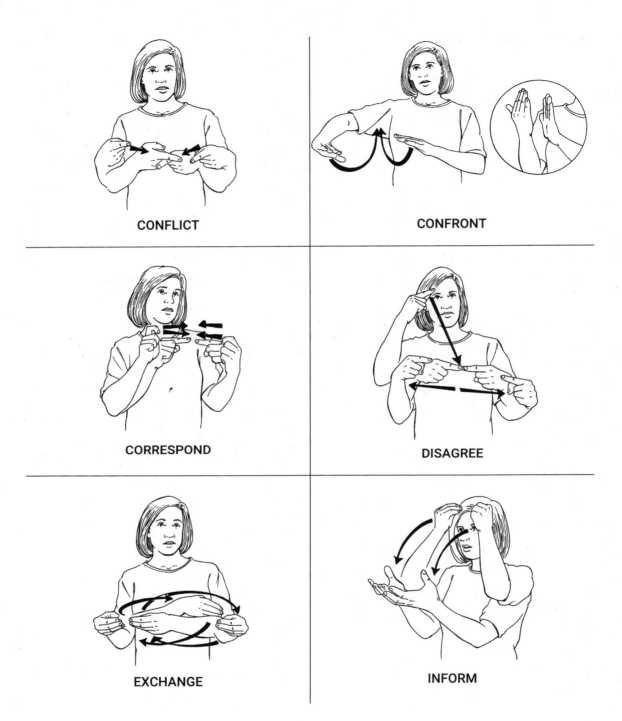

CONFLICT

CONFRONT

CORRESPOND

DISAGREE

EXCHANGE

INFORM

Practice Activity

1. Place a check mark in the column to indicate whether the main characteristic of the following verbs

   (a) can indicate the subject and object of a sentence,

   (b) uses a nondominant hand to indicate the object of a sentence,

   (c) can indicate the movement from a source to a goal, or

   (d) marks them as reciprocal verbs.

   Although some verbs have more than one of the following characteristics, select only the main one.

	Indicate subject and object	Nondominant hand shows the object	Movement from source to goal	Reciprocal verbs
1. BOTHER				
2. LOOK				
3. TRANSFER				
4. PAY				
5. ARGUE				
6. SUPPORT				
7. RUN				
8. INFORM				
9. QUIT				
10. DRIVE				

LESSON 13: THE DEAF TEACHER

Signing Dialogue

1. **Daveed:** **YOU TEACH COMPUTER SCIENCE YOU?**

    Do you teach computer science?

YOU | TEACH

COMPUTER | SCIENCE | YOU

2. **Vinay:** **NO, ME STUDENT. SCHOOL TEACHER SHOW-UP NOT-YET.**

No, I'm a student. The school teacher hasn't shown up yet.

NO ME

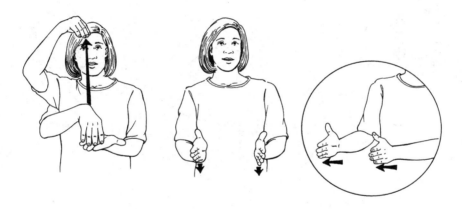

STUDENT

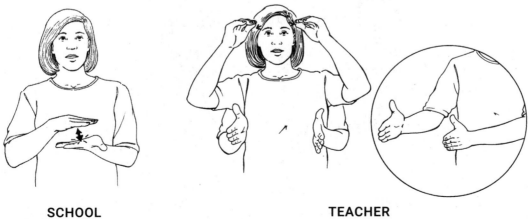

SCHOOL TEACHER

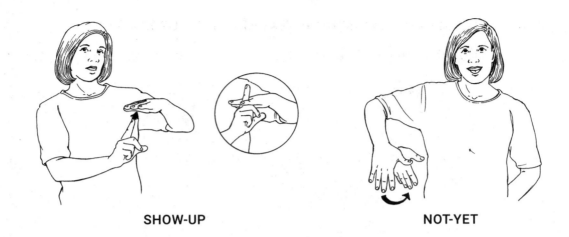

SHOW-UP   NOT-YET

3. **Daveed:**   **TEACHER MEET FINISH YOU?**

Have you met the teacher?

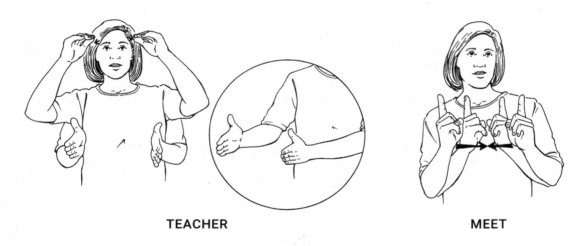

TEACHER   MEET

FINISH   YOU

4. **Vinay:** **MEET (shake head) NOT-YET ME.**

No, I haven't met her yet.

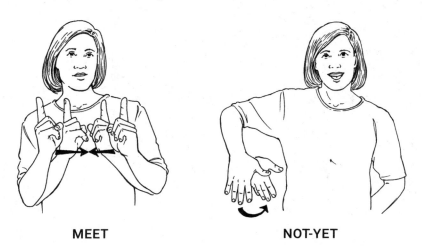

MEET   **NOT-YET**

ME

5. **Daveed:** **ME HEARD, TEACHER point-right, SHE-point-right DEAF.**

I heard that the teacher's deaf.

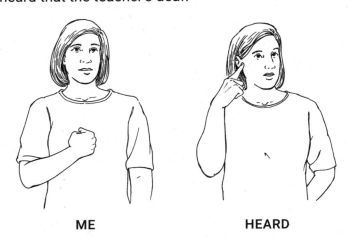

ME   **HEARD**

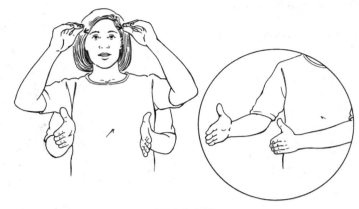

TEACHER

point-right

SHE-point-right

DEAF

6. **Vinay:**   **REALLY? SHE-point-left DEAF?**

Oh, really? She's deaf?

REALLY   SHE-point-left

DEAF

7. **Daveed:**   **(nod head) SHE-point-right DEAF. YOU DIDN'T-KNOW?**

Yes, she is deaf. You didn't know that?

SHE-point-right   DEAF

YOU   DIDN'T-KNOW

8. **Vinay:**   **(shake head) ME DIDN'T-KNOW.**

No, I didn't know.

ME   DIDN'T-KNOW

Breaking Down the Dialogue

Simple Yes/No Questions

Four yes/no questions were asked:

1. YOU TEACH COMPUTER SCIENCE YOU?
2. TEACHER MEET FINISH YOU?
3. SHE-point-left DEAF?
4. SHE-point-right DEAF, YOU DIDN'T-KNOW?

In sentence 1, the sign YOU can be used to ask a yes/no question, as shown in the following:

topic:	YOU TEACH COMPUTER SCIENCE
question:	YOU?

Repeating the pronoun in a sentence is a common ASL grammatical device.

In sentence 2, the FINISH sign can be placed after a verb—TEACHER MEET FINISH YOU?—or before a verb—TEACHER YOU FINISH MEET?—to ask if an action has been completed. The meaning of both sentences is the same: "Have you met the teacher?" Note that in this variation of the sign MEET, there is no pronoun incorporated into its movement. Instead, the signer makes the general sign for MEET.

In sentence 3, the sign SHE is made by pointing to the left. This pointing is referring to a place in the signing space where the teacher was established.

Sentence 4 uses the negative sign DIDN'T-KNOW to ask a question. The negative sign is placed at the end of the question. The sign SHE is made by pointing to the right in order to be consistent with where the teacher was placed in the signing space. That is, in the dialogue, Daveed first placed the teacher to the right side of his signing space in the sentence, ME HEARD, TEACHER point-right, SHE-point-right DEAF. Therefore, when he signs SHE again he must point to the same spot. More about pronominalization is found below.

Negation

To negate a thought, you first describe the topic and then add the appropriate negative sign.

topic:	SCHOOL TEACHER SHOW-UP
negative:	NOT-YET.

The sign NOT-YET does not always need to be placed at or near the end of a sentence. In the sentence

MEET (shake head) NOT-YET ME.

it would also be correct to sign

ME NOT-YET MEET.

The meaning in both cases is the same. The nonmanual signals that accompany the use of NOT-YET depend upon the situation. Sometimes the signer will shake the head while signing NOT-YET to emphasize the negative. If the signer is exasperated that someone has not shown up, then she or he might open the mouth slightly while wrinkling the nose.

Pronominalization

Pointing with the index finger is critical to the identification of pronouns in ASL. It can be used when a person is not present as long as the pronoun to which it refers has been established in the signing space. After a signer points to a spot to refer to someone or something, that spot becomes a reference point for that person or thing:

TEACHER point-right, SHE-point-right DEAF.

The dialogue has indicated to point to the right side; however, this was an arbitrary choice. The point can also be to the left side, and the meaning of the sentence will remain the same. A notation was made to "point-right" after the first occurrence of the pronoun SHE to remind you on which side of the signing space the teacher was placed. After a signer locates a person in the signing space, then the other signer can refer to that person by simply pointing to the same location. When the pointing instruction stands alone as in the above signed sentence, then it is made in addition to the sign that precedes it. That is, in the phrase, TEACHER point-right, there are two hand gestures—TEACHER and a point to the right. But when the pointing gesture is linked to the pronoun as in SHE-point-right, there is only one hand gesture—the point to the right, which is the sign for SHE.

Note that if Daveed points to his right side and Vinay wants to talk about the teacher, he would point to the same side, *which would be his LEFT side* if he and Daveed are facing each other. Think of the signers Daveed and Vinay as being mirror images of each other when trying to picture what the signing space looks like.

What's the Sign?

DEAF

The sign DEAF can be made either by moving the index finger from the mouth to the ear, as shown in the illustration in this book, or by moving the index finger from the ear to the mouth.

DIDN'T-KNOW

In Lesson 8, you learned the sign KNOW and DIDN'T KNOW. To form the sign DIDN'T-KNOW, the sign KNOW is turned away from the body. This characteristic of turning the hand away is referred to as *negative incorporation*. The sign DIDN'T-KNOW is the same as the signs DON'T KNOW and DOESN'T KNOW.

AGENT-sign

The AGENT-sign is shown in the following diagram and is used to make a noun out of a verb using the formula VERB + AGENT-sign = NOUN:

LEARN + AGENT-sign = LEARNER or STUDENT

TEACH + AGENT-sign = TEACHER

Compare the signs for LEARN and TEACH with the signs for STUDENT (LEARNER) and TEACHER and you will note that the verb signs are not formed in precisely the same manner when the noun is made. Their movements are slightly modified to accommodate the formation of the AGENT-sign.

TRUE

The sign TRUE can be interpreted in many different ways, but the basic meaning is that something or someone is a reality.

ASL Synonyms

Some signs can be used to mean other things.

Sign	Also used for
NOT-YET	LATE
SHE	HE, HER (nonpossessive form), HIM, IT
SHOW-UP	APPEAR, POP-UP
TEACHER	INSTRUCTOR, PROFESSOR
TRUE	ACTUAL, CERTAIN, REAL, REALLY, REALITY, SURE

Practice Activities

1. MODEL FOR SIMPLE YES/NO QUESTIONS

    Signer A: 1. Describe the topic;

                    2. sign YOU at the end of the sentence.

                Topic: YOU TEACH COMPUTER SCIENCE

                Question: YOU?

    Signer B: 1. Answer the question with the sign NO;

                    2. describe who you are.

                Topic: YOU TEACH COMPUTER SCIENCE YOU?

                Question: ME STUDENT.

Practice

    Signer A: YOU TEACH COMPUTER SCIENCE YOU?

    Signer B: NO, ME STUDENT.

2. MODEL FOR SIMPLE YES/NO QUESTIONS AND NEGATION

    Signer A: 1. Describe the topic;

                    2. shake the head and add the appropriate negative sign (NOT-YET).

                Topic: SCHOOL TEACHER SHOW-UP

                Negation: NOT-YET.

    Signer B: 1. Describe the topic;

                    2. ask a yes/no question using the sign FINISH.

                Topic: TEACHER YOU MEET

                Question: FINISH YOU?

Signer A: 1.   Describe the action related to the topic;

                2.   shake head and use the sign NOT-YET to negate the action.

Action:	MEET
Negation:	(shake head) NOT-YET ME.

Practice

Signer A: SCHOOL TEACHER SHOW-UP NOT-YET.

Signer B: TEACHER YOU MEET FINISH YOU?

Signer A: MEET (shake head) NOT-YET ME.

3.   MODEL FOR PRONOMINALIZATION

Signer A: 1.   Sign the noun TEACHER;

                2.   point to the right side (or left side) of the signing space after making the noun sign;

                3.   point again to the same spot to indicate the pronoun SHE;

                4.   describe the teacher.

Noun:	TEACHER
Locate the noun:	point-right,
Pronoun:	SHE-point-right
Description:	DEAF.

Signer B: 1.   Respond to Signer A's comment about the teacher;

                2.   point to the location where the TEACHER was placed in the signing space by Signer A;

                3.   ask a yes/no question with the sign DEAF.

Response:	REALLY?
Pronoun:	SHE-point-left
Question:	DEAF?

Signer A: 1. Answer the question affirmatively by nodding your head;
2. point to the location where TEACHER was placed in the signing space;
3. describe her;
4. ask a yes/no question.

Answer:	(nod head)
Pronoun:	SHE-point-right
Description:	DEAF.
Question:	YOU DIDN'T-KNOW?

Signer B: 1. Respond to the question.

Response:	(shake head) ME DIDN'T-KNOW.

Practice

Signer A: TEACHER point-right, SHE-point-right DEAF.

Signer B: REALLY? SHE-point-left DEAF?

Signer A: (nod head) SHE-point-right DEAF, YOU DIDN'T-KNOW?

Signer B: NO, ME DIDN'T-KNOW.

4. MASTERY LEARNING

When you feel comfortable signing these phrases, practice signing the entire dialogue shown at the beginning of this lesson. Practice the dialogue until you can sign the part of each character smoothly while using the appropriate facial grammar.

5. FURTHER PRACTICE

Use the following dialogue to review signs for descriptive terms introduced in previous lessons.

Signer A: TEACHER-point-right, SHE-point-right DEAF.

Signer B: REALLY? SHE-point-left DEAF?

Signer A: (nod head) SHE DEAF.

LESSON 14: THE INTERPRETER

Signing Dialogue

1. **Claire:** **TEACHER SHOW-UP, YAY!**

   The teacher has shown up!

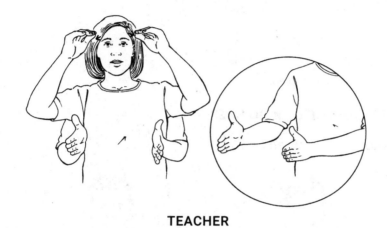

TEACHER

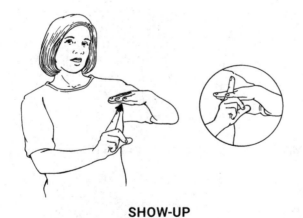

SHOW-UP

YAY

2. **Oliver:** **WOMAN THERE, WHO SHE?**

Who is that woman?

WOMAN   **THERE**

WHO   **SHE**

3. **Claire:** **WOMAN THERE, SHE INTERPRETER.**

That woman is an interpreter.

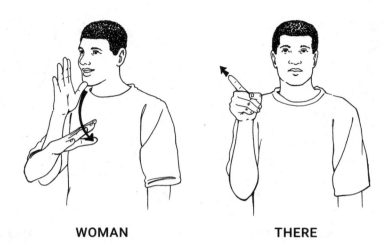

WOMAN

THERE

SHE

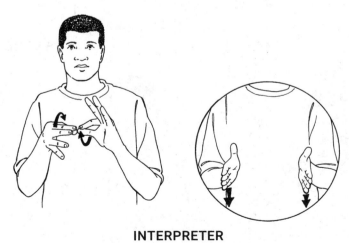

INTERPRETER

4. **Oliver:** **INTERPRETER, DO-what?**

What does an interpreter do?

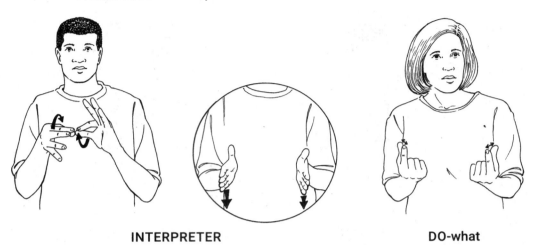

INTERPRETER   DO-what

5. **Claire:** **DEAF HEARING COMMUNICATE HOW? INTERPRETER INTERPRET.**

Deaf and hearing people communicate because an interpreter interprets.

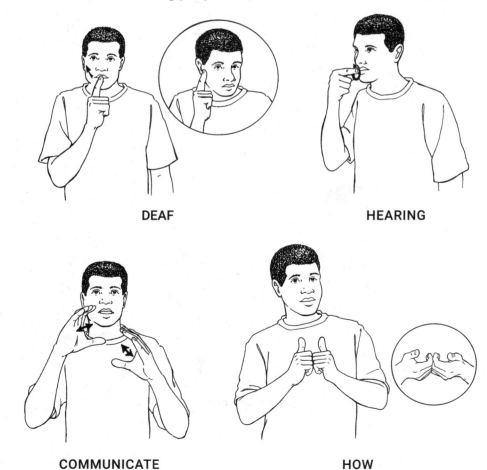

DEAF   HEARING

COMMUNICATE   HOW

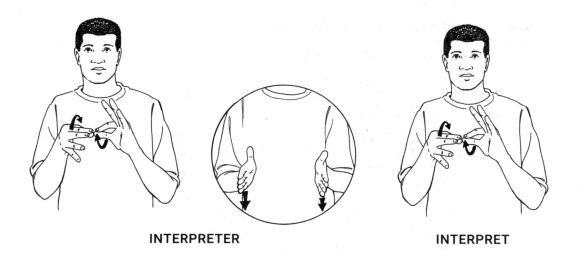

INTERPRETER   INTERPRET

6. **Oliver:**   **OH-I-see, SHE INTERPRET.**

I get it, she interprets.

OH-I-see   SHE

INTERPRET

7. **Claire:** **(nods head) LEARN+ YOU, FINALLY!**

Yes, you are finally learning.

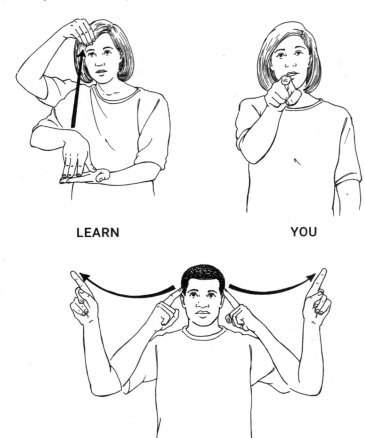

LEARN   YOU

FINALLY

8. **Oliver:** **SILLY YOU. ME LEARN ALWAYS.**

You are being silly. I am always learning.

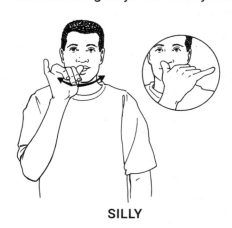

SILLY

YOU   ME

LEARN   ALWAYS

Breaking Down the Dialogue

Use of the Sign YAY

The sign for YAY can be used to show excitement. The students are excited to see the teacher. It typically is used in applause or celebration.

TEACHER SHOW-UP, YAY!

Alternate Sign Choice Can Be the Use of the Sign FINALLY

The sign for FINALLY can be used alone to mean "It's about time" or "It finally happened" or some other close approximation to these meanings. It can also be used after an action to show that the action has finally taken place. It typically follows the action to which it is referring.

INTERPRETER SHOW-UP, FINALLY!

The sign FINALLY is often made with the signer mouthing the expression "Pah!"

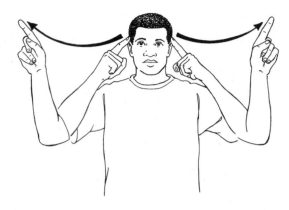

FINALLY

Information-seeking Questions

The signer describes the topic and then signs the wh-question.

Topic	Wh-question
WOMAN THERE	WHO SHE?
INTERPRETER,	DO-what?

Pronominalization

When a person is present, pronouns can be signed by directly pointing to that person. This pointing behavior is represented by the sign THERE. In the dialogue, the Deaf teacher and the interpreter are visible to the two signers. Therefore, to talk about the woman interpreter, the signer uses the sign THERE to point directly at her. Because the woman is now placed in the signing space, the signer can point to this place when referring to the woman with the pronoun SHE. In the following two sentences

WOMAN THERE, WHO SHE?

WOMAN THERE, SHE INTERPRETER.

the signs THERE and SHE are made in exactly the same manner.

Rhetorical Questions

In the rhetorical question

DEAF HEARING COMMUNICATE HOW? INTERPRETER INTERPRET.

HOW is not directly translated into English. Rather, it is translated to the conjunction *because*. One translation of this sentence is "Deaf and hearing people communicate because an interpreter interprets." When signing HOW, (1) *the head tilts forward* and (2) *the eyebrows are raised* because the question is a rhetorical one.

SILLY YOU

The translation of SILLY YOU is "You are being silly." It can be used with other phrases or by itself. The face should relay the feelings of the signer who is signing this phrase.

Temporal Aspect: Progressive Form of a Verb

The progressive form of some verbs can be indicated by repeating the sign. This repetition is indicated by the plus sign (+) placed after the sign.

progressive form:	LEARN+
translation:	learning

What's the Sign?

FINALLY

A nonmanual signal that often accompanies the sign FINALLY is *a voiceless expression of the syllable "Pah" with the mouth held open for a few seconds while the final position of the sign is also held.* This signal, along with holding the hands in the final position of the sign, helps to emphasize the relief that a person feels when something has finally taken place.

HEARING

The sign for HEARING refers to a hearing person. This sign is not used to refer to the act of hearing. This sign is also used for SAY and SPEAK. The connection in the meaning of the sign stems from the fact that a hearing person normally speaks, which distinguishes him or her from a Deaf person, who normally uses sign language.

INTERPRET/INTERPRETER

Some verbs can be made into a noun by adding the AGENT-sign at the end of the verb sign. Thus, INTERPRET + AGENT-sign = INTERPRETER.

OH-I-see

The sign for OH-I-see can be translated to "Oh, I see what you mean," "I get it," "Now I understand," and other close approximations to these meanings. It is often used to indicate to another signer that someone is following or understanding what's being said. A nonmanual signal that is suitable to this sign is to (1) *tilt the head back slightly* and (2) *raise the eyebrows slightly.*

ASL Synonyms

Some signs can be used to mean other things.

Sign:	HEARING
Also used for:	PRONOUNCE, SAY, SPEAK

 Practice Activities

1. MODEL FOR INFORMATION-SEEKING QUESTIONS AND PRONOMINALIZATION

   Signer A: 1. Describe the topic of the question;

   2. ask a wh-question using the sign WHO.

Topic:	WOMAN THERE,
Question:	WHO SHE?

   Signer B: 1. Respond to the question by indicating the subject (you must select an imaginary place in the signing space when signing THERE);

   2. describe the subject.

Subject:	WOMAN THERE,
Identity:	SHE INTERPRETER.

   Practice

   Signer A: WOMAN THERE, WHO SHE?

   Signer B: WOMAN THERE, SHE INTERPRETER.

2. MODEL FOR INFORMATION-SEEKING QUESTIONS AND RHETORICAL QUESTIONS

   Signer A: 1. Describe the subject of the sentence;

   2. ask a question with the DO-what sign.

Subject:	INTERPRETER,
Question:	DO-what?

Signer B: 1. Begin the rhetorical question by describing a topic;
             2. end the rhetorical question by asking a question with the sign HOW;
             3. answer the question.

Topic: DEAF HEARING COMMUNICATE

Question: HOW?

Answer: INTERPRETER INTERPRET.

Practice

Signer A: INTERPRETER, DO-what?

Signer B: DEAF HEARING COMMUNICATE HOW? INTERPRETER INTERPRET.

3. FURTHER PRACTICE SENTENCES

Signer A: OH-I-see, SHE INTERPRET.

Signer B: (nods head) LEARN+ YOU, FINALLY!

Signer A: SILLY YOU, ME LEARN ALWAYS.

4. MASTERY LEARNING

When you feel comfortable signing these phrases, practice signing the entire dialogue shown at the beginning of this lesson. Practice the dialogue until you can sign the part of each character smoothly using the appropriate facial grammar.

5. FURTHER PRACTICE

The following dialogue is to help you practice fingerspelling. Substitute a fingerspelled name, occupation, or descriptive term for the italicized word.

Signer A: WOMAN THERE, WHO SHE?

Signer B: WOMAN THERE, SHE *R-E-P-O-R-T-E-R*.

Signer A: SHE *R-E-P-O-R-T-E-R*?

Signer B: YES, SHE *R-E-P-O-R-T-E-R*.

LESSON 15: UNDERSTANDING COMMUNICATION

Signing Dialogue

1. **Jenson:** **DEAF TEACHER, SHE SIGN FINGERSPELL FAST.**

   The Deaf teacher signs and fingerspells fast.

DEAF

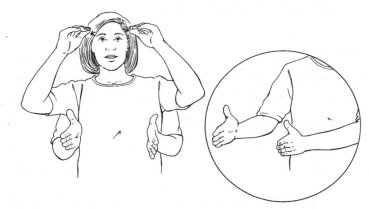

TEACHER

SHE

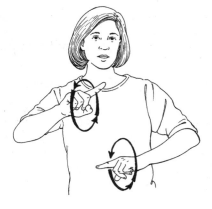

SIGN

FINGERSPELL   FAST

2.   **Grace:**   **SHE SIGN, YOU UNDERSTAND SHE?**

Do you understand her signing?

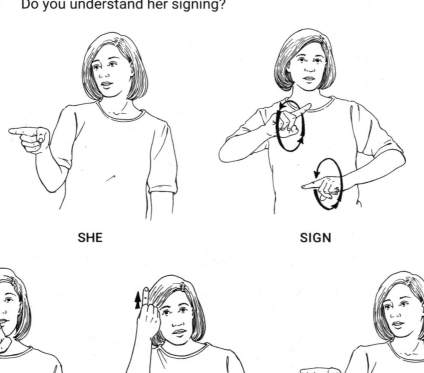

SHE   SIGN

YOU   UNDERSTAND   SHE

3. **Jenson:** **NO, ME UNDERSTAND LITTLE-BIT.**

No, I just understand a little bit.

NO

ME

UNDERSTAND

LITTLE-BIT

4. **Grace:** **SUPPOSE YOU SKILL SIGNER, YOU UNDERSTAND SHE?**

If you were a skilled signer, would you understand her?

SUPPOSE

YOU

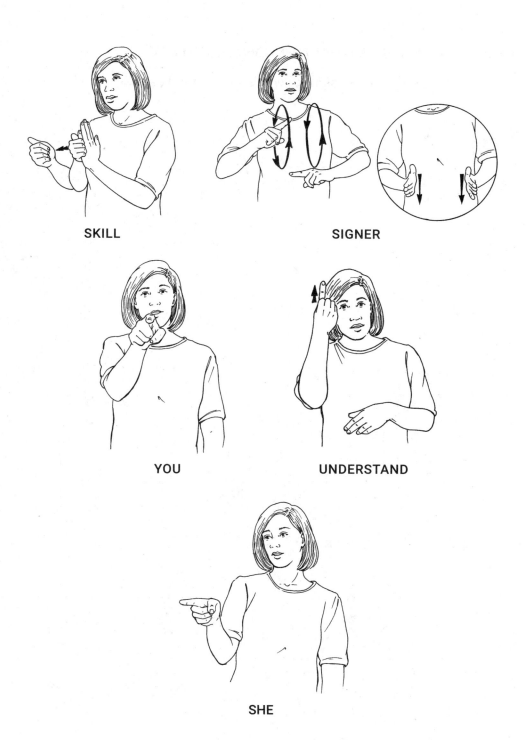

SKILL   SIGNER

YOU   UNDERSTAND

SHE

5. **Jenson:** **IF ME SKILL SIGNER, ME UNDERSTAND EASY.**

If I were a skilled signer, I would understand easily.

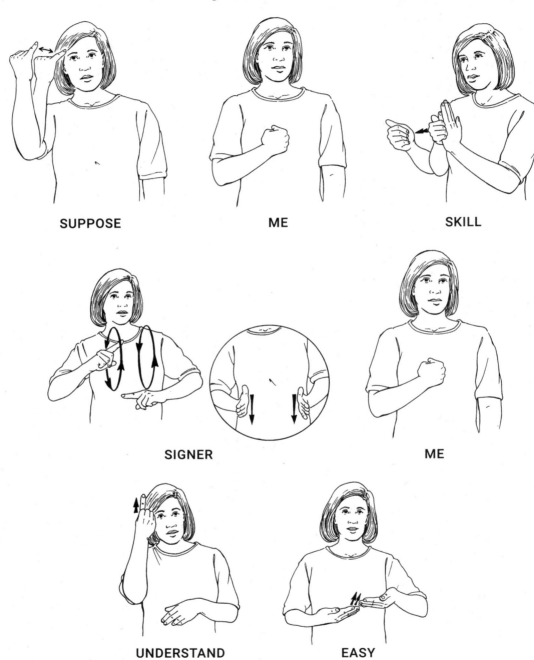

SUPPOSE   ME   SKILL

SIGNER   ME

UNDERSTAND   EASY

6. **Grace:** **SUPPOSE YOU INEPT SIGNER, DO-what YOU?**

What would you do if you were an incapable signer?

SUPPOSE   YOU

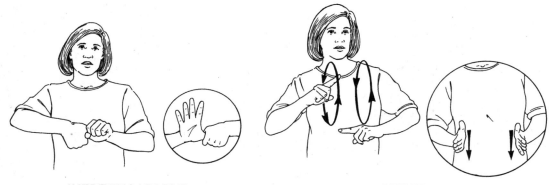

INEPT/INCAPABLE   SIGNER

DO-what   YOU

7. **Jenson:** **ME INEPT SIGNER, ME SIGN PRACTICE.**

If I were an incapable signer, I would practice my signing.

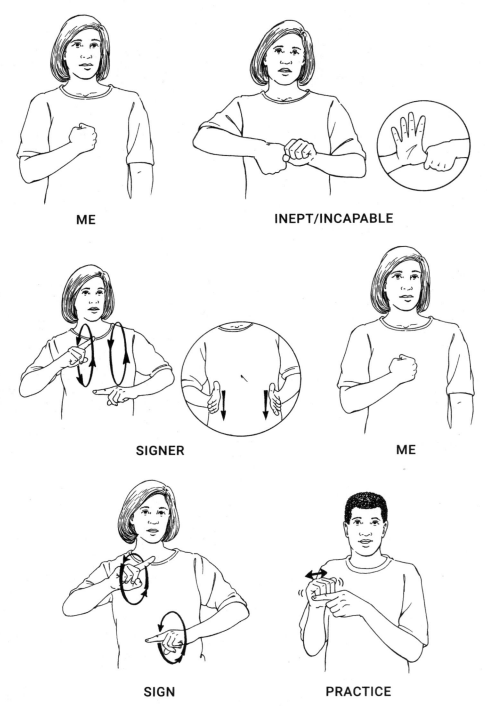

ME   INEPT/INCAPABLE

SIGNER   ME

SIGN   PRACTICE

8. **Grace:**   **RIGHT! TOMORROW, DO-what YOU?**

Right! What are you doing tomorrow?

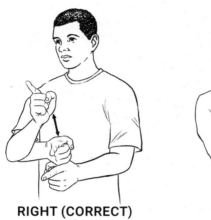

RIGHT (CORRECT)

TOMORROW

DO-what

YOU

9. **Jenson:** **TOMORROW, TWO-OF-US SIGN PRACTICE.**

Let's practice signing tomorrow.

TOMORROW   TWO-OF-US

SIGN   PRACTICE

10. Grace: ALL-RIGHT. TOMORROW me-PICK-UP-you.

Alright. I will pick you up tomorrow.

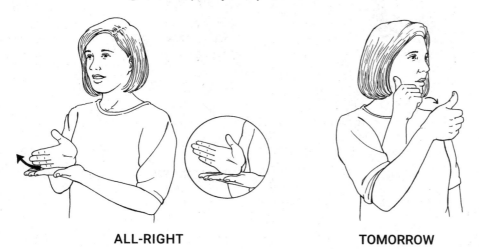

ALL-RIGHT   TOMORROW

me-PICK-UP-you

11. Jenson: GOOD. SEE YOU TOMORROW.

That's good. I will see you tomorrow.

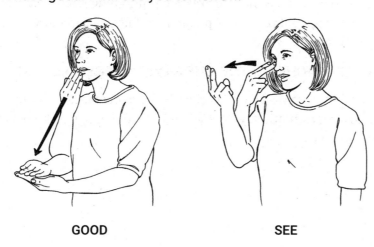

GOOD   SEE

YOU   TOMORROW

12. **Grace:**   **BYE.**

     Bye.

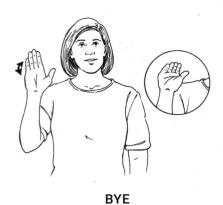

BYE

Breaking Down the Dialogue

Pronominalization

In this dialogue, you are practicing how to create a pronoun when the person is present. You must imagine that the Deaf teacher is present so that you can point to her when signing THERE in the sentence:

DEAF TEACHER THERE, SHE SIGN FINGERSPELL FAST.

Where you pointed when signing THERE is exactly the same place to point when signing the pronoun SHE. In a real situation, where you point will change if the person being referred to by pointing moves.

Conditional Sentences

The dialogue contains two sentences with conditional clauses with the sign SUPPOSE and two sentences where the nonmanual signals are the clue that the clause is conditional. The sign SUPPOSE is placed at the beginning of the sentence, followed by the condition, and then either a question or a comment related to the condition.

Conditional clause	Question/comment
SUPPOSE YOU SKILL SIGNER,	YOU UNDERSTAND SHE?
SUPPOSE YOU INEPT SIGNER,	DO-what YOU?
ME SKILL SIGNER,	ME UNDERSTAND EASY.
ME INEPT SIGNER,	ME SIGN PRACTICE.

When translating, the conditional clause can be placed at the beginning or the end of the sentence.

Translation: Conditional clause at the beginning of the sentence:

If you were a skilled signer, would you understand her?

If you were an incapable signer, what would you do?

If I were a skilled signer, I would understand easily.

If I were an incapable signer, I would practice signing.

Translation: Conditional clause at the end of the sentence:

Would you understand her if you were a skilled signer?

What would you do if you were an incapable signer?

I would easily understand if I were a skilled signer.

I would practice signing if I were an incapable signer.

Information-seeking Questions

When asking a wh-question using the DO-what sign, place the sign for the time adverb at the beginning of the sentence:

TOMORROW DO-what YOU?

A translation for this is "What are you doing tomorrow?"

Tense with Time Adverbs

Placing a sign for indicating time at the beginning of a sentence is a common way for showing tense in ASL. Note the placement of the sign TOMORROW in each of the following sentences and the corresponding translation:

Sentence indicating time	Translation
TOMORROW DO-what YOU?	What are you doing tomorrow?
TOMORROW, YOU ME SIGN PRACTICE.	You and I will practice signing tomorrow.
TOMORROW me-PICK-UP-you.	I will pick you up tomorrow.

However, in common expressions of departure such as "See you later," "See you in a while," and "See you tomorrow," the sign for time comes at the end of the sentence:

SEE YOU TOMORROW.   I will see you tomorrow.

What's the Sign?

SHE/HER

When HER is used as the objective form of SHE, it is signed in the same manner as SHE. This is the way it is signed in the dialogue. When it is used as the possessive form of SHE, then it is signed with an open hand. The English gloss for the objective form is SHE, and for the possessive form it is HER.

INEPT/INCAPABLE

The sign for INEPT (not skilled) should be accompanied by a facial expression that emphasizes the awkwardness or lack of skill of the person being described. A common facial expression is to puff the cheeks while making the sign.

SEE

There are many signs to describe the different ways of looking at something. The handshape is typically the V handshape with the two fingers representing the eyes.

SIGNER

The sign for SIGNER is made by making the AGENT-sign after SIGN. The AGENT-sign changes the meaning of a verb to a noun.

PICK-UP

PICK-UP is a directional verb. In the phrase me-PICK-UP-you, the signer reaches toward the addressee and makes the sign.

ASL Synonyms

Some signs can be used to mean other things.

Sign	Also used for
FAST	QUICK, RAPID
FINGERSPELL	SPELL
INEPT	INCAPABLE, INCOMPETENT, UNSKILLED
LITTLE-BIT	TINY
SKILL	EXPERT, PROFICIENT
UNDERSTAND	COMPREHEND

 Practice Activities

1. MODEL FOR SIMPLE YES/NO QUESTIONS AND PRONOMINALIZATION

   Signer A: 1. Describe the person;
   2. sign THERE by pointing to the person or pointing ahead to the left side (or the right side) as if the person is present;
   3. point again to the same spot to indicate the pronoun SHE;
   4. make a comment about the person.

Description:	DEAF TEACHER
Point:	THERE (point ahead to the left side),
Pronoun:	SHE (point ahead to the left side)
Comment:	SIGN FINGERSPELL FAST.

Signer B: 1. Point in the same direction that Signer A did when placing the Deaf teacher in the signing space;

    2. describe an action for the subject pronoun SHE;

    3. ask a yes/no question.

Pronoun:	SHE (point in the same direction that Signer A did)
Action:	SIGN,
Question:	YOU UNDERSTAND SHE?

Signer A: 1. Respond to the question by signing NO;

    2. make a follow-up comment to the negative response.

Negative:	NO,
Comment:	ME UNDERSTAND LITTLE-BIT.

Practice

Signer A: DEAF TEACHER THERE, SHE SIGN FINGERSPELL FAST.

Signer B: SHE SIGN, YOU UNDERSTAND SHE?

Signer A: NO, ME UNDERSTAND LITTLE-BIT.

2. MODEL FOR CONDITIONAL SENTENCES

Signer A: 1. Ask a question with a conditional clause (introduce the conditional clause by signing SUPPOSE);

    2. state the condition;

    3. make a question about the condition.

a.	Introduce:	SUPPOSE
	Condition:	YOU SKILL SIGNER,
	Question:	YOU UNDERSTAND SHE?
b.	Introduce:	SUPPOSE
	Condition:	YOU INEPT SIGNER,
	Question:	DO-what YOU?

Signer B: 1. State the condition;

    2. make a comment about the condition.

    a. Condition: ME SKILL SIGNER,

       Comment: ME UNDERSTAND EASY.

    b. Condition: ME INEPT SIGNER,

       Comment: ME SIGN PRACTICE.

Practice

Signer A: SUPPOSE YOU SKILL SIGNER, YOU UNDERSTAND SHE?

Signer B: ME SKILL SIGNER, ME UNDERSTAND EASY.

Signer A: SUPPOSE YOU INEPT SIGNER, DO-what YOU?

Signer B: ME INEPT SIGNER, ME SIGN PRACTICE.

3. MODEL FOR TENSE WITH TIME ADVERBS

Signer A: 1. Indicate the time;

    2. ask a DO-what question.

    Time: TOMORROW,

    Question: DO-what YOU?

Signer B: 1. Indicate the time;

    2. make a comment.

    Time: TOMORROW,

    Comment: YOU ME SIGN PRACTICE.

Signer A: 1. Make a remark;

    2. indicate the time;

    3. make a comment.

    Remark: ALL-RIGHT.

    Time: TOMORROW

    Comment: me-PICK-UP-you.

Signer B:	1. Make a remark;
	2. make a comment;
	3. indicate the time.

Remark:	GOOD.
Comment:	SEE YOU
Time:	TOMORROW.

Practice

Signer A:	TOMORROW, DO-what YOU?
Signer B:	TOMORROW, YOU ME SIGN PRACTICE.
Signer A:	ALL RIGHT. TOMORROW me-PICK-UP-you.
Signer B:	GOOD. SEE YOU TOMORROW.

4. MASTERY LEARNING

When you feel comfortable signing these phrases, practice signing the entire dialogue shown at the beginning of this lesson. Practice the dialogue until you can sign the part of each character smoothly while making the appropriate nonmanual signals.

5. FURTHER PRACTICE

Create a dialogue with conditional sentences similar to the ones shown in this lesson. Keep the sentences and dialogue short. Write the English gloss and the English translations for your ASL sentences. Practice signing the dialogue with a partner.

 Video Quiz Visit online.barronsbooks.com for scored practice on directional verbs and communicating.

Grammar Practice

Translate each of the following sentences to ASL, sign it, and then write the English gloss of the signs you used in your translation.

Note that there may be other ways of translating these sentences than the ones shown here.

1. I don't care if you have finished studying.

2. It snowed yesterday.

3. I will meet you here tomorrow afternoon at one o'clock.

4. What are you doing if it snows tomorrow?

5. How do I contact you if I forget your name?

6. What's the name of the video?

7. Must I practice ASL?

8. He hasn't shown up for class yet.

9. The interpreter signs in ASL.

10. She's a skillful signer.

CHAPTER 9

Relations

Learning Objectives

In this chapter, you will learn:

- How to apply the following grammar rules to create sentences: topic/comment, simple yes/no questions, pronominalization, information-seeking questions, ordering of simple sentences
- How to use pairs of opposites to describe people, places, and courses
- How to use TEACH as a directional verb
- New signs that describe family relations
- New name signs for cities
- New signs for occupations

LESSON 16: OPPOSITES

Signing Dialogue

Describing People

1. **Kaylia:** **YOUR TEACHER, DEAF HEARING WHICH?**

   Is your teacher deaf or hearing?

YOUR   TEACHER

DEAF   HEARING   WHICH

2. **James:** **MY TEACHER, DEAF.**

My teacher is deaf.

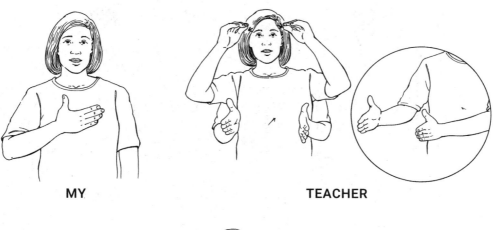

MY   TEACHER

DEAF

Opposites

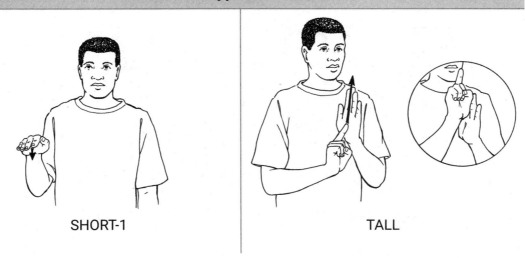

SHORT-1   TALL

Opposites

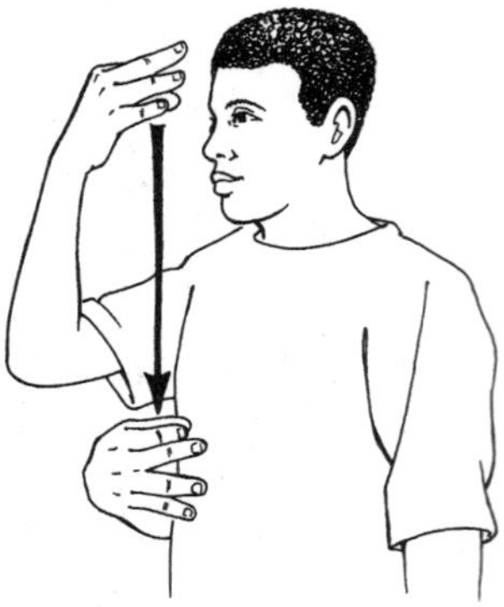

THIN

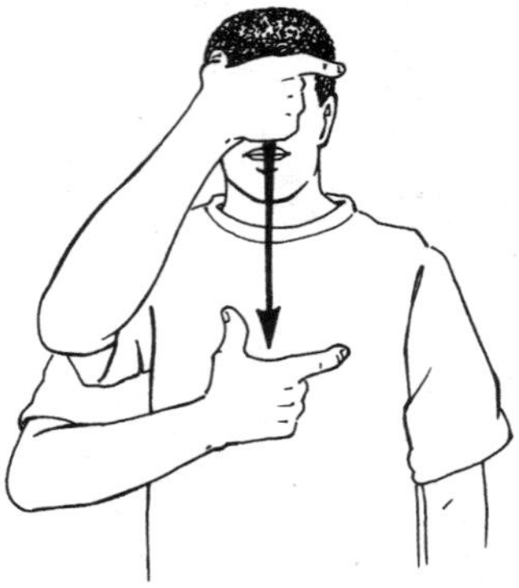

THICK

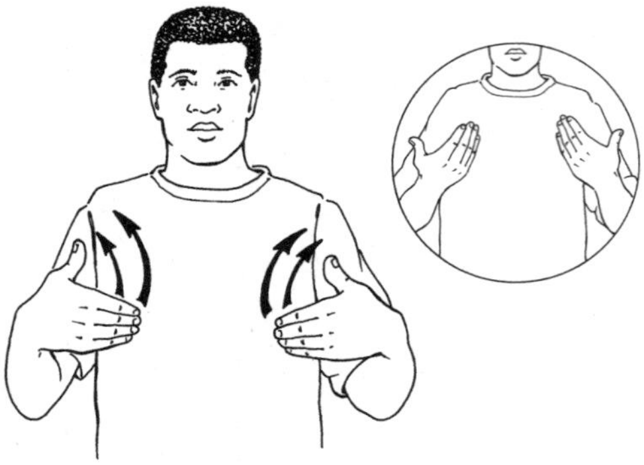

YOUNG

OLD

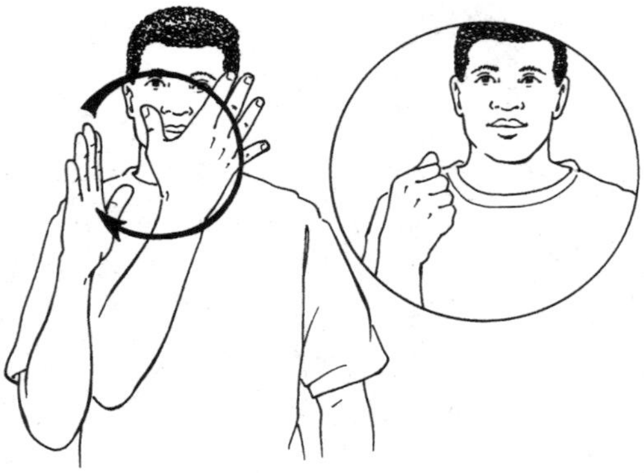

BEAUTIFUL

UGLY

Opposites	
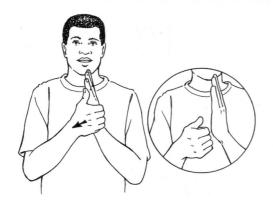 SKILLED	 INEPT
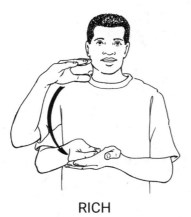 RICH	 POOR
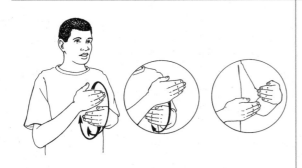 KIND	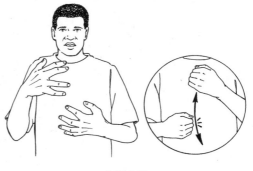 MEAN

Opposites

POLITE

RUDE

STRONG

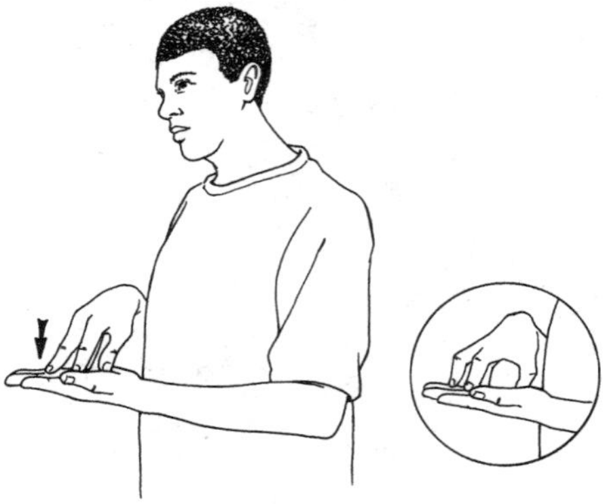

WEAK

Describing a Room

3. **Chai-Ling:** **YOUR ROOM, SMALL LARGE WHICH?**

Is your room small or large?

YOUR   ROOM

SMALL   LARGE   WHICH

4. **Michelle:** **MY ROOM, LARGE.**

My room is large.

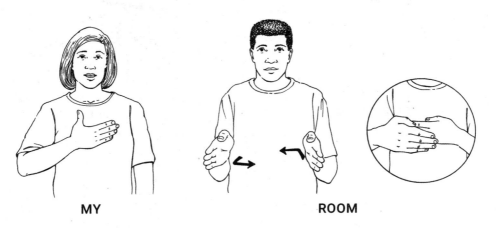

MY   ROOM

LARGE

More Opposites

QUIET

NOISY

EMPTY

FULL

More Opposites

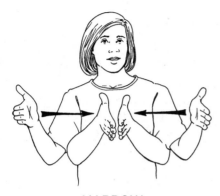

NARROW

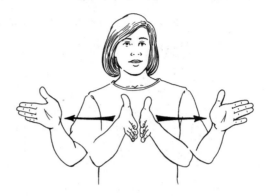

WIDE

BRIGHT

DARK

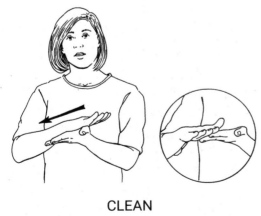

CLEAN

DIRTY

Describing a Course

5. **Alec:** **YOUR ASL COURSE, FASCINATING DULL WHICH?**

Is your ASL course fascinating or dull?

YOUR

ASL

COURSE

FASCINATING

DULL

WHICH

6. **Armen:** **ASL COURSE, FASCINATING.**

My ASL course is fascinating.

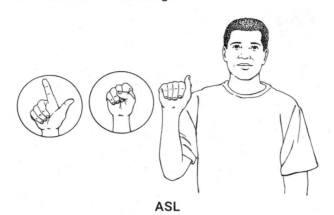

ASL

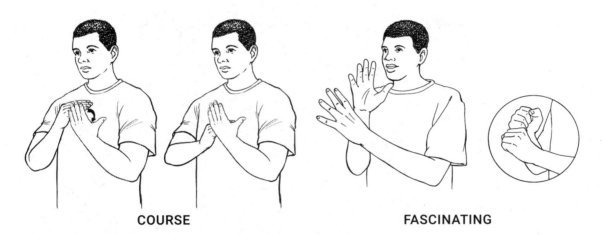

COURSE   FASCINATING

Even More Opposites

EASY

DIFFICULT

Even More Opposites

SLOW

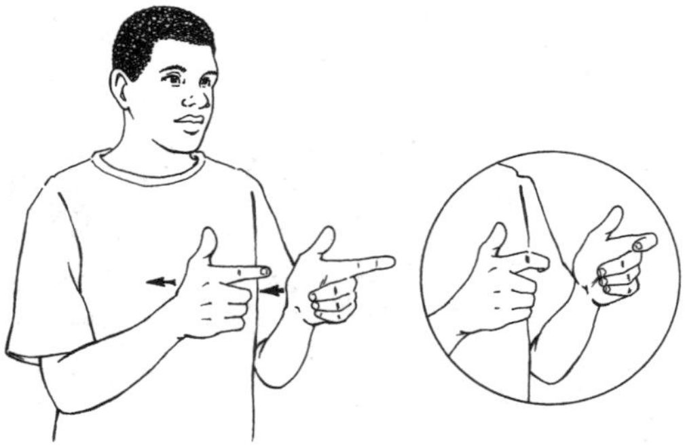

FAST

IMPORTANT

WORTHLESS

SHORT-2

LONG

| Even More Opposites |
| FASCINATING | DULL |

Breaking Down the Dialogue

Information-seeking Questions

The sign WHICH can be used to present a choice of answers to a question. It is particularly helpful when the choice involves opposites as in the following sentences:

YOUR TEACHER, DEAF HEARING WHICH?

YOUR ROOM, SMALL LARGE WHICH?

YOUR ASL COURSE, FASCINATING DULL WHICH?

The subject is first identified, followed by the descriptive terms (the adjectives), and then the sign WHICH.

Topic/Comment

You can describe things in the following manner:

MY TEACHER, DEAF.

MY ROOM, LARGE.

MY ASL COURSE, FASCINATING.

The topic or the subject is at the beginning of the sentence followed by a comment about it. Note that Rule #8 (ordering of simple sentences) could also be applied to these sentences. However, by using the topic/comment rule, you will signal what the topic is by (1) *raising the eyebrows* and (2) *tilting the head slightly forward*, (3) *pausing slightly at the end of the topic*, and then (4) *signing the comment*. Rule #8 does not specifically call for this use of nonmanual signals, although it does not bar their use either.

What's the Sign?

SHORT-1

The meaning of the SHORT-1 sign refers to a physical characteristic of something—height.

SHORT-2

The sign for SHORT-2 refers to the length of time and cannot be used interchangeably with the sign SHORT-1.

ASL Synonyms

Some signs can be used to mean other things.

Sign	Also used for
SHORT-1	DIMINUTIVE, LITTLE, SMALL
THIN	GAUNT, LEAN, LANK, SKINNY, SLIM
YOUNG	YOUTH
OLD	AGE
BEAUTIFUL	GORGEOUS, HANDSOME, LOVELY, PRETTY
SKILLED	ADEPT, COMPETENT, EXPERT, PROFICIENT
INEPT	INEXPERIENCED, UNSKILLED, INCAPABLE
RICH	AFFLUENT, FORTUNE, WEALTH, WEALTHY
POOR	POVERTY
MEAN	CRUEL
KIND	BENEVOLENT, GENEROUS, HUMANE
POLITE	COURTEOUS, COURTESY, GENTLE, MANNERS
RUDE	CURT, DISCOURTEOUS, IMPOLITE, MEAN
STRONG	STRENGTH, POWERFUL
SMALL	LITTLE, MINIATURE, TINY
LARGE	BIG, GIGANTIC, HUGE, IMMENSE, MASSIVE
QUIET	CALM, SERENE, SILENT, TRANQUIL

Sign	Also used for
NOISY	LOUD
EMPTY	AVAILABLE, BARE, NAKED, NUDE, VACANT
WIDE	BROAD
BRIGHT	BRILLIANT, CLEAR
CLEAN	NICE
DIRTY	FILTHY, POLLUTED
EASY	EFFORTLESS, SIMPLE
DIFFICULT	HARD
FAST	QUICK, RAPID, SWIFT
IMPORTANT	CRITICAL, CRUCIAL, VALID, VALUABLE, WORTHWHILE, WORTHY
WORTHLESS	IRRELEVANT, POINTLESS, USELESS
SHORT-2	BRIEF, BREVITY, FLEETING, TEMPORARY
FASCINATING	APPEALING, ATTRACTIVE
DULL	BORING, DRY, TEDIOUS, TIRESOME
COURSE	LESSON

 ## Practice Activities

1. MASTERY LEARNING

   Practice asking and answering questions by substituting signs from the list of opposites in the model shown in the dialogue at the beginning of this lesson. Be sure to use the correct nonmanual signals associated with asking a wh-question and forming a topic/comment sentence.

2. FURTHER PRACTICE

   Write ten sentences that use the sign WHICH to ask a question. Sign these sentences to a partner who must then answer them.

LESSON 17: RELATIONS AND PLACES

Signing Dialogue

1. **Naomi: STUDENT YOU?**

   Are you a student?

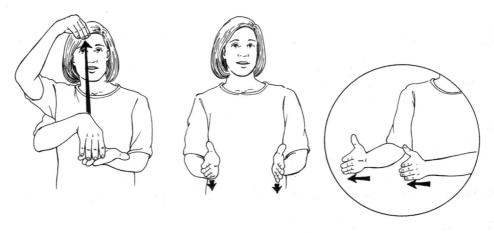

STUDENT

YOU

2. **Bob:** **YES, ME STUDENT. YOUR CLASS, ME TAKE-UP.**

Yes, I am a student. I am taking your class.

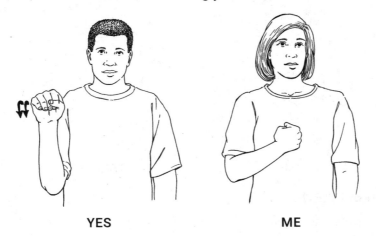

| YES | ME |

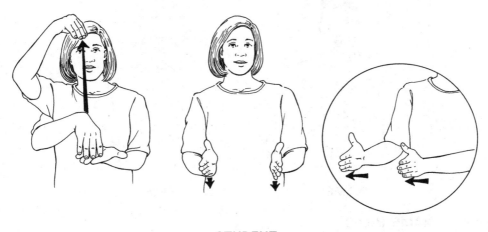

STUDENT

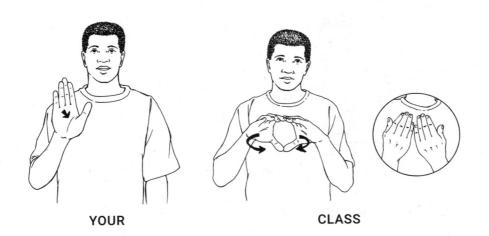

| YOUR | CLASS |

ME

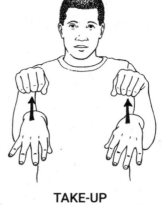

TAKE-UP

3. **Naomi: NAME YOU?**

What is your name?

NAME

YOU

4. **Bob: NAME, B-O-B.**

My name is BOB.

NAME

5. **Naomi:** **YOU LEARN ASL HOW?**

How did you learn ASL?

YOU   LEARN

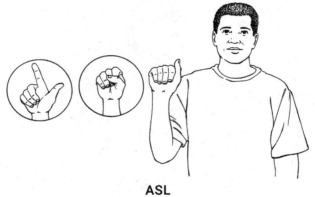

ASL

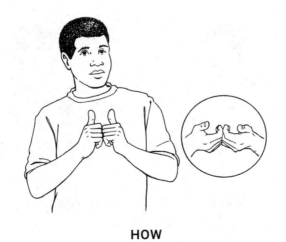

HOW

6. **Bob:** **MY BROTHER point-left, HE DEAF. ME SMALL, he-TEACH-me.**

My brother's deaf and he taught me when I was little.

MY	BROTHER	point-left

HE	DEAF	ME

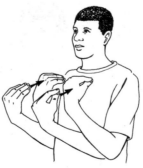

SMALL   he-TEACH-me

7. **Naomi: YOUR BROTHER LIVE WHERE?**

    Where does your brother live?

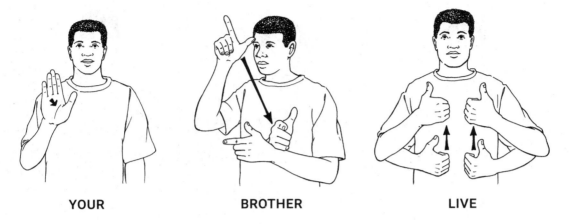

YOUR	**BROTHER**	**LIVE**

WHERE

8. **Bob: HE LIVE BOSTON.**

    He lives in Boston.

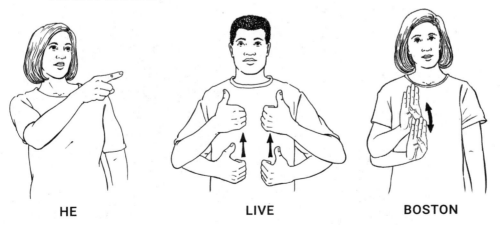

HE	**LIVE**	**BOSTON**

9. **Naomi:** **YOUR BROTHER LIVE BOSTON?**

Your brother lives in Boston?

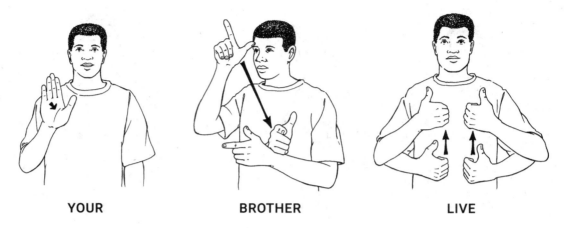

| YOUR | BROTHER | LIVE |

BOSTON

10. **Bob:** **YES, HE ENGINEER.**

Yes, he's an engineer.

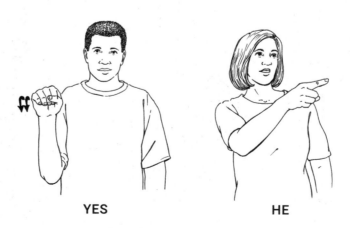

| YES | HE |

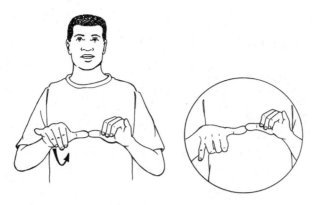

ENGINEER

11. **Naomi:** **MY BROTHER, ENGINEER SAME.**

My brother is an engineer, too.

MY   BROTHER

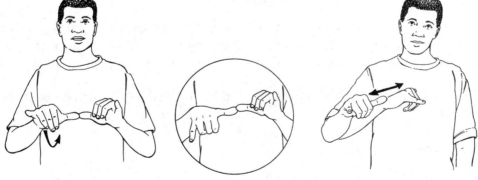

ENGINEER   SAME

12. **Bob:** **COOL!**

Hey, that's cool!

COOL

Breaking Down the Dialogue

Simple Yes/No Questions

1. YOU STUDENT YOU?
2. YOUR BROTHER LIVE BOSTON?

The sign YOU is often used to ask a simple yes/no question as shown in question 1. The question "Are you a student?" could also be asked as follows:

YOU STUDENT?

STUDENT YOU?

In both examples, the nonmanual signals for asking a yes/no question will typically accompany the last sign. However, with a short sentence a signer could send the proper nonmanual signals throughout the sentence.

In question 2, a topic is described, YOUR BROTHER, followed by a question about the topic, LIVE BOSTON?

Topic/Comment

Five sentences use the topic/comment rule:

ME NAME, B-O-B.

YOUR CLASS, ME TAKE-UP.

MY BROTHER point left, HE DEAF.

ME SMALL, he-TEACH-me.

MY BROTHER, ENGINEER SAME.

Information-seeking Questions

When asking a wh-question, you set up the topic and then use the wh-sign.

Topic	Wh-sign
YOU LEARN ASL	HOW?
YOUR BROTHER LIVE	WHERE?

Pronominalization

In the sentence

MY BROTHER point-left, HE DEAF.

where do you point to sign HE? You point to the left because that is where BROTHER was placed in the signing space.

Ordering of Simple Sentences

The sentences

HE LIVE BOSTON.

HE ENGINEER.

are examples of a simple sentence structure.

What's the Sign?

BROTHER

An older sign for brother and one that is still used in many places is a compound sign where the signs BOY and SAME are combined. The illustration for BROTHER shown in this lesson is a more common sign. To illustrate the difference between the two types of signs, the next lesson shows the sign SISTER being made by signing GIRL and SAME. You should, however, select one handshape for signing BROTHER and SISTER and use it consistently.

COOL

The COOL sign is used to mean one of the following or something similar: "Awesome," "That's neat," "That's super." It is *not* to be used to mean a temperature (e.g., "a cool day").

BOSTON

Many name signs for cities will use the handshape for the initial letter of the city's name.

SMALL

The sign SMALL is used in the sense of a young child. The signer is indicating the height of a child rather than the size of an object.

he-TEACH-me

TEACH is a directional verb. The sign originates in the location where the pronoun "he" is placed in the signing space. The fingertips are turned toward the signer to indicate who is being taught.

ASL Synonyms

Some signs can be used to mean other things.

Sign	Also used for
SAME	TOO, ALSO
ENGINEER	DRAFTING, MEASURE
LIVE	ADDRESS
TEACH	EDUCATE, EDUCATION, INSTRUCT, INSTRUCTION
COOL	NEAT, AWESOME

 ## Practice Activities

1. MODEL FOR TOPIC/COMMENT AND SIMPLE YES/NO QUESTIONS

   Signer A: 1. Describe the topic;
                2. ask the question using the sign YOU.

                Topic: YOU STUDENT
                Question: YOU?

Signer B: 1. Respond to the question with the sign YES;

2. repeat the topic;

3. describe a topic;

4. make a comment about the topic.

Response:	YES,
Topic:	ME STUDENT.
Topic:	YOUR CLASS,
Comment:	ME TAKE-UP.

Practice

Signer A: YOU STUDENT YOU?

Signer B: YES, ME STUDENT. YOUR CLASS, ME TAKE-UP.

2. MODEL FOR ASKING FOR THE NAME OF SOMEONE

Signer A: 1. Sign the topic;

2. sign the pronoun YOU.

Topic:	NAME
Pronoun:	YOU?

Signer B: 1. Repeat the topic;

2. fingerspell your name.

Topic:	ME NAME,
Name:	B-O-B.

Practice

Signer A: NAME YOU?

Signer B: ME NAME, B-O-B.

3. MODEL FOR TOPIC/COMMENT, INFORMATION-SEEKING QUESTIONS, AND PRONOMINALIZATION

a. HOW

Signer A: 1. Describe the topic;

2. ask a question using the sign HOW.

Topic:	YOU LEARN ASL
Question:	HOW?

Signer B: 1. Describe the topic;

2. make a comment about the topic.

Topic:	MY BROTHER point-left,
Comment:	HE DEAF.
Topic:	ME SMALL,
Comment:	he-TEACH-me.

Practice

Signer A: YOU LEARN ASL HOW?

Signer B: MY BROTHER, HE DEAF. ME SMALL, he-TEACH-me.

b. WHERE

Signer A: 1. Describe the topic;

2. ask a wh-question with the sign WHERE.

Topic:	YOUR BROTHER LIVE
Comment:	WHERE?

Signer B: 1. Repeat the topic;

2. name the place where the person lives.

Topic:	HE LIVE
City:	BOSTON.

Practice

Signer A: YOUR BROTHER LIVE WHERE?

Signer B: HE LIVE BOSTON.

4. MODEL FOR TOPIC/COMMENT AND SIMPLE YES/NO QUESTIONS

Signer A: 1. Describe the topic;
             2. ask a yes/no question about the topic.

             Topic: YOUR BROTHER
             Question: LIVE BOSTON?

Signer B: 1. Respond affirmatively to the yes/no question,
             2. describe the subject.

             Response: YES,
             Description: HE ENGINEER.

Signer A: 1. Describe the topic;
             2. make a comment about the topic.

             Topic: MY BROTHER,
             Comment: ENGINEER ALSO.

Signer B: 1. Make a remark relating to what Signer B has just said.

             Remark: COOL!

Practice

Signer A: YOUR BROTHER LIVE BOSTON?

Signer B: YES, HE ENGINEER.

Signer A: MY BROTHER, ENGINEER ALSO.

Signer B: COOL!

5. MASTERY LEARNING

When you feel comfortable signing these phrases, practice signing the entire dialogue shown at the beginning of this lesson. Practice the dialogue until you can sign the part of each character smoothly while using the appropriate nonmanual signals.

6. FURTHER PRACTICE

With a partner, place two people in your signing space and describe them using signs learned. Then ask a question about a person you have just described and see if your partner can answer it. For example:

Signer A: MY BROTHER point-left, MY TEACHER point-right.

              HE-point-left LITTLE, SHE-point-right TALL.

              SHE-point-right WHAT?

Signer B: SHE-point-left TALL.

Signer A: LITTLE WHO?

Signer B: HE-point-right LITTLE.

When Signer B answers the question, he or she must use the same location that Signer A used to establish the people in the signing space. For example, if both signers are facing each other, then when Signer A points to his or her right to indicate the teacher, Signer B must point to his or her left in order to refer to this teacher. That is, both signers point to the same spot in space.

LESSON 18: RELATIONS, CITIES, AND OCCUPATIONS

NOTE: This is a repeated dialogue from Lesson 17. Only newly introduced signs are illustrated in this dialogue.

Signing Dialogue

1. **Abbie:** **STUDENT YOU?**

   Are you a student?

2. **Juniper:** **YES, ME STUDENT. YOUR CLASS, ME TAKE-UP.**

   Yes, I am a student. I am taking your class.

3. **Abbie:** **NAME YOU?**

   What is your name?

4. **Juniper:** **NAME, J-U-N-I-P-E-R.**

   My name is Juniper.

5. **Abbie:** **YOU LEARN ASL HOW?**

   How did you learn ASL?

6. **Juniper:** **MY SISTER point-right, SHE DEAF. ME SMALL, she-TEACH-me.**

   My sister's deaf and she taught me when I was little.

SISTER

BROTHER and SISTER

Just as BROTHER can be signed two ways, with BOY moving to L handshapes or two L handshapes the whole time, SISTER can as well. As shown here, SISTER is signed by moving from the sign for GIRL to L handshapes hitting.

7. **Abbie:** **YOUR SISTER LIVE WHERE?**

Where does your sister live?

8. **Juniper:** **SHE LIVE SAN FRANCISCO.**

She lives in San Francisco.

SAN FRANCISCO

9. **Abbie:** **YOUR SISTER LIVE SAN FRANCISCO?**

Your sister lives in San Francisco?

SAN FRANCISCO

10. **Juniper:**   **YES, SHE DOCTOR.**

Yes, she's a doctor.

DOCTOR

11. **Abbie:**   **MY SISTER, DOCTOR SAME.**

My sister is a doctor, too.

12. **Juniper:**   **WOW!**

Wow!

WOW

ASL TIP

WOW

WOW can be signed a few different ways. It can be fingerspelled with great emphasis, or with a hand waving motion by the head/face area, or with the hand waving motion placed farther down toward the chest/side of body.

Mastery Learning

The signing dialogue for this lesson is taken from the previous lesson, except the sign for a family relation (BROTHER), a city (BOSTON), and an occupation (ENGINEER) are replaced with the signs for other family relations, cities, and occupations. Proceed slowly through each sentence and each new sign.

The purpose of this lesson is to use a sentence structure that will allow you to become familiar with new signs for family relations, cities, and occupations. You will also practice dialogue from memory—illustrations will be provided in the dialogue for new signs only.

English sentences are not provided for the short dialogues below, as you will practice writing the English in the Practice Activity.

More Family Relations

13. **Rebecca:** **YOU LEARN ASL HOW?**

    Rachel: MY SISTER, SHE DEAF. ME SMALL, she-TEACH-me.

14. **Rebecca:** **YOUR SISTER LIVE WHERE?**

    Rachel: SHE LIVE DETROIT.

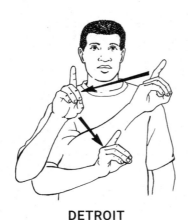

DETROIT

15. **Rebecca:** **YOUR SISTER LIVE DETROIT?**
Rachel: YES, SHE LAWYER.

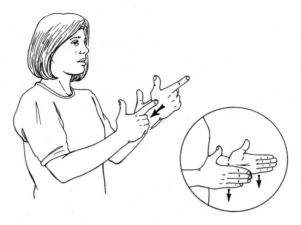

LAWYER

16. **Rebecca:** **MY SISTER, LAWYER TOO.**

Family

AUNT

COUSIN

Family

FATHER

GRANDFATHER

GRANDMOTHER

MOTHER

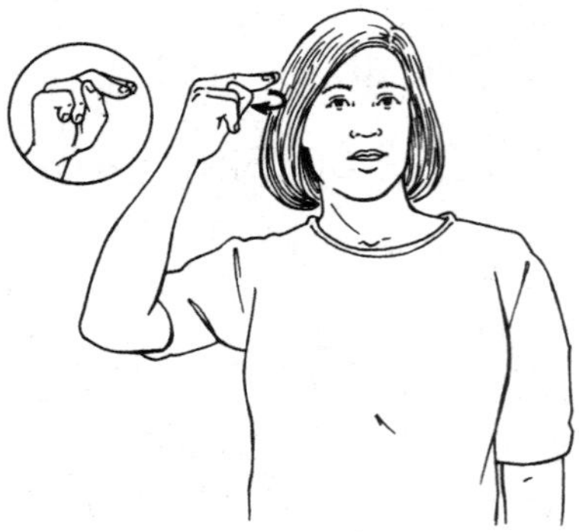

NEPHEW

NIECE

HUSBAND   WIFE   UNCLE

FAMILY

Switch Out the Cities and Occupation

17. **Rebecca: YOUR SISTER LIVE WHERE?**

    Rachel: SHE LIVE CHICAGO.

CHICAGO

18. **Rebecca:** **YOUR SISTER LIVE CHICAGO?**

Rachel: YES, SHE PILOT.

PILOT

Cities	

ATLANTA

BALTIMORE

Cities

CITY

EDMONTON

HOUSTON

LOS-ANGELES

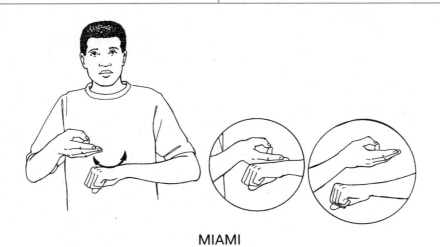

MIAMI

States, Provinces, and Cities

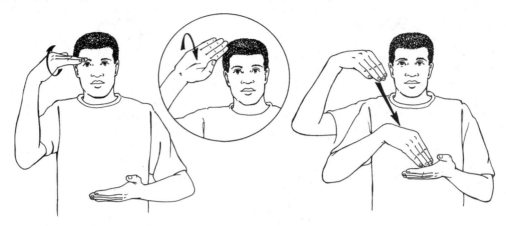

MONTREAL

NEW-ORLEANS

NEW-YORK

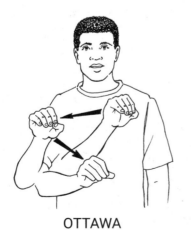

OTTAWA

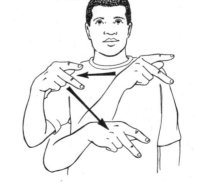

PHILADELPHIA

States, Provinces, and Cities

PITTSBURGH

ROCHESTER

SEATTLE

VANCOUVER

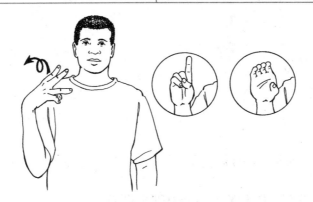

WASHINGTON, D.C.

ASL TIP

Cities

It is always best to first fingerspell the city you are referring to when you are out of town. Not everyone knows the sign for particular cities if they are not from that area. Example: TORONTO and POLAND have the same sign. Fingerspell for clarity until city, state, or country are identified.

CITY, COUNTRY, and STATE signs may vary from region to region.

19. **Rebecca:** **YOUR SISTER LIVE TORONTO, CANADA?**

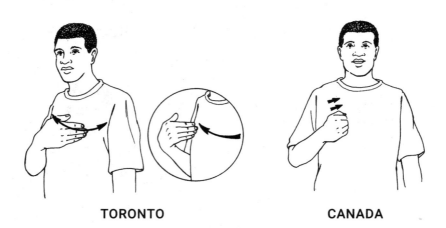

TORONTO CANADA

20. **Rachel:** **YES, SHE POLICE OFFICER.**

POLICE OFFICER

21. **Rebecca:** **MY SISTER, POLICE OFFICER TOO.**

Professions

CARPENTER

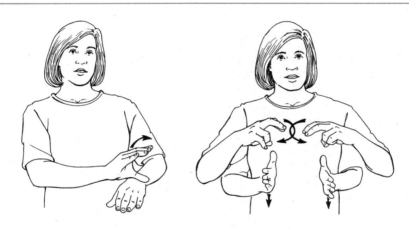

COMPUTER-ANALYST

DOCTOR

NURSE

Professions

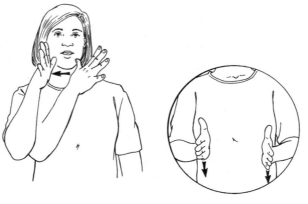

FARMER

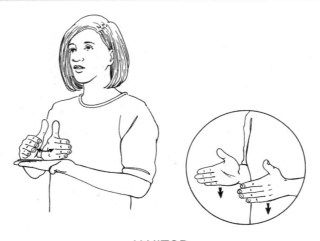

JANITOR

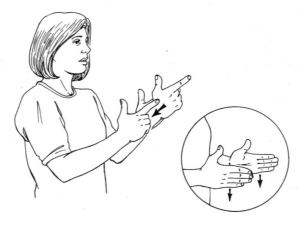

LAWYER

Professions	
 OCCUPATION	 PILOT

PLUMBER/MECHANIC

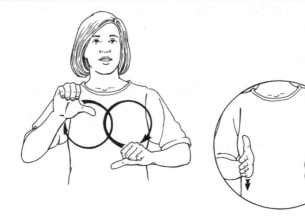

SCIENTIST

SECRETARY, RECEPTIONIST,
OFFICE ASSISTANT

 Practice Activities

NOTE: There are no new ASL sentence structures introduced in the dialogue for this lesson. Do not try to learn all the signs in a single day. Select a few to learn every day until you have gone through all the lessons. You can also refer to this lesson on a need-to-know basis, especially for signs for cities that you do not use in your daily conversations. Do practice the sentences until you feel comfortable signing them. As always, remember to use your nonmanual signals.

1. FURTHER PRACTICE

   Create a dialogue that uses signs from previous lessons. In your dialogue, have one person ask another person about his or her relatives, their occupations, and where they live. This is a good opportunity to fingerspell the city or occupation you do not know the sign for.

2. WRITE THE ENGLISH

   Write the proper English sentences from the ASL structure sentences provided.

 Video Quiz Visit online.barronsbooks.com for scored practice on relations.

CHAPTER 10

Role Shifting

> **Learning Objectives**
>
> In this chapter, you will learn:
> - Role-shifting techniques
> - Body- and gaze-shifting techniques
> - New signs

LESSON 19: ROLE-SHIFTING TECHNIQUES

NOTE: There is no Video Quiz for this chapter. Practice signing the provided sentences as you go along.

Role Shifting

The imagination is a great asset in ASL. To become someone else while signing, you must be able to create an image in your mind of what it is like to be this person. If you are repeating something that this person has said, then you try to say it the way it was originally said. Even though repeating something might just mean repeating the signs, there are times when you will want to mimic the body movements and facial expressions that accompanied the original message. In this way, you personalize the message—you let people know that this is how someone else acted. Welcome to acting class. I mean . . . ASL class.

Body- and Gaze-Shifting

Body- and gaze-shifting help indicate "what was said" and "who said it" or "what was done" and "who did it." This is accomplished through movement on the horizontal or vertical plane and the direction of a signer's gaze. The basic principle of this technique is that what a signer says or does is a direct reflection of what someone else has said or done. By shifting the body into a particular position, a signer becomes a certain person where the identity of this person is derived from the context of the conversation. To do this, you must have an image of what a person said and how this person acted. Read the following and imagine how you might sign it:

LONG-AGO ME CHILD, MY MOTHER she-SCOLD-me WHY?

ME WATCH T-V TOO-MUCH.

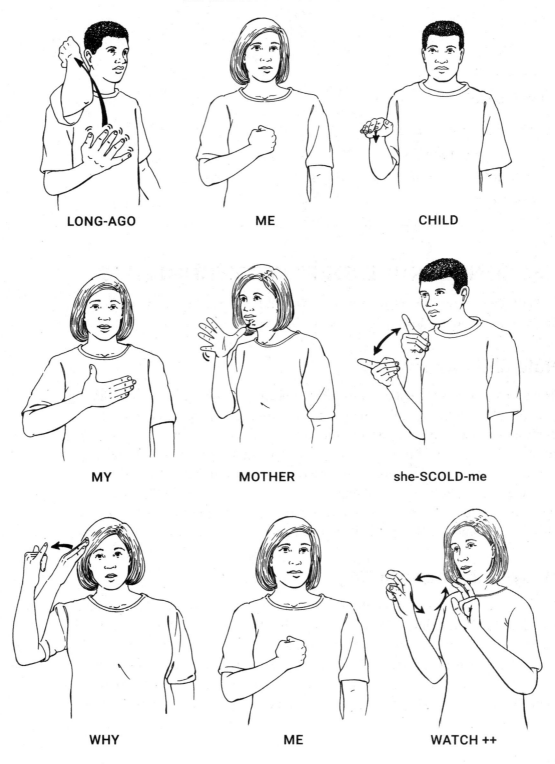

LONG-AGO	ME	CHILD
MY	MOTHER	she-SCOLD-me
WHY	ME	WATCH ++

TOO-MUCH

SHE SAY, "YOU T-V WATCH++ EYES DETERIORATE."

ME LISTEN, REFUSE.

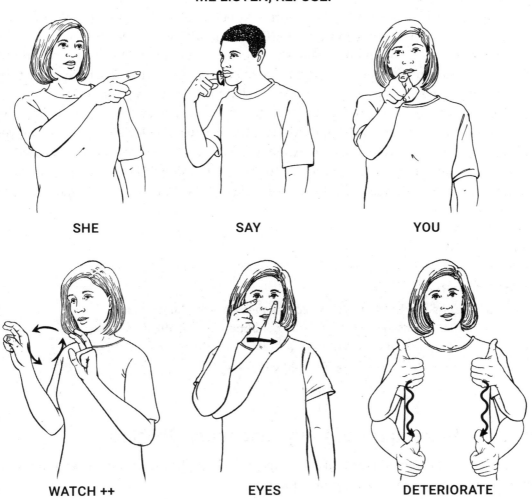

SHE   SAY   YOU

WATCH ++   EYES   DETERIORATE

| ME | LISTEN | REFUSE |

One way of signing this story is to turn the shoulders to the right and gaze slightly upward while signing she-SCOLD-me. You look upward because you have become the child you once were, and you are portraying your mother as being taller than you at that time. Because your mother was taller, you sign she-SCOLD-me with your index finger coming down toward your head as if your mother were shaking her finger at you. When you looked to the right, you placed your mother in the right side of your signing space. Therefore, you turn the shoulders to the left (because you are to the left of her in the signing space) and gaze slightly downward (because your mother was taller than you when you were a child) when saying what your mother said. To sign the last phrase, you sign LISTEN while leaning your head slightly to the right to indicate to whom you were listening (your mother). Finally, to demonstrate your act of defiance, you look to the left and sign REFUSE. You have now personalized the story—you assumed the role of yourself as a child and of your mother during that time.

ASL TIP

Time Duration

Some time signs can be changed to express the concept of time. For example, WATCH++ prompts the signer to continuously hold the sign while moving it in an up and down circular movement. This shows time duration, indicating WATCHING something for a long period of time.

The Four Techniques of Body- and Gaze-Shifting

There are four basic techniques that will help you master the art of shifting your body and eyes when you are personalizing your signing.

Movement Along the Horizontal Plane

Movement to the right or left, also known as moving along the horizontal plane, typically identifies "who" is talking. This movement can be made by:

1. Turning the shoulders and head to the right or left
2. Turning the head in either direction
3. Turning the whole body to the right or left
4. Gazing to the right or left

In the following story, the image is of a woman who is looking at a doctor holding a needle and becomes dizzy:

WOMAN point-left, she-LOOK-right DOCTOR N-E-E-D-L-E HAVE.

SHE DIZZY.

WOMAN   **point-left**   **she-LOOK-right**

DOCTOR   **HAVE**

SHE   DIZZY

To sign this story, you turn the shoulder to the right while signing she-LOOK-right DOCTOR NEEDLE HAVE because the woman has been placed in the left side of the signing space. You return to a normal pose with eye contact with the addressee when signing the rest of the sentence. To top off this story, you should also look dizzy when signing DIZZY.

Movement Along the Vertical Plane

Movement of the head and gazing up and down, also known as movement along the vertical plane, illustrate the different height or status of a person and the different height of an object.

WOMAN point-left, she-LOOK-up BUILDING TALL.

SHE DIZZY.

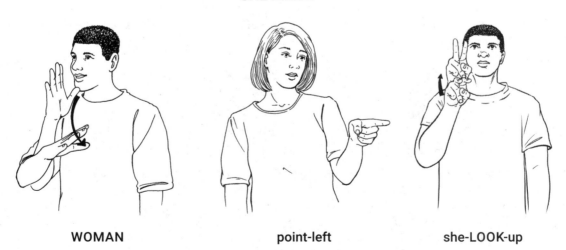

WOMAN   point-left   she-LOOK-up

BUILDING

TALL

SHE

DIZZY

This story is similar to the previous one except this time instead of looking at a doctor holding a needle, the woman is looking up at a tall building. To sign this, you should look to the right and gaze upward while signing she-LOOK-up BUILDING TALL. You should return to a normal signing position and look at the addressee when signing SHE DIZZY.

In the story about the child who watched too much TV, we will see that the signer looks down when saying what his mother had said to him as a child. The signer looks down to convey the image of a mother looking down at her shorter child.

Positions Relating to Directional Movements

Directional movements are related to the use of directional verbs, which you learned about previously. The directional movement refers to the movement of a sign that indicates the subject and object of a sentence. When signing a directional verb, your head and eyes should look in the direction that the verb is moving. You may also want to turn your body in that direction depending upon the amount of emphasis you wish to give to the sentence you are signing.

But gazing with directional verbs also depends on whether a signer is going to personalize a story. With the sentence "He asked her to please help him study," we get the following translation:

he-ASK-her, STUDY she-HELP-him PLEASE.

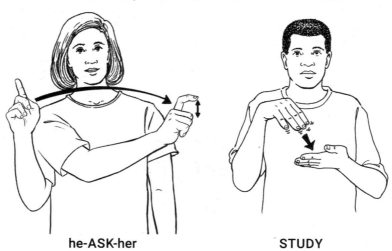

he-ASK-her   STUDY

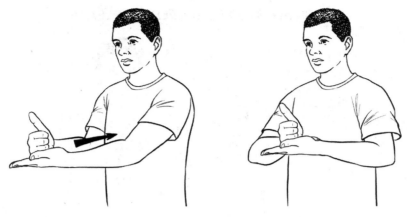

she-HELP-him

PLEASE

If you are not going to personalize this sentence, there is no need to shift the body. You can simply gaze in the direction that the directional verbs move. The sign he-ASK-her moves from wherever the person represented by "he" was placed in the signing space to wherever the person represented by "her" was placed. If "he" is on the left side and "her" is on the right, then the sign moves from the left to the right side, and you should gaze toward the right side. The right side is also referred to as the goal of the directional verb; therefore, gazing toward the goal is a good rule of thumb when using directional verbs. Similarly, you should gaze to the left for she-HELP-him. In the final part of the sentence, you can continue gazing to the right or you can resume a normal position with eye contact with your addressee.

Now, let's change this sentence to "He asked her, 'Will you please help me with my studying?'" which we can translate to:

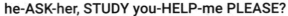

he-ASK-her, STUDY you-HELP-me PLEASE?

he-ASK-her   STUDY

you-HELP-me   PLEASE

If you keep the same placements in the signing space for the two pronouns, you shift your body to the right when signing he-ASK-her. Then you will personalize the question by continuing to face the right side while signing the entire question. Because you have become the person referred to by the pronoun "he," you sign you-HELP-me from the right side toward yourself.

Comparison

The visual and spatial qualities of ASL provide a convenient means of making comparisons. This is done by locating objects in the signing space and then using body- and gaze-shifting to establish a comparison. A signer in the process of comparing two dogs might place one of them in the right side of the signing space and the other in the left side. Then, for example, by gazing downward to the right and smiling, the signer indicates some degree of affection or feelings toward that particular dog. A downward gaze to the left accompanied with a frown would make it obvious that the signer is not as pleased with that dog as with the other.

Practice Activities

Beside each sentence, write the direction in which you might shift your body and gaze when signing. Remember that, unless otherwise stated, it does not matter whether you select the right or left side of the signing space as long as you remember where you have placed people or objects in the signing space. For example:

> She told her little brother, "Don't eat chips in bed." *Look to the right and downward.*

> But he responded back to her, "Go away." *Look to the left and upward.*

1. I looked and saw a police officer standing outside my car window. He didn't look happy.

2. "Look. Can you see the bird on the roof?"

3. The teacher told John, "Thank you for doing such fine work."

4. The child asked the teacher, "Can I be a frog in the play?"
   The teacher responded, "No, because you were a frog last year."

5. I watched the kite fly in the air.

6. I was shocked when I saw him standing beside me.

7. I was lying on the ground when my aunt came up and said, "The grass is wet. Please stand up."

8. The game is canceled for tomorrow.

9. I told my dog, "Sit and I will feed you."

10. I looked over my shoulder and saw my classmate.

Time

Learning Objectives

In this chapter, you will learn:

- How to apply the following grammar rules to create sentences: tense with time adverbs, simple yes/no questions, long yes/no questions, information-seeking questions, rhetorical questions, ordering of simple sentences, negation
- The plural forms of time adverbs
- How to incorporate numbers into time adverbs
- New signs for time adverbs in a self-created dialogue
- How to use one technique for indicating time in ASL
- The days of the week

LESSON 20: THE TIME LINE
Signing Dialogues

Past Tense Dialogue

1. **Michael:** **YESTERDAY, DO-what YOU?**

   What did you do yesterday?

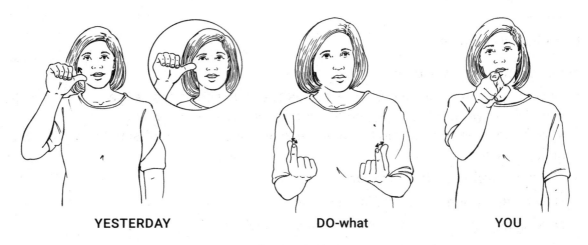

| YESTERDAY | DO-what | YOU |

2. **Lisa:** **YESTERDAY, ME BOOK READ.**

   I read a book yesterday.

| YESTERDAY | ME |

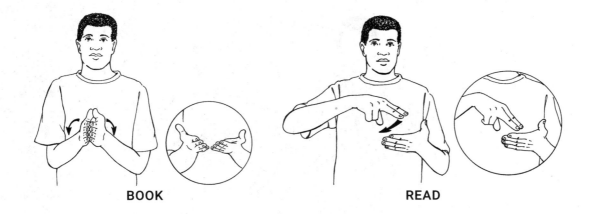

BOOK

READ

Past Tense

BEFORE

LONG-TIME-AGO

PAST (BEFORE)

RECENTLY

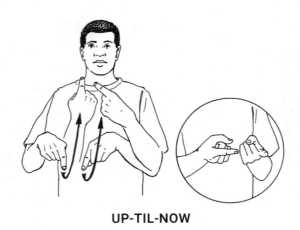

UP-TIL-NOW

Present Tense Dialogue

3. **Sebastian:** **TODAY, DO-what YOU?**

What are you doing today?

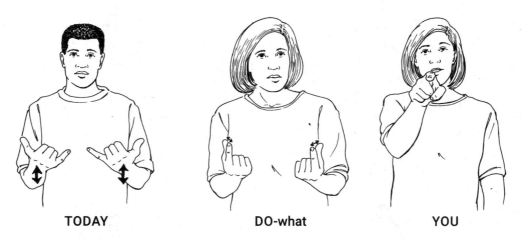

TODAY   DO-what   YOU

4. **Kelsey:** **TODAY, ME STORY WRITE.**

I am writing a story today.

TODAY   ME

STORY   WRITE

Present Tense

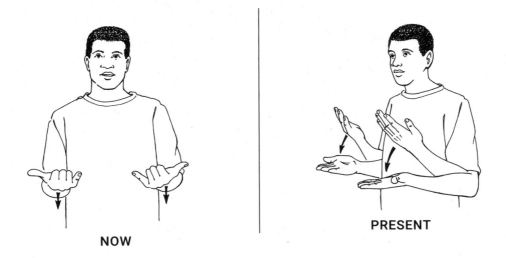

NOW   PRESENT

Future Tense Dialogue

5. **Manpreet:** **TOMORROW, DO-what YOU?**

What are you doing tomorrow?

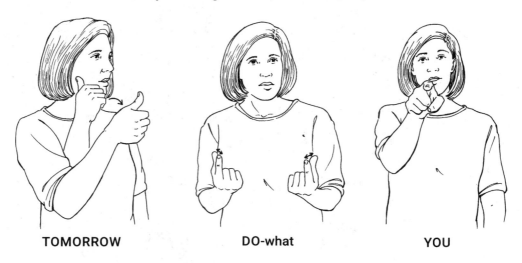

TOMORROW   DO-what   YOU

6. **Jamilla:** **TOMORROW, ME PICTURE DRAW.**

I will draw a picture tomorrow.

TOMORROW   ME

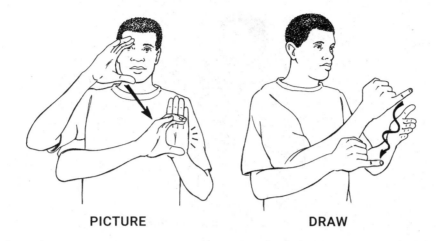

PICTURE DRAW

Future Tense

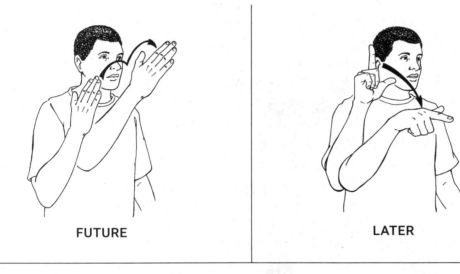

FUTURE LATER

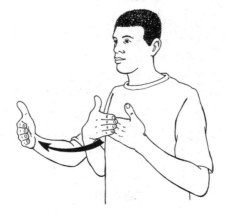

FROM-NOW-ON

IN-A-WHILE

AFTER

Writing

POETRY

MAGAZINE

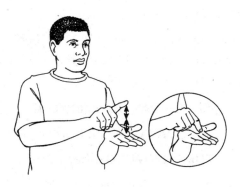

NEWSPAPER

Breaking Down the Dialogue

The Time Line

The body and the signing space combine to indicate time in ASL. The body represents the present time. Movement of signs to the back of the body represents action and events that took place in the past or the past tense. Movement to the front of the body represents action and events that have yet to occur or the future. Thus, the time line runs from the front to the back of the body. The position of signs for time adverbs illustrates their relationship to the time line.

Tense with Time Adverbs

Signs in ASL are not marked for time. You indicate time by first signing a time adverb, which establishes the time for the forthcoming sentences. After you sign the time adverb, the tense remains the same until it is changed. The master dialogue has the following time adverbs:

YESTERDAY, ME BOOK READ.

TODAY, ME STORY WRITE.

TOMORROW, ME PICTURE DRAW.

Information-seeking Questions

The wh-questions in this lesson take into account Rule #2, because each one of them begins with a time adverb at the beginning of the question, which establishes the tense for the question. The three wh-questions in the dialogue are

YESTERDAY, DO-what YOU?

TODAY, DO-what YOU?

TOMORROW, DO-what YOU?

Facial Grammar

Nonmanual signals can clarify the intended time frame. One set of signals is used to indicate that something happened close in time. These signals include *raising the shoulders and moving them forward a bit*, *tightening the muscles around the mouth* (either with or without the mouth open), and *tilting the head to the side or forward*. These signals would be appropriate if you used the sign RECENTLY to indicate that something just happened a few moments ago. It would not be correct to use these signals to talk about something that happened recently in a more general sense such as "She recently moved into her new home."

Another set of nonmanual signals is used to show that something happened or will happen in the distant past or future. These signals are *the puffed cheeks* with *the eyebrows either raised or squeezed together*. Examples of sentences in which these signals can be used are "It was a long time ago when the buffaloes roamed freely across the prairie" and "It will be in the very distant future before people are able to travel outside our solar system."

What's the Sign?

BEFORE

Two signs for "before" are shown in this lesson. The sign BEFORE that is shown in the illustration refers to an event or action that occurred or will occur before a specific point in time. Examples of when it is used are "I arrived there before she did," "Dinosaurs inhabited the earth before human beings," and "I will arrive there before 5:00 this afternoon."

The other sign for "before" is made in the same manner as the sign PAST. It refers to something that occurred in the past, as illustrated in the sentences "I have met you before" and "I can't remember where I used to put my books before."

AFTER

The sign AFTER refers to an event or action that occurred or will occur after a specific point in time. Thus, it refers to something that happened after something else did. Examples of how it is used are "I will meet you after the game" and "The school closed after the blizzard came."

ASL Synonyms

Some signs can be used to mean other things.

Sign	Also used for
DRAW	ART, ARTISTIC, ILLUSTRATE, ILLUSTRATION
MAGAZINE	ARTICLE, BROCHURE, CATALOG, PAMPHLET
NEWSPAPER	PRINT
PAST	AGO, BEFORE, FORMER
PICTURE	PHOTO, PHOTOGRAPH
POETRY	POEM
PRESENT	CONTEMPORARY, CURRENT, CURRENTLY, PRESENTLY
NOW	AT-ONCE, IMMEDIATE
IN-A-WHILE	SHORTLY
STORY	NARRATIVE, NOVEL, PARABLE, PHRASE, PROSE, TALE
UP-TIL-NOW	SINCE

Practice Activities

1. MASTERY LEARNING

   Practice signing the three dialogues substituting signs from this lesson. When signing the questions, be sure to use the appropriate nonmanual signals.

2. FURTHER PRACTICE

   Use selected directional verb signs to create ten sentences that include signs for time adverbs learned in this lesson. Write an English translation for each of your sentences. Sign your sentences to a partner. Recall that the illustrations for directional verbs in this book are for the neutral position of the sign. In the following examples, the subject and object of the sentence are incorporated into the movement of the verb sign. Check with a teacher/Deaf mentor to ensure that you are making the sign in the correct manner. Examples follow:

   a. TODAY, TEACHER (point-right) BOOK you-GIVE-her.
      Give the book to the teacher today.

   b. LONG-TIME-AGO, B-E-T-T-Y (point-left) she-INFORM-me SCHOOL, SHE ENJOY.
      A long time ago, Betty informed me that she enjoyed school.

   c. NEXT-WEEK, YOU ME SIGNS, TEACH-each-other.
      Next week, you and I will teach each other signs.

LESSON 21: TALKING ABOUT TIME

Signing Dialogue

1. **Ella:** **FINALLY! ME WAIT, ONE-HOUR.**

   Finally. I waited for one hour.

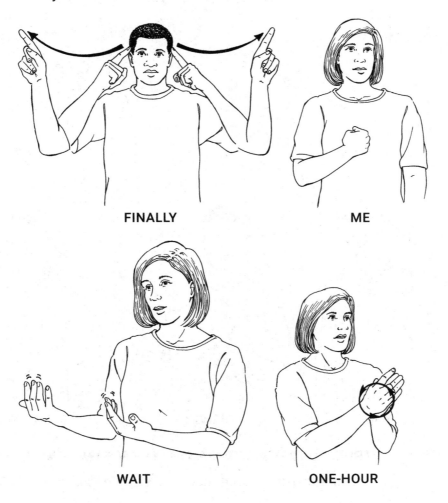

FINALLY

ME

WAIT

ONE-HOUR

2. **Angela:** **YOU WAIT WHY? YOU ARRIVE EARLY.**

You waited because you arrived early.

| YOU | WAIT | WHY |

| YOU | ARRIVE | EARLY |

3. **Ella:** **TRUE. SUNDAY ACCOMPANY-me MOVIE WANT YOU?**

That's true. Do you want to come with me to a movie on Sunday?

| TRUE | SUNDAY | ACCOMPANY-me |

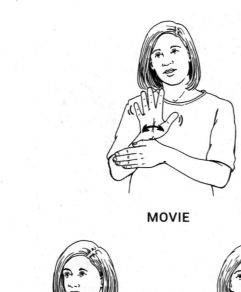

MOVIE

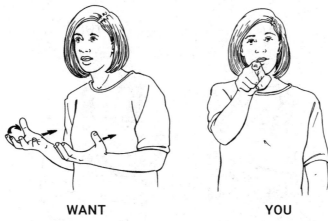

WANT   YOU

4. **Angela:** **CAN'T. THIS WEEK, BUSY.**

I can't. I'm busy this week.

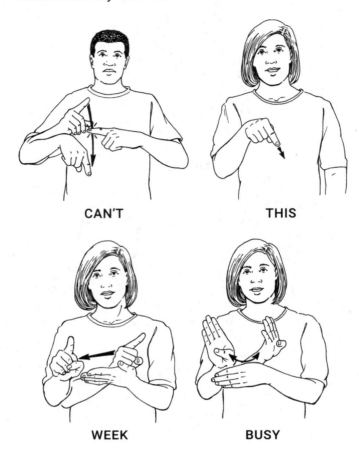

CAN'T	THIS

WEEK	BUSY

5. **Ella:** **NEXT MONTH, YOU BUSY?**

Are you busy next month?

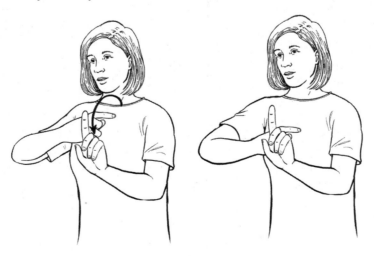

NEXT-MONTH

YOU   BUSY

6. **Angela:** **NO. NEXT MONTH, MY SCHEDULE AVAILABLE.**

No. Next month my schedule is available.

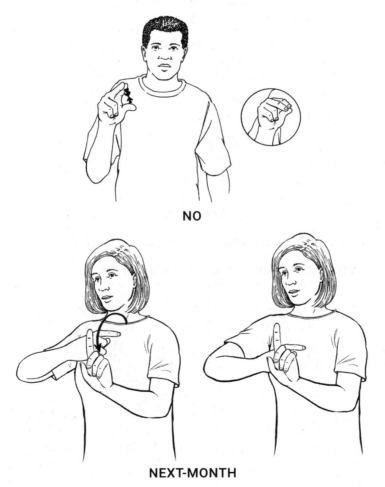

NO

NEXT-MONTH

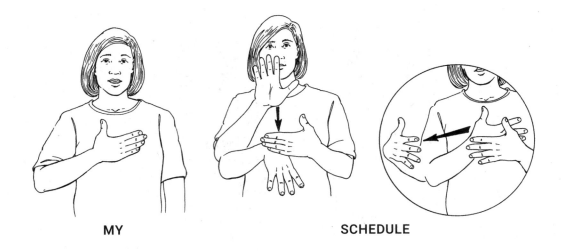

MY   SCHEDULE

AVAILABLE

7.   **Ella:**   **YOU LUCKY. THIS YEAR, MY SCHEDULE FULL.**

You're lucky. This year my schedule is full.

YOU   LUCKY

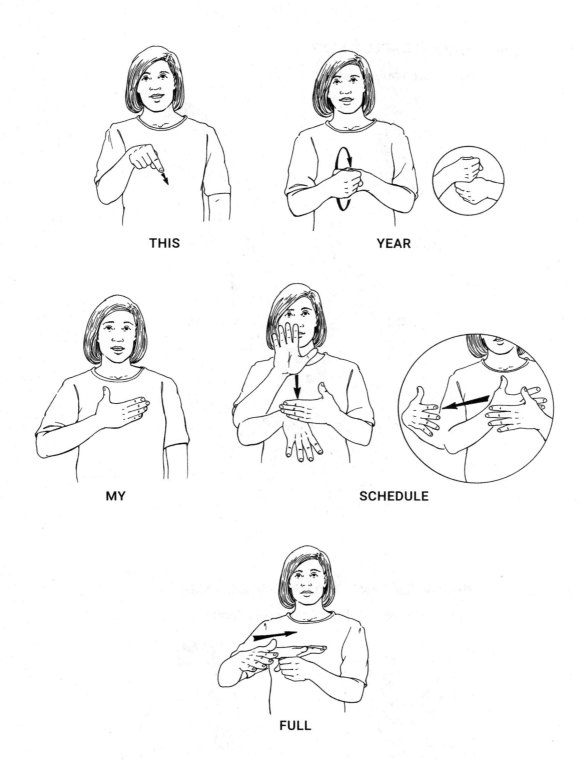

THIS YEAR

MY SCHEDULE

FULL

8. **Angela:** **YOU AVAILABLE WHEN?**

    When are you available?

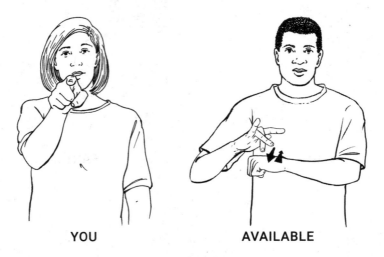

YOU   AVAILABLE

WHEN

9. **Ella:** **NEXT-WEEK CAN'T. IN-THREE-WEEKS MONDAY?**

    I can't next week. How about on a Monday in three weeks?

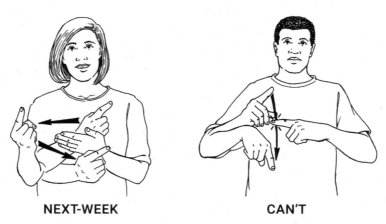

NEXT-WEEK   CAN'T

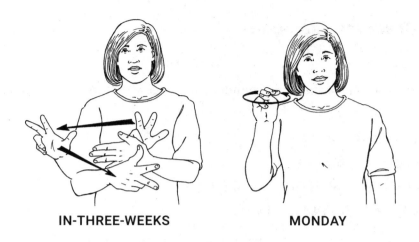

IN-THREE-WEEKS   MONDAY

10.   **Angela: GOOD. SEE YOU IN-THREE-WEEKS.**

Good. I will see you in three weeks.

GOOD   SEE

YOU   IN-THREE-WEEKS

Breaking Down the Dialogue

Topic/Comment

The dialogue illustrates how the topic/comment sentence structure can be used to talk about time:

1. ME WAIT, ONE HOUR.
2. THIS WEEK, ME BUSY.
3. NEXT MONTH, MY SCHEDULE AVAILABLE.
4. THIS YEAR, MY SCHEDULE FULL.

In each of these sentences, the time adverb is placed at the beginning of the sentence. This strategy also establishes the tense in sentences 2, 3, and 4. Using the topic/comment structure for these sentences places the emphasis on the comment that is made in each one of them. Because time in the dialogue is important, the nonmanual signals associated with the topic/comment sentence structure are used to highlight the time adverbs.

In sentence 1, the time adverb ONE HOUR is used to make a comment about how long Ella waited for Angela to show up.

Tense with Time Adverbs

1. NEXT MONTH, YOU BUSY?
2. IN-THREE-WEEKS MONDAY?

In sentence 1, the topic is first described (NEXT MONTH) followed by a yes/no question about it (YOU BUSY?). In sentence 2, all the signs are used to ask a question about a particular time. There is no need to include movie in the question because the dialogue is about finding a day to go and see a movie.

Long Yes/No Questions

Time, topic, and question are combined in the following yes/no question:

time:	SUNDAY
topic:	ACCOMPANY-me MOVIE
question:	WANT YOU?

Information-seeking Questions

The wh-question in the dialogue places the sign WHEN at the end of the sentence:

YOU AVAILABLE WHEN?

Rhetorical Questions

The following rhetorical question was used to explain why Ella had waited for one hour:

YOU WAIT WHY? YOU ARRIVE EARLY.

The question is first asked and then an answer is given immediately.

Ordering of Simple Sentences

A common salutary remark when departing is illustrated in the sentence

SEE YOU IN-THREE-WEEKS.

The signed phrase SEE YOU is followed by the time adverb IN-THREE-WEEKS. Another simple sentence in the dialogue was

YOU LUCKY.

Negation

The dialogue provides three examples of negation. In two of the instances, Angela signs CAN'T or NO in response to a question. When responding to a yes/no question, a simple YES or NO or another negative sign is often sufficient. In the second instance, Ella explains that she can't do something next week:

NEXT-WEEK CAN'T.

The negative sign CAN'T is placed at the end of the sentence.

What's the Sign?

NEXT-WEEK

The sign for NEXT-WEEK uses the time line to represent the concept of one week from now. The sign WEEK is made and then the hand moves forward beyond the stationary hand (i.e., into the future).

IN-THREE-WEEKS

This is an example of how numbers are incorporated into a sign. The sign NEXT-WEEK is made with the 3 handshape. This is a common linguistic device in ASL.

NEXT-MONTH

The sign for NEXT-MONTH can be done as one large movement combining the sign for MONTH and a movement forward indicating a movement forward in time.

ASL Synonyms

Some signs can be used to mean other things.

Sign	Also used for
NEXT-WEEK	IN-ONE-WEEK, a-WEEK-from-now

 Practice Activities

1. MODEL FOR TOPIC/COMMENT AND RHETORICAL QUESTIONS

    Signer A:
    1. Initiate the conversation with a remark;
    2. describe a topic;
    3. make a comment about the topic.

Remark:	FINALLY!
Topic:	ME WAIT,
Comment:	ONE HOUR.

    Signer B:
    1. Ask a rhetorical question;
    2. answer the question.

Rhetorical question:	YOU WAIT WHY?
Answer:	YOU ARRIVE EARLY.

Practice

Signer A: FINALLY! ME WAIT, ONE HOUR.

Signer B: YOU WAIT WHY? YOU ARRIVE EARLY.

2. MODEL FOR TOPIC COMMENT, LONG YES/NO QUESTIONS, AND NEGATION

Signer A:
1. Make a remark about a previous comment;
2. establish the time frame by signing a time adverb;
3. describe the topic;
4. ask a yes/no question about the topic.

Remark:	TRUE.
Time:	SUNDAY
Topic:	ACCOMPANY-me MOVIE
Question:	WANT YOU?

Signer B:
1. Respond to the yes/no question with a negative;
2. describe a topic;
3. make a comment about the topic.

Response:	CAN'T.
Topic:	THIS WEEK,
Comment:	BUSY.

Practice

Signer A: TRUE. SUNDAY ACCOMPANY-me MOVIE WANT YOU?

Signer B: CAN'T. THIS WEEK, BUSY.

3. MODEL FOR TOPIC/COMMENT, SIMPLE YES/NO QUESTIONS, AND ORDERING OF SIMPLE SENTENCES

Signer A:
1. Describe a topic;
2. ask a yes/no question about the topic.

Topic:	NEXT MONTH,
Question:	YOU BUSY?

Signer B:
1. Respond to the yes/no question with a negative;
2. describe a topic;
3. make a comment about the topic.

Response:	NO.
Topic:	NEXT MONTH,
Comment:	MY SCHEDULE EMPTY.

Signer A:	1. Make a remark using a simple sentence structure;
	2. describe a topic;
	3. make a comment about the topic.

Remark:	YOU LUCKY.
Topic:	THIS YEAR,
Comment:	MY SCHEDULE FULL.

Practice

Signer A:	NEXT MONTH, YOU BUSY?
Signer B:	NO. NEXT MONTH, MY SCHEDULE EMPTY.
Signer A:	YOU LUCKY. THIS YEAR, MY SCHEDULE FULL.

4. MODEL FOR SIMPLE YES/NO QUESTIONS, INFORMATION-SEEKING QUESTIONS, ORDERING OF SIMPLE SENTENCES, AND NEGATION

| Signer A: | 1. Describe the topic; |
| | 2. ask a wh-question about the topic. |

| Topic: | YOU AVAILABLE |
| Question: | WHEN? |

Signer B:	1. Describe the topic;
	2. sign a negative about the topic;
	3. ask a new question by proposing a new date of when you will be available.

Topic:	NEXT-WEEK
Negative:	ME CAN'T.
Question:	IN-THREE-WEEKS MONDAY?

Signer A:	1. Make a remark about what Signer B asked;
	2. describe an action;
	3. state a time adverb.

Remark:	GOOD.
Action:	SEE YOU
Time:	IN-THREE-WEEKS.

Practice

Signer A: YOU AVAILABLE WHEN?

Signer B: NEXT-WEEK ME CAN'T. IN-THREE-WEEKS MONDAY?

Signer A: GOOD. SEE YOU IN-THREE-WEEKS.

5. MASTERY LEARNING

When you feel comfortable signing these phrases, practice signing the entire dialogue shown at the beginning of this lesson. Practice the dialogue until you can sign the part of each character smoothly while using the appropriate facial grammar.

6. FURTHER PRACTICE

Create five time-related sentences. Write the English gloss for the ASL sentences and the English translations. Sign your sentences to a partner who will write down the English translation to compare with your translations. Two examples are:

a. IN-THREE-WEEKS, SCHOOL FINISH.
    School is finished in three weeks. OR In three weeks, school will be finished.

b. me-HELP-you WHEN? ONE MONTH AGO?
    When did I help you? Was it one month ago?

ASL TIP

English Translation
Remember that there is usually more than one way to translate an ASL sentence into English. However, while the wording of the translations might be different, the meaning of all translations should be the same.

LESSON 22: TIME ADVERBS

Days of the Week

The most correct way to sign the days of the week (except SUNDAY) are with the palm in—facing the body. However, they are pictured palm out so that you can see them better. Either way is acceptable.

SUNDAY

MONDAY

TUESDAY

WEDNESDAY

"T" handshape moving to an "H" handshape.

THURSDAY

FRIDAY

SATURDAY

Time Regularity

To show the concept of regularity, the form of some time signs can be changed. The sign for WEDNESDAY or SATURDAY can be changed to convey *every* Wednesday or *every* Saturday by moving the hand down vertically while holding the sign.

EVERY-WEDNESDAY

EVERY-SATURDAY

Past and Future Form

The following signs use the time line to refer to time that is either in the past (the hand moves toward the back of the shoulder) or future (the hand moves to the front of the body).

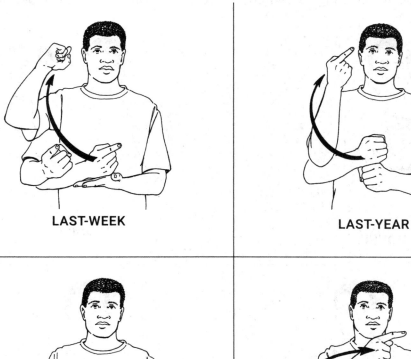

LAST-WEEK

LAST-YEAR

NEXT-WEEK

NEXT-YEAR

Adverbial Form -LY

To create the adverb form -LY, the movement of the dominant hand is repeated in HOUR, WEEK, and MONTH. The sign YEARLY is made by repeating the sign for NEXT-YEAR. The sign DAILY is made by repeating the sign for TOMORROW. This shows time repetition.

HOURLY

DAILY

MONTHLY

WEEKLY

YEARLY

Incorporating Numbers into Hours, Days, Weeks, and Months

The numbers 1–9 can be used with the signs for HOUR, DAY, WEEK, and MONTH to represent the concepts one hour, two hours, . . . nine hours; one day, two days, . . . nine days; one week, two weeks, . . . nine weeks; and one month, two months, . . . nine months. Some people also use this technique to sign one year, two years, and so forth, while others first sign the number and then the sign YEAR—in other words, they do not incorporate the number into the sign for year.

1–9 HOURS (see illustrations for 3 HOURS and 7 HOURS)

1–9 DAYS (see illustrations for 4 DAYS and 6 DAYS)

1–9 WEEKS (see illustrations for 5 WEEKS and 9 WEEKS)

1–9 MONTHS (see illustrations for 2 MONTHS and 8 MONTHS)

3 HOURS

7 HOURS

4 DAYS

6 DAYS

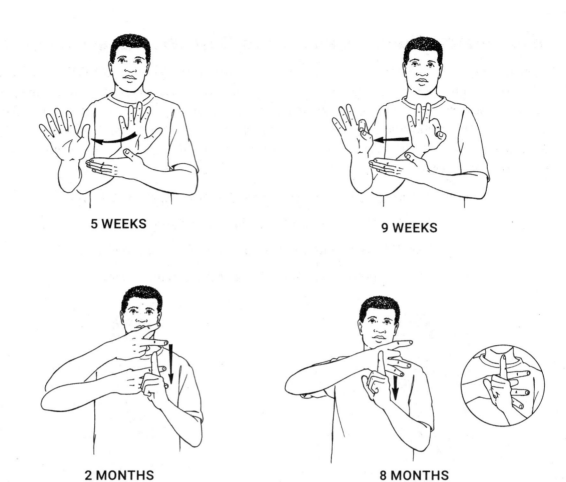

5 WEEKS

9 WEEKS

2 MONTHS

8 MONTHS

The signs for 1–9 WEEKS can be incorporated into the signs for

    a. NEXT-WEEK to give:
       IN-1-WEEK, IN-2-WEEKS, . . . IN-9-WEEKS

    b. LAST-WEEK to give:
       1-WEEK-AGO, 2-WEEKS-AGO, . . . 9-WEEKS-AGO

More Time Adverbs

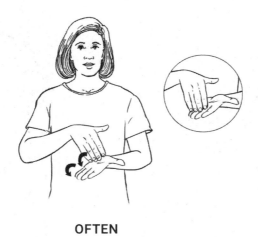

OFTEN

SOMETIMES

NOON

DAY

NIGHT

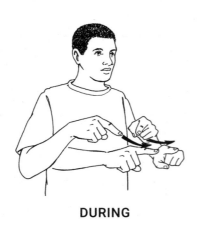

DURING

UNTIL

 Practice Activity

Select signs learned in any of the previous lessons to create dialogues that incorporate the signs learned in this lesson. Use any or all of the ASL grammar rules. Keep your sentences short, and write the rule number next to each one. An example of a dialogue is provided for you below.

Signer A:	HELLO C-A-M-E-R-O-N, SCHOOL START WHEN?
	Hello Cameron, when does school start?
Signer B:	SCHOOL START, IN-4-WEEKS TUESDAY.
	School starts on Tuesday in four weeks.
Signer A:	NEXT-WEEK THURSDAY, STUDY YOU WANT?
	On Thursday next week, do you want to study?
Signer B:	NEXT-WEEK THURSDAY FINE. SEE-you-LATER.
	Next week on Thursday is fine with me. See you later.

 Video Quiz Visit online.barronsbooks.com for scored practice on ASL expressions related to time.

Grammar Practice

Translate each of the following sentences to ASL by writing the English gloss of the signs used in the translation and signing it.

Note that there may be other ways of translating these sentences than the ones shown here.

1. Can I borrow your book?

2. I study ASL every day because my sister is deaf.

3. I start working at seven o'clock Monday morning.

4. Do you feel hot or cold?

5. I live in Philadelphia.

6. My cousin is a computer analyst.

7. My room is dark and quiet.

8. What time did you finish writing the poem?

9. What is the name of your uncle?

10. Is that woman over there an engineer or a doctor?

CHAPTER 12

Classifiers

Learning Objectives

In this chapter, you will learn:

○ How to apply the following grammar rules to create sentences: tense with time adverbs, simple yes/no questions, information-seeking questions, rhetorical questions, ordering of simple sentences, negation

○ All about classifiers: what they are, how to write them, how to use them, the handshapes used to form them, and how movements can affect their meaning

○ How to use the directional verb LOOK/WATCH, ASK

○ Negation in a sentence using the sign DON'T-WANT

LESSON 23: INTRODUCTION TO CLASSIFIERS

The Beauty of Classifiers

Classifiers are not unique to ASL or any other sign language. The spoken language Navajo uses classifiers in ways almost identical to ASL. Japanese uses classifiers when counting people, objects, and events. But native speakers of English may find classifiers difficult because English has no classifier system. This chapter introduces some common ASL classifiers. These classifiers and others can be used to outline the shape of a building, pattern of a dress, flow of tap water, ray of a sunbeam, limp of a hurt athlete, scattering of many ants, and so forth. We might even say that classifiers have a sense for the dramatic. At the very least, your knowledge of classifiers will help you paint images in the air. Again, welcome to visual arts and acting class. I mean … ASL class.

What Are Classifiers and How Do We Write Them?

Classifiers are a set of signs used to describe (a) a physical characteristic of a noun and/or (b) the movement or location of a noun. Classifiers make signing more like art. They do this by representing the following:

- Object's size and shape
- Depth
- Texture
- Movement
- Location

The important feature of a classifier is the handshape. In this text, signs that serve as classifiers are identified in *three* parts.

1. The first part is the symbol cl-, which denotes that the sign is a classifier.

2. The second part gives the handshape of a number or letter. If only one letter or number is shown such as cl-F or cl-2, then only the dominant hand is used to make the sign. If a specific hand is to be used, then it will be specified using the term *right* or *left* to indicate which hand is used to make the classifier. In cl-F(right), for example, the right hand is used. If a double letter or double number is shown such as cl-LL or cl-33, both hands are classifiers.

3. The third part tells us what characteristic or action of a noun the classifier is representing. Although a classifier is representing a characteristic or an action of a noun, it is *not* the sign for that noun. An example of a classifier is shown in the following illustration.

The handshape of the classifier cl-1:go-past-me tells us that the signer is referring to a person or an animal because the 1 handshape is used to represent a person or an animal. The movement of the handshape relative to the signer shows a person or an animal going past the signer.

The classifier by itself does not identify the subject or object of a sentence. This must be done by adding more information, as in the following sentences:

1. MY NEPHEW cl-1:go-past-me.
2. YOUR HORSE cl-1:go-past-me.

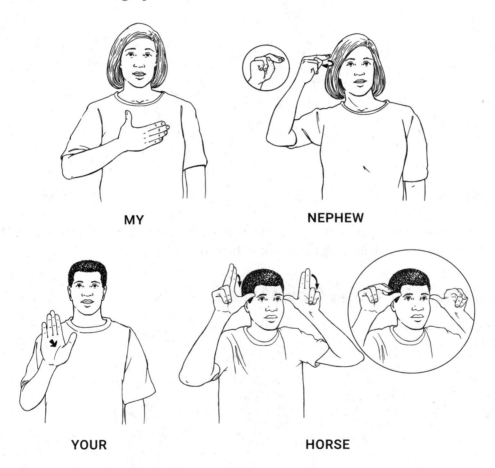

MY

NEPHEW

YOUR

HORSE

In sentence 1, we know that the signer is talking about his or her nephew going past him or her. In sentence 2, the subject is the addressee's horse. More information can be added to these phrases to indicate the time that both events occurred.

3. ONE-HOUR AGO, MY NEPHEW cl-1:go-past-me.

   My nephew went past me an hour ago.

4. YESTERDAY, YOUR HORSE cl-1:go-past-me.

   Yesterday, your horse went past me.

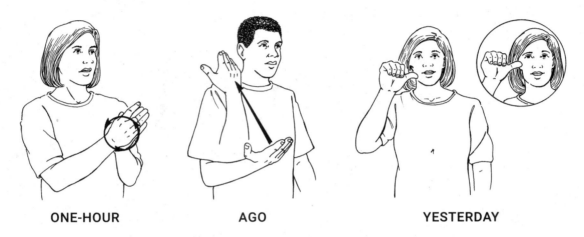

| ONE-HOUR | AGO | YESTERDAY |

In sentences 1–4, the classifier cl-1:go-past-me describes an action associated with the subject of the sentence. The classifier is not in fact the sign for GO.

A Basic Rule for Using Classifiers

RED PEN cl-1:on-shelf.
The red pen is on the shelf.

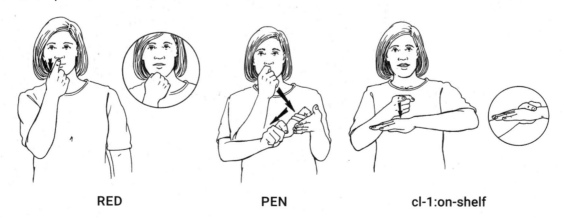

| RED | PEN | cl-1:on-shelf |

STEAK (MEAT) cl-LL:large.
The steak is large.

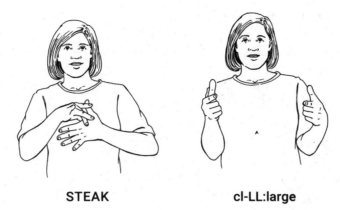

STEAK **cl-LL:large**

It must be clear what a classifier is representing before it can be used. Thus, the basic sentence pattern for using classifiers is:

noun(s)/classifier

In the first part of the sentence, the signer identifies the subject, object, or both. Examples of how the noun(s)/classifier rule is used follow:

There are lots of people going to the movie.

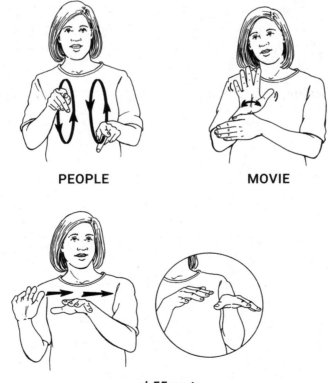

PEOPLE **MOVIE**

cl-55:go-to

The classifier for indicating a horde of people moving in a particular direction is used to represent the movement of people.

There is a little bit of milk in the glass.

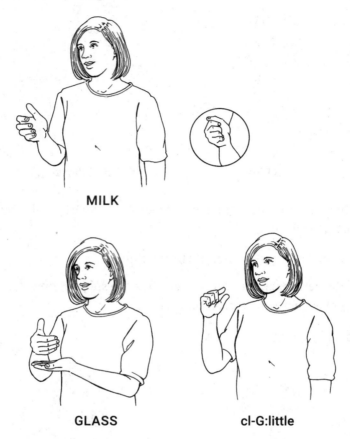

MILK

GLASS

cl-G:little

The classifier for indicating a small quantity is used to show how much milk is left in a glass.

Bob followed Ted (in a vehicle).

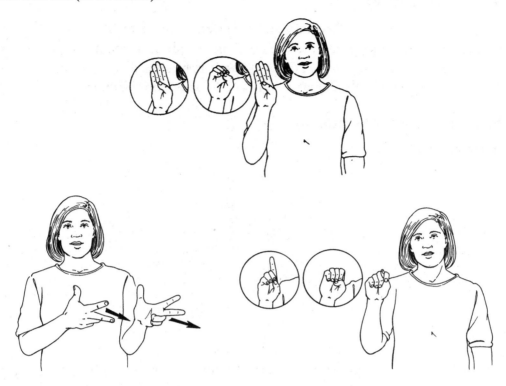

Car, Van, Truck, Bus, Boat, Bicycle, or Any Other Type of Motor Vehicle

The movement of a classifier for a person or an animal in the signing space is not a random event. Each movement is a clear representation of an action that someone or something has done, is doing, or will be doing. When watching a signer, you must pay attention to the location of the classifier in the signing space and especially to where the movement of the classifier ends.

ASL TIP

Location in the Signing Space
The final location of the classifier marks the location of the subject or object in the signing space. The signer can later refer to the subject or object of a sentence simply by pointing to a place where they were marked in the signing space.

Types of Classifiers

Following is a list of common classifiers and the physical characteristic of a noun that they represent. Most classifiers can represent more than one physical characteristic. For example, the phrase "a small, round object on the table" can be signed using a single classifier that describes the size (small), shape (round), and location (on the table).

Classifiers that Describe Motor Vehicles

Motor vehicle (cl-3)

The 3 handshape is held horizontally. This is used for a car, van, truck, bus, boat, bicycle, or any other type of motor vehicle.

Examples of how this classifier is used: In all of the examples, only the classifier is shown and not the signs for the nouns.

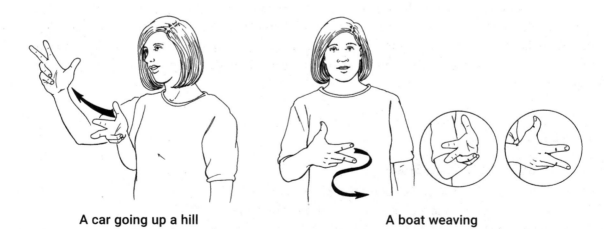

A car going up a hill   A boat weaving

Two motor vehicles (cl-33)

Both 3 handshapes are held horizontally. This can be used for two cars, two vans, two buses, two boats, or two of any other type of motor vehicle.

Examples of how this classifier is used:

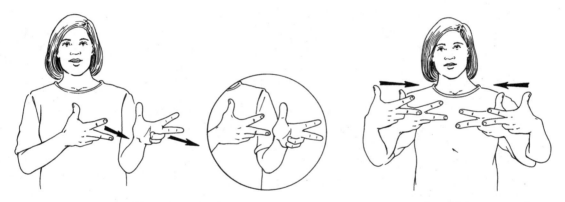

One car following another car

Two trucks driving toward each other

Classifiers that Show the Action of People or Things

Person or animal (cl-1)

The 1 handshape is held vertically. This can be used for a person or an animal.

451

Examples of how this classifier is used:

A person turning away   **A person falling down**

Two people or two animals (cl-11 or cl-2)

cl-11

Both 1 handshapes are held vertically. This can be used for two people or two animals.

cl-2

The 2 handshape is held vertically. This can be used for two people or two animals.

Examples of how these classifiers are used:

One person turning away from
another person

Two people moving forward

Many people in a line (cl-44)

Both 4 handshapes are held vertically. This can be used for a stream of people or animals.

Examples of how this classifier is used:

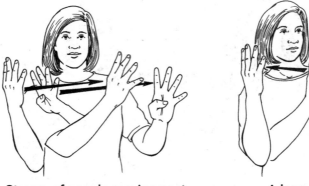

Stream of people moving past   **A long lineup**

Large quantity of things moving in a specific direction (cl-55)

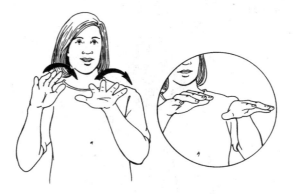

Both 5 handshapes are held with palms down. This can be used for hordes of people, animals, bicycles, cars, and so forth moving toward a common place.

Examples of how this classifier is used:

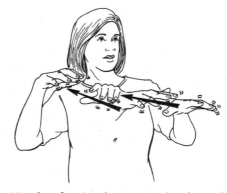

Horde of people coming together   **Horde of animals moving backward**

Person standing or walking (cl-V)

The V handshape is held upside down. This can be used for a person standing or walking.

Examples of how this classifier is used:

A person falling off of a platform

A person walking up a spiral staircase

Chair, person, or animal seated (cl-bent V)

The bent V handshape is held horizontally. This can be used for a chair, a person sitting, or an animal sitting.

Examples of how this classifier is used:

A person sitting next to a tree

A person sitting on a platform

Classifiers that Show the Size and Shape of Things

Cylindrical objects (cl-1/)

Finger pointing or the 1 handshape is held horizontally or upright. This can be used for a pen, pencil, straw, log, or telephone pole.

Examples of how this classifier is used:

A pen on top of a table

A straw in a cup

Flat objects (cl-B)

The B handshape is held with the thumb next to the index finger. This can be used for a bed, sheet of paper, kite, tile, board, or leaf.

Examples of how this classifier is used:

A leaf falling off a tree

A person lying on a bed

Small, flat, and round objects (cl-F)

The F handshape is held horizontally or vertically. This can be used for a coin, button, medal, pendant, or watch.

Examples of how this classifier is used:

A button on a shirt   **A small badge on the chest**

Large, flat, and round (cl-LL)

Two L handshapes are used to form the outline of a horizontal circle. This can be used for a plate, steak, large hole, frisbee, or discus.

Examples of how this classifier is used:

The size of a child-size Frisbee **The size of an adult-size Frisbee**

Small container-like objects (cl-C)

The C handshape is held horizontally. This can be used for a glass, bottle, vase, can, cup, or pen holder.

Examples of how this classifier is used:

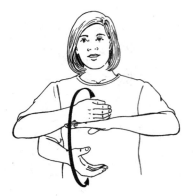 

A glass falling off a shelf   **Raising a bottle above the head**

Larger size container-like objects (cl-CC)

Two C handshapes are used to form the outline of a container. This can be used for a paint can, garbage can, large bowl, melon, or pumpkin.

Examples of how this classifier is used:

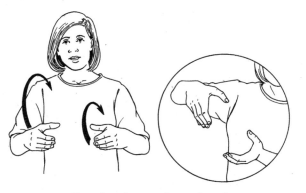 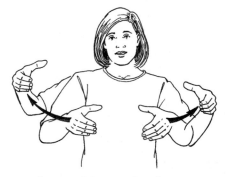

Pouring from a large bowl   **A pumpkin growing larger**

Flat surfaces (cl-BB)

Two B handshapes are held horizontally and pulled apart. This can be used for a tabletop, stage, shelf, or floor.

Examples of how this classifier is used:

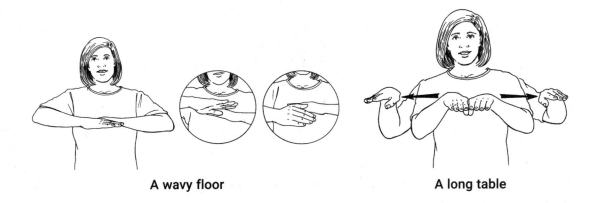

A wavy floor　　　　　　　　　　**A long table**

Classifiers that Show the Amount

Small amount (cl-G)

The G handshape can be used for a small amount of liquid or solid, a small height of a stack of things, or a small insect.

Examples of how this classifier is used:

The amount of water in a container

Comparing the height of two piles of paper

Medium amount (cl-L)

The L handshape can be used for a medium amount of liquid or solid, a medium height of a stack of things, or something that grows.

Examples of how this classifier is used:

The height of grass

The height of a stack of paper on a shelf

Large amount (cl-BB/)

Two B handshapes with one held above the other can be used for a large amount of liquid or solid, a high height of a stack of things, or something that grows.

Examples of how this classifier is used:

The increasing height of a stack of books

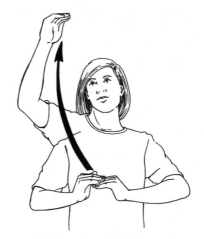

How high something has grown

Classifiers that Show a Stationary Object

Stationary object (cl-A)

The A handshape held with the thumb up. This can be used for a house, vase, lamp, building, statue, or grain bin.

Examples of how this classifier is used:

Two houses side by side   Two lamps apart from each other

Classifiers that Show the Flow of Things

Flow of liquid (cl-4>)

The 4 handshape is held vertically with fingers pointed to the side—the hand moves up and down. This can be used to indicate the flow of liquid, a bleeding nose, a running tap, or running water.

Examples of how this classifier is used:

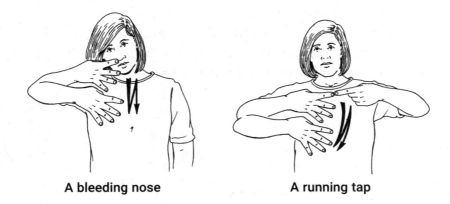

A bleeding nose   A running tap

Flow of objects (cl-44/)

Two 4 handshapes—hands moving back and forth to the side—can also be done with one palm facing up and the other palm facing down. This can be used to indicate the flow of objects moving along a conveyor belt or assembly line or logs moving down a river.

Examples of how this classifier is used:

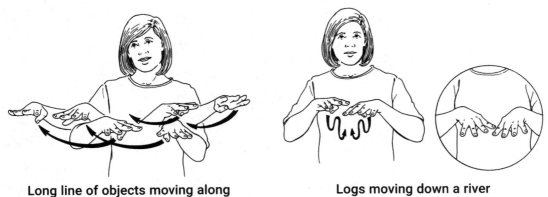

Long line of objects moving along   Logs moving down a river

Plurals

Many classifiers that represent a person, an animal, or a thing can be moved to indicate plurality. Often, both hands are used when the plural form of a classifier is being made. The following illustrations show the plural form of three classifiers. Compare each of them with the singular form of the classifier shown in the preceding section.

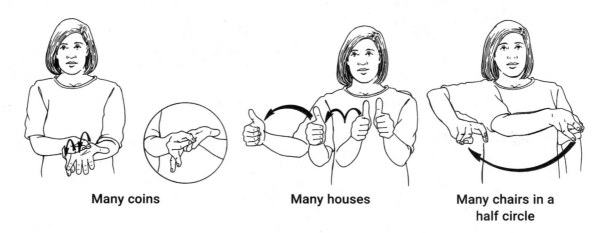

Many coins   **Many houses**   **Many chairs in a
                                                    half circle**

Notice that in the illustration of many chairs in a half circle, the classifier describes the object (chair), the number of objects (many), and the location of the objects relative to each other (aligned in a half circle).

Practice Activity

Write the symbol for the classifier that is most appropriate for representing each of the following phrases.

1. A herd of deer

2. A large leak in a water pipe

3. A pedestrian crossing the street

4. The size of a barrel

5. The stillness of a calm sea

6. The waves of a rough ocean

7. Two bottles of water

8. A fallen telephone pole

9. Two people standing side by side

10. Three lamps in a row

11. A lineup of people

12. A one-inch stack of paper

13. A large pothole

14. A kite in the air

15. A boat rocking from side to side

LESSON 24: A DIALOGUE WITH CLASSIFIERS

Telling a story in ASL typically includes the use of many classifiers. This is a simple story to start your practice.

Signing Story

YESTERDAY, MAN cl-1:WALK-past-me.

Yesterday, a man walked past me.

YESTERDAY   MAN

WALK-past-me

ME WATCH-go-past. ME KNOW HIM?

I watched him as he went past. Did I know him?

ME   WATCH-go-past   ME

KNOW   HIM

ME CALL-OUT, D-A-V-E!

I called out, "Dave!"

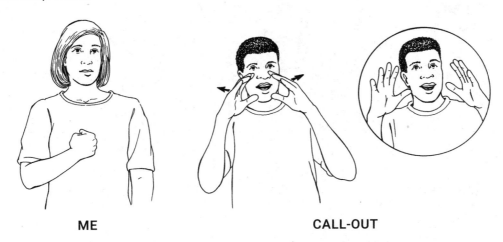

ME   CALL-OUT

469

cl-1:he-TURN-TOWARD-me, cl-1:CAME-UP-to-me. me-LOOK-at-him.

He turned and came up to me. I looked at him.

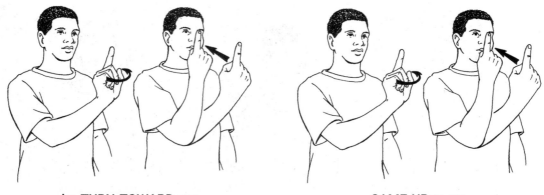

he-TURN-TOWARD-me　　　　　　　　**CAME-UP-to-me**

me-LOOK-at-him

MISTAKE ME. DON'T-KNOW HIM.

I had made a mistake. I didn't know him.

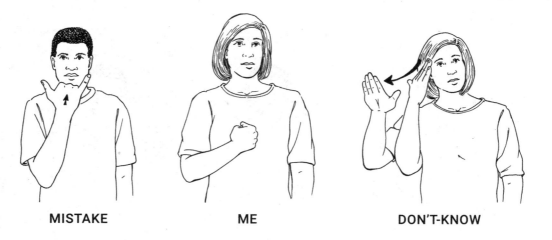

MISTAKE　　　　　　**ME**　　　　　　**DON'T-KNOW**

HIM

ME SAY, ME MISTAKE SORRY.

I said, "I am sorry, I have made a mistake."

ME **SAY** **ME**

MISTAKE **SORRY**

cl-1:he-TURN-AWAY, cl-1:he-MOVE-AWAY.
He turned and went away.

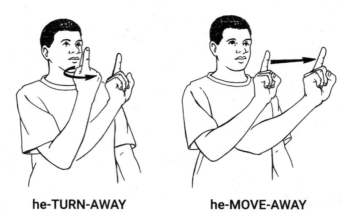

he-TURN-AWAY   he-MOVE-AWAY

The Classifiers

Main classifier cl-1: (upright 1 handshape to refer to a person in the story)

Breaking Down the Story

Telling a Story

You tell a story in ASL by stringing thoughts together in the order that they occur. In the master story, a sequence of events is used to describe a case of mistaken identity. The first sign of the story is YESTERDAY, which establishes the tense for the entire story. Therefore, the English translation is written in the past tense.

Classifiers

The precise meaning of a classifier depends upon the context of the sentence in which it is used. How this is accomplished is shown in the following discussion of the classifiers used in the dialogue.

cl-1:WALK-past-me

The cl-1:WALK-past-me classifier tells us nothing about what walked past. You move an upright index finger past your face, but does the finger represent a woman, child, teacher, friend, or some kind of animal? We don't know unless we add context to the situation in which the classifier is used. In the story, context is added:

MAN cl-1:WALK-past-me.

Now we know that it was a man who walked past. When did he walk past?

YESTERDAY, MAN cl-1:WALK-past-me.

At this point, a translation is possible.

A man walked past me yesterday.

A classifier is a powerful linguistic tool in ASL. Using the classifier cl-1:WALK-past-me, you can indicate many different kinds of movements and show the relative distance between the subject and object. For example, to show that the man ran past quickly, you move the hand fast. To show that the man walked past close by, you keep the hand close to the face as it is moved past. To show that the man walked past at a distance, you keep the hand away from the body as it is moved past.

cl-1:he-TURN-TOWARD-me

The subject and tense of this sentence have already been established in the story. Therefore, a translation of this classifier could be "He turned toward me" or "The man turned toward me" or some other close approximation.

cl-1:CAME-UP-to-me

Two possible translations are "He came up to me" and "He walked up to me."

cl-1:he-TURN-AWAY

An appropriate translation is "He turned away from me."

cl-1:he-MOVE-AWAY

A couple of possible translations are "He walked away from me" and "He moved away from me."

Gaze-shifting

Gaze-shifting is the movement of the eye and is an important part of ASL (see Chapter 10, "Body- and Gaze-Shifting"). In the story, eye gazing is used to emphasize the relationship between you, the signer, and the man you are talking about. In the first sentence,

YESTERDAY, MAN cl-1:WALK-past-me.

you sign YESTERDAY, MAN, and then turn your head slightly to watch the upright finger as it moves past the face. If you are a right-handed person, the sign cl-1:WALK-past-me will start at the right side of the signing space, and at this point you should be looking directly at it. As the finger moves across the face you follow it by keeping your eyes on it. The head also will move slightly to follow the movement of the finger. In the practice activity, the eye gazing is described for each of the classifiers used in the story.

In the sentence,

ME WATCH-go-past.

you repeat the eye gaze of the previous sentence, but this time you watch the hand signing WATCH-go-past. At the start, the fingertips of this sign (for a right-handed signer) will be pointing to the right side of the signing space. The sign will then move across the face just as the classifier cl:WALK-past-me did.

Indicating that You Have Made a Mistake

The phrase

MISTAKE ME

is a common one used to indicate that a person has made a mistake and is usually translated as "I have made a mistake" or "I was wrong." In the story, the meaning is "I had made a mistake" to account for the fact that the signer is telling a story in the past tense. More generally, English translations of ASL should always attempt to capture the sense of what the signer is trying to say. In the phrase

MISTAKE ME. DON'T-KNOW HIM.

a good translation might be "Whoops, I didn't know him" or "Oh no, I didn't know him," and facial expressions will help determine which one it might be. Recall that signs are glossed in English because of the necessity of facilitating discussions of ASL grammar and vocabulary. These English glosses are shown in uppercase print and are sometimes only a suitable approximation of what a sign means.

Indicating a Verbatim Remark or Question

In the sentence

ME SAY, ME MISTAKE SORRY.

a correct translation is

I said, "I am sorry, I have made a mistake."

The signed phrase ME SAY is translated to "I said" because the time frame was established by the signing of YESTERDAY at the beginning of the story. What the signer said, however, is translated in the present tense because the signer is telling us exactly what she or he had said a day earlier.

What's the Sign?

KNOW

The sign KNOW is made with the fingertips touching the forehead once. In some instances, when a signer wants to emphasize that he or she "really knows something," the forehead can be tapped more than once.

LOOK

There are many signs to describe the different ways of looking at something. The hand-shape is typically the V handshape with the two fingers representing the eyes. In the story, you use the sign for LOOK in the sense of trying to recognize someone. An appropriate facial expression for this would be for you to (1) *bend your head forward slightly* and (2) *raise your eyebrows*.

MAN

Signs for MALE are made by the forehead. Compare this with signs for females, which are made by the chin.

WATCH-go-by

The WATCH-go-by sign is a variation of the sign WATCH. The difference between the two is that in the sign WATCH the fingertips move forward, whereas in WATCH-go-by, the fingertips move from one side to the other side to indicate that the eyes moved as something went by. In both cases, your eye gaze should follow the direction indicated by the sign.

ASL Synonyms

Some signs can be used to mean other things.

Sign	Also used for
CALL-OUT	YELL
HIM	HE, SHE, HER, IT
MAN	GENTLEMAN
MISTAKE	ERROR, WRONG
SAY	HEARING, PRONOUNCE, SPEAK, SPEECH

Practice Activities

1. MODEL FOR GAZE-SHIFTING, CLASSIFIERS CL-1:, SIMPLE YES/NO QUESTIONS, AND ORDERING OF SIMPLE SENTENCES

Signer: cl-1:WALK-past-me

1. Place the time adverb sign at the beginning of the sentence to establish the tense of the story;
2. sign the subject of the story;
3. sign the classifier *using eye gazing* to emphasize the sign's movement. Mentally note where you stopped the sign in the signing space.

Time: YESTERDAY

Subject: MAN

Gaze: cl-1:WALK-past-me (eyes follow the sign as it moves across the signing space)

Signer: WATCH-go-past

1. Use gaze-shifting to emphasize what the signer did (the sign should stop moving at the same point where the sign cl-1:WALK-past-me ended);
2. ask a yes/no question *raising the eyebrows* and *tilting the head forward*.

Gaze: ME WATCH-go-past (eyes follow the sign WATCH-go-past)

Question: ME KNOW HIM?

Practice

Signer: [eyes follow the sign]

YESTERDAY MAN cl-1:WALK-past-me

[eyes follow the sign]

ME WATCH-go-past, ME KNOW HIM?

2. MODEL FOR CLASSIFIERS CL-1:, GAZE-SHIFTING, AND ORDERING OF SIMPLE SENTENCES

Signer: 1. Describe an action (the sign CALL-OUT will move in the direction of where the sign WATCH-go-past ended in the previous sentence; the eyes should be looking in the same direction);
2. fingerspell the name of the person called.

Action: ME CALL-OUT,
Name: D-A-V-E!

Signer: cl-1:he-TURN-TOWARD-me.
1. Make sign where sign WATCH-go-past ended.

Signer: cl-1:CAME-UP-to-me.
1. Use this sign to follow through from the previous sign. There should be a slight pause after the sign cl-1:he-TURN-TOWARD-me, and then the sign cl-1:CAME-UP-to-me is made. The eyes watch the movement of both classifiers.

Signer: me-LOOK-at-him.
1. Describe an action (the eyes look in the direction of the man).

Practice

Signer: ME CALL-OUT, D-A-V-E!
[eyes watch the hand movement]
cl-1:he-TURN-TOWARD-me.
[eyes watch the hand moving toward the signer]
cl-1:CAME-UP-to-me.
[eyes look in the direction where the man is placed in the signing space]
me-LOOK-at-him.

3. MODEL FOR INDICATING THAT YOU HAVE MADE A MISTAKE

Signer: 1. Describe the topic;
           2. make a comment about the mistake.

        Topic: MISTAKE ME.
        Comment: ME DON'T-KNOW HIM.

Signer: 1. Describe an action;
           2. apologize for making the mistake.

        Action: ME SAY,
        Apology: ME MISTAKE SORRY.

Signer: 1. Describe an action that the man did;
           2. describe another action that the man did.

        Action 1:   cl-1:he-TURN-AWAY,
        Action 2:   cl-1:he-MOVE-AWAY.

Practice

Signer: MISTAKE ME.
           ME DON'T-KNOW HIM.
           ME SAY, ME MISTAKE SORRY.
           cl-1:he-TURN-AWAY,
           cl-1:he-MOVE-AWAY.

4. MASTERY LEARNING

When you feel comfortable signing these phrases, practice signing the entire story shown at the beginning of this lesson. Practice the story until you can sign the classifiers and use the appropriate eye gazes comfortably.

5. FURTHER PRACTICE

Rewrite and practice the story making the following substitutions:

a. Substitute   MAN WOMAN   for   MAN

                   cl-2   for   cl-1

b. Substitute   C-A-R   for   MAN

                   cl-3   for   cl-1

                   S-T-O-P   for   C-A-M-E-R-O-N

LESSON 25: EXPLORING WITH CLASSIFIERS

More Practice with Classifiers

A classifier can take on a variety of meanings depending upon how it is moved. When two classifiers are used, the number of meanings multiplies. Assigning a single word or a combination of words to represent these meanings in print is difficult. Furthermore, small changes in the movement of a classifier can drastically change the meaning of a sign. Therefore, even though it is important that you learn the handshape associated with a classifer, it is impractical for you to memorize the many meanings that a classifier can have.

What should you do? You need to *explore* the uses of classifiers using *images* of situations and practice how to sign these images. In this way, you will be able to develop a *sense* of how a classifier is used. This would then prepare you for using the classifier when the situation arises.

The Two Master Classifiers

1. cl-1: (upright 1 handshape to represent a person or animal)
2. cl-2: (upright 2 handshape to represent two persons or two animals)

Practice Activities

For each exploration sentence, do the following:

1. Close your eyes and

   - imagine the scene that each sentence describes.
   - replace the image of one of the persons (or animals) with a classifier.
   - use the classifier to make the movement described in the sentence.
   - imagine looking at the scene being described to practice eye gazing and head movements.
   - sign the sentence. Recall that the pronoun is incorporated into each classifier.

2. Open your eyes and

   - sign the sentence using appropriate eye gazing and head movements.

   Hint #1. In some cases, it can be more convenient to switch hands rather than make a one-handed sign with the same hand all the time. For a right-handed person, signs that move off to the right side of the body are easily made with the right hand. Similarly, signs that move to the left side of the body can be made with the left hand.

   Hint #2. Placement of a classifier in the signing space can show the relative size of a person or an animal when compared to the signer. When the classifier cl:1 is used to represent the movement of a dog, the hand is often positioned lower than it would be when representing a person. In the former case, the hand would move at about chest height and in the latter it would move at about the same height as the head.

   Hint #3. When twisting the hand to indicate that someone or something turned away, twist counterclockwise for signs made with the right hand and clockwise for signs made with the left hand.

 Practice Sentences

Use one hand with the classifier cl-1.

1. She came straight to me.

2. I went off to the right.

3. She went off to the left.

4. She walked up to me and then turned away.

5. He came to me from my left side.

6. She came to me from my right side.

7. I walked straight ahead and then came straight back.

8. I walked straight ahead and then turned to the right.

9. I walked ahead, stopped, and then continued walking ahead.

10. The dog ran past me quickly.

11. The cat came up to me.

12. The dog came straight up to me and then turned and walked away to the left.

Use two hands with the classifier cl-1.

1. I went to the right and she went to the left. (**Hint:** Use two hands with your right hand representing you and your left hand representing the other person.)

2. He came up to me from the right side, and she came up to me from the left side.

3. They walked right past each other.

4. I followed her. (**Hint:** Place one hand behind the other, then move both of them forward.)

5. I walked around her. (**Hint:** Hold the left hand stationary, then move the other hand in a semicircle around it.)

6. I walked up to her and then turned and moved off to the right.

7. The dog followed the cat to the right and then the left.

8. I went up to her, and then the two of us went to the right.

9. We walked right past one another.

10. I walked in circles.

Use the classifier cl-2.

1. Two people came up to me on my right side.

2. I approached the two of them. (**Hint:** You must use two classifiers in this sentence: cl-1: and cl-2:. The phrase "the two of them" is made with cl-2, while the pronoun "I" is represented by cl-1.)

3. I walked right past the two of them.

4. Two people came up to me and then turned around and walked away.

5. Two people turned away from me, walked in a big circle, and then came back to me.

6. I walked up to them. ("Them" is two people.)

7. The two of them were walking past me; they stopped and then continued walking.

8. The two of them turned away quickly.

9. The two of them hopped past me. (**Hint:** Keep the fingertips pointing up.)

10. Two people followed me. (**Hint:** "Two people" will be represented by cl-2, and "me" will be represented by cl-1.)

LESSON 26: CONVERSATIONS WITH CLASSIFIERS

Signing Dialogue

1. **Alexa:** **MAN THERE, WHO HE?**

   Who is that man?

MAN

THERE

WHO

HE

2. **Kieran:** **ME DON'T-KNOW. you-MEET-him WANT YOU?**

I don't know. Do you want to meet him?

ME   DON'T-KNOW   you-MEET-him

WANT   YOU

3. **Alexa:** **YES. ME WANT me-MEET-him.**

Yes, I do want to meet him.

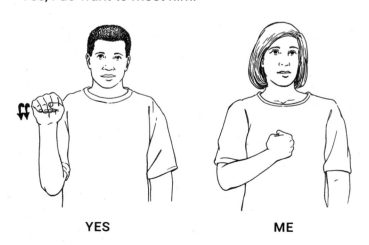

YES   ME

WANT   **me-MEET-him**

4.   **Kieran: YOU cl-1:you-GO-to-him, you-ASK-him NAME.**

Go up to him and ask for his name.

YOU   **you-GO-to-him**

you-ASK-him   **NAME**

5. **Alexa:** **cl-1:me-GO-to-him, me-ASK-him NAME? ME DON'T-WANT.**

I don't want to go and ask him for his name.

me-GO-to-him   me-ASK-him   NAME

ME   DON'T-WANT

6. **Kieran:** **YOU DON'T-WANT, WHY-NOT?**

Why don't you want to?

YOU   DON'T-WANT   WHY-NOT

7. **Alexa:** **ME SHY.**

   I'm shy.

ME SHY

8. **Kieran:** **YOU SHY? DOUBT-IT.**

   I doubt that you are shy.

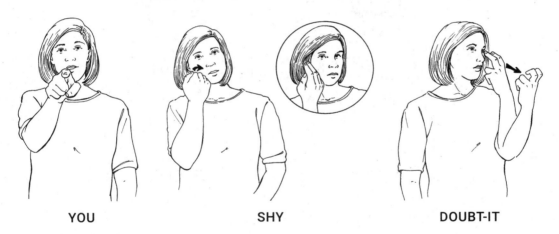

YOU SHY DOUBT-IT

9. **Alexa:** **TWO-of-us, cl-2:we-GO-to-him ASK-him, WHY-NOT?**

Why don't the two of us go up and ask him for his name?

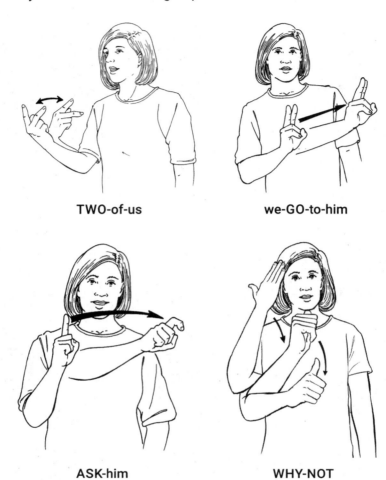

TWO-of-us   we-GO-to-him

ASK-him   WHY-NOT

10. **Kieran:** **SURE. cl-2:we-GO-to-him, NAME ASK-him.**

Sure. The two of us can go and ask him for his name.

SURE   we-GO-to-him

NAME   ASK-him

Breaking Down the Dialogue

Information-seeking Questions

The signer describes the topic and then signs the wh-question.

Topic	Wh-question
MAN THERE,	WHO HE?
YOU DON'T-WANT,	WHY-NOT?
TWO-of-us, cl-2:we-GO-to-him ASK-him,	WHY-NOT?

The meaning for the sign WHY-NOT is along the line of "why don't you?" or "why don't we?" depending upon the subject of the sentence.

Simple Yes/No Questions

As with many ASL yes/no questions, the question follows the topic.

topic:	YOU-MEET-him
question:	WANT YOU?

Using the Sign WANT

The sign WANT can come before or after the person or thing that is desired:

ME WANT me-MEET-him.

me-MEET-him, WANT ME.

Directional Verbs

The directional verb GO is incorporated into the movement of the classifiers cl-1 and cl-2. In the story, there are also two other directional verbs: ASK-him and MEET-him. The object of both sentences is "him" or the man in the story. The subject depends on the context of the sentence. The translations for just the directional verb phrases are shown here. They differ slightly from the translations in the story because the story has more information added to the sentences.

ASL	Translation
you-MEET-him WANT YOU?	Do you want to meet him?
ME WANT me-MEET-him.	I want to meet him.
you-ASK-him NAME.	You ask him for his name.
me-ASK-him NAME?	I ask him for his name?

In the dialogue, the classifier cl:1 is used to identify the subject and object associated with two of the foregoing phrases as follows:

YOU cl-1:you-GO-to-him, you-ASK-him NAME.

cl-1:me-GO-to-him, me-ASK-him NAME? ME DON'T-WANT.

Negation

To negate a thought, you describe a topic and then add a negative sign.

topic:	cl-1:me-GO-to-him, me-ASK-him NAME?
negative:	ME DON'T-WANT.

Ordering of Simple Sentences

Sentences that use descriptive terms to describe the subject can follow a simple subject-adjective order as seen in the following sentence:

ME SHY.

Rhetorical Questions

In the following sentences, a rhetorical question is asked and then answered:

YOU SHY? ME DOUBT-IT.

cl-1:me-GO-to-him, me-ASK-him NAME? ME DON'T-WANT.

What's the Sign?

ASK

The sign ASK is a directional verb. The direction of its movements indicates the subject and object of a sentence. For the sign ASK-him, the hand moves toward a place in the signing space where the person represented by HIM is placed. The subject of the phrase could be "me" as in me-ASK-him or "you" as in you-ASK-him, depending upon the context of the sentence. The subject can vary to take on other pronouns, too.

DON'T-WANT

The sign for DON'T-WANT is another example of negative incorporation. The sign WANT is made, and then the hands are turned away to show that something is not wanted.

SHY

Signs for feelings can be accompanied by facial expressions that clue in on the feelings. While signing SHY, a person could (1) *raise the right shoulder* and (2) *tilt the head slightly toward the same shoulder* to emphasize the withdrawal characteristic of a person being shy.

WHY-NOT

The sign WHY-NOT is a combination of the signs WHY and NOT.

ASL Synonyms

Some signs can be used to mean other things.

Sign	Also used for
ASK	INQUIRE, QUESTION
WANT	DESIRE
DOUBT-IT	SKEPTICAL

 Practice Activities

1. MODEL FOR DIRECTIONAL VERB ASK AND INFORMATION-SEEKING QUESTIONS

    Signer A: 1. Describe the topic;
    2. ask a wh-question about the topic.

    Topic: MAN THERE,
    Question: WHO HE?

    Signer B: 1. Respond to the question;
    2. use the directional verb MEET to describe a topic;
    3. use the sign WANT to ask a yes/no question.

    Response: ME DON'T-KNOW.
    Topic: you-MEET-him
    Question: WANT YOU?

    Signer A: 1. Respond to the question affirmatively;
    2. describe what the signer wants to do.

    Response: YES.
    Describe action: ME WANT me-MEET-him.

Practice

Signer A:	MAN THERE, WHO HE?
Signer B:	ME DON'T-KNOW. you-MEET-him WANT YOU?
Signer A:	YES. ME WANT me-MEET-him.

2. MODEL FOR CLASSIFIER CL-1, DIRECTIONAL VERB ASK, RHETORICAL QUESTIONS, AND NEGATION

Signer A:　　1. Use the classifier cl-1: to describe an action with a subject (YOU) and object (HIM);

2. use the sign ASK to indicate a second action.

Action 1:	YOU cl-1:you-GO-to-him,
Action 2:	you-ASK-him NAME.

Signer B:　　1. Use the classifier cl-1: to describe an action with a subject (ME) and object (HIM);

2. repeat the question with the sign ASK moved in a direction that identifies the subject (ME) and object (HIM) of the sentence;

3. answer the question with the negative sign DON'T-WANT.

Action:	cl-1:me-GO-to-him,
Question:	me-ASK-him NAME?
Response:	ME DON'T-WANT.

Practice

Signer A:	YOU cl-1: you-GO-to-him, you-ASK-him NAME.
Signer B:	cl-1:me-GO-to-him, me-ASK-him NAME? ME DON'T-WANT.

3. MODEL FOR INFORMATION-SEEKING QUESTIONS, RHETORICAL QUESTIONS, AND ORDERING OF SIMPLE SENTENCES

Signer A: 1. Describe the topic;
            2. ask a wh-question using the sign WHY-NOT.

         Topic: YOU DON'T-WANT,
         Question: WHY-NOT?

Signer B: 1. Respond to the question with a simple sentence.

         Response: ME SHY.

Signer A: 1. Ask a rhetorical question;
            2. answer the question.

         Rhetorical question: YOU SHY?
         Answer: ME DOUBT-IT.

Practice

Signer A: YOU DON'T-WANT, WHY-NOT?

Signer B: ME SHY.

Signer A: YOU SHY? ME DOUBT-IT.

4. MODEL FOR CLASSIFIER CL-2, DIRECTIONAL VERB ASK, AND INFORMATION-SEEKING QUESTIONS

Signer A: 1. Use the classifier cl-2: to describe the first action of the subject (TWO-of-us) and the relationship of this action to the object of the sentence (HIM);
            2. use the directional verb ASK to describe the second action of the subject and to indicate the object (HIM) in a sentence;
            3. ask a wh-question using the sign WHY-NOT.

         Action 1:   TWO-of-us, cl-2:we-GO-to-him
         Action 2:   ASK-him,
         Question: WHY-NOT?

Signer B: 1. Respond to the question;

2. use the classifier cl-2: to describe an action with a subject (TWO-of-us) and object (HIM);

3. describe the topic.

Response: SURE.

Action: cl-2:we-GO-to-him,

Topic: NAME ASK-him.

Practice

Signer A: TWO-of-us, cl-2: we-GO-to-him ASK-him, WHY-NOT?

Signer B: SURE. cl-2: we-GO-to-him, NAME ASK-him.

5. MASTERY LEARNING

When you feel comfortable signing these phrases, practice signing the entire dialogue shown at the beginning of this lesson. Practice the dialogue until you can sign the part of each character smoothly.

6. FURTHER PRACTICE

Create ten ASL sentences that use a classifier. Write the English gloss for these sentences, and then sign each sentence to a partner who will translate them back to English.

 Video Quiz Visit online.barronsbooks.com for scored practice on classifiers.

CHAPTER 13

Sports

Learning Objectives

In this chapter, you will learn:

- How to apply the following grammar rules to create sentences: topic/comment, tense with time adverbs, simple yes/no questions, information-seeking questions, rhetorical questions, ordering of simple sentences, negation
- How to use the directional verbs FLY-to, TEASE, ARRIVE, and GO-to
- The classifier cl:55 to convey many people going to a particular place
- How to use the sign FINISH to indicate an action occurred in the past and the command "stop"
- New signs to describe sports and leisure activities

LESSON 27: GOING TO THE WORLD GAMES FOR THE DEAF

Signing Dialogue

1. **Desire:** **HELLO Z-A-N-E, YOU EXCITED WHY?**

   Hello Zane, why are you excited?

HELLO   YOU

EXCITED   WHY

2. **Zane:**   **ME EXCITED WHY? NEXT-WEEK JAPAN me-FLY-to-there.**

I am excited because I am flying to Japan next week.

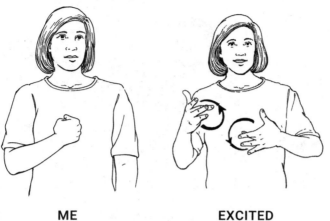

ME	EXCITED

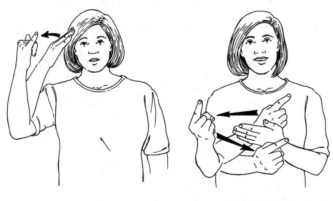

WHY	NEXT-WEEK

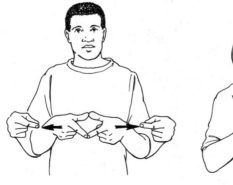

JAPAN	me-FLY-to-there

3. **Desire:** **JAPAN you-FLY-to-there, FOR-FOR?**

Why are you flying to Japan?

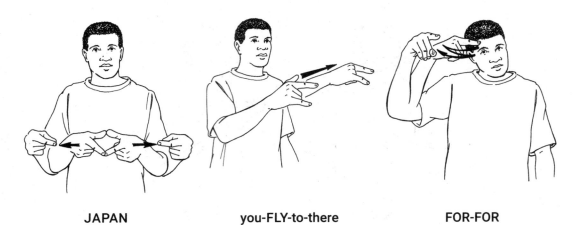

JAPAN you-FLY-to-there FOR-FOR

4. **Zane:** **JAPAN HOST WORLD GAMES DEAF, W-G-D.**

Japan is hosting the World Games for the Deaf.

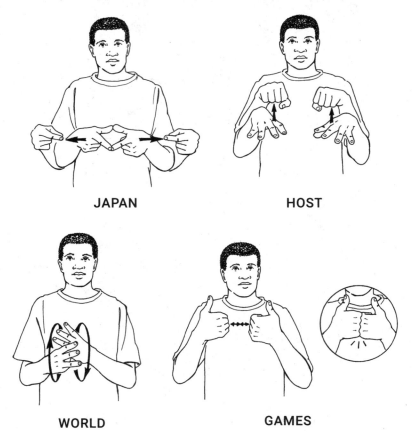

JAPAN HOST

WORLD GAMES

DEAF

5. **Desire:**　　**W-G-D MEAN?**

What does WGD mean?

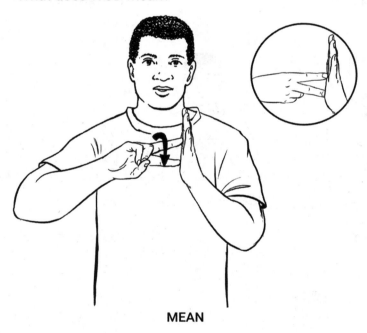

MEAN

6. **Zane:** **W-G-D SIMILAR OLYMPICS EXCEPT ATHLETE ALL DEAF.**

The WGD is similar to the Olympics except all of the athletes are Deaf.

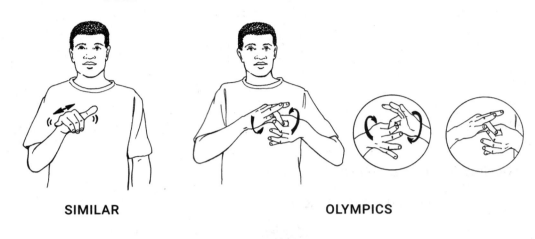

SIMILAR   OLYMPICS

EXCEPT   ATHLETE

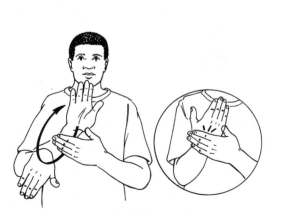

ALL   DEAF

7. **Desire:** **ATHLETE ALL DEAF, INTERESTING.**

That's interesting that all of the athletes are Deaf.

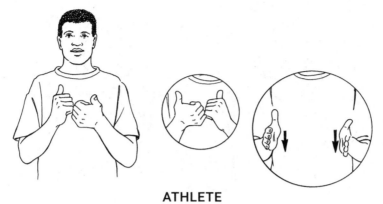

ATHLETE

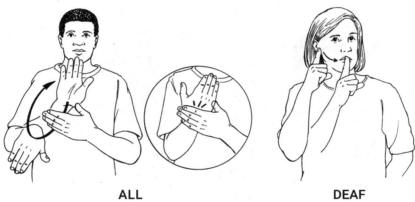

ALL   DEAF

INTERESTING

8. **Zane:** **SUPPOSE YOU HEARING, YOU W-G-D COMPETE, CAN'T.**

If you are a hearing person, then you can't compete in the WGD.

SUPPOSE	YOU
HEARING	YOU
COMPETE	CAN'T

Breaking Down the Dialogue

Information-seeking Questions

In the dialogue, Desire begins the conversation with a wh-question:

YOU EXCITED WHY?

In this type of question, the wh-question sign comes at or near the end of the sentence.

In the following sentence

JAPAN you-FLY-to-there, FOR-FOR?

Desire uses the sign FOR-FOR to ask a why question. The sign FOR-FOR always translates to "why" or "why did you do that" in English. The dialogue contains another information-seeking question:

W-G-D MEAN?

The nonmanual signals for information-seeking questions provide the clue that the sentence W-G-D MEAN? is a question.

Ordering of Simple Sentences

The following is an example of a subject-verb-object (SVO) ordering of a sentence:

JAPAN HOST WORLD GAMES DEAF, W-G-D.

You fingerspell W-G-D at the end of the sentence to indicate how you will be referring to the World Games for the Deaf.

Rhetorical Questions

In the dialogue, Zane uses a rhetorical question to explain why he is excited:

ME EXCITED WHY? NEXT-WEEK JAPAN me-FLY-to-there.

In the second part of this sentence, the time adverb (see Rule #2) is placed at the beginning of the response to the rhetorical question.

Directional Verb FLY-to

a. JAPAN me-FLY-to-there.
b. JAPAN you-FLY-to-there.

The starting and ending positions of the directional verb FLY-to indicate the subject and object of the sentence. In both sentences a and b, the ending position of the sign FLY-to shows the location of the object of the sentence (JAPAN) in the signing space for each signer.

Preposition: EXCEPT

The following sentence consists of two phrases joined by the preposition EXCEPT:

W-G-D SIMILAR OLYMPICS EXCEPT ATHLETE ALL DEAF.

Topic/Comment

In the sentence

ATHLETE ALL DEAF, INTERESTING.

a topic is first described followed by a comment.

Conditional Sentences

In the following sentence, the condition is first signed followed by the outcome of this condition:

SUPPOSE YOU HEARING, YOU W-G-D COMPETE, CAN'T.

As with all conditional sentences, you (1) *raise your eyebrows* and (2) *tilt the head forward* while stating the condition. The second part of the sentence

YOU W-G-D COMPETE, CAN'T

is an example of Rule #10, negation, which states that the negative sign typically comes at or near the end of the sentence. For the second part of the sentence, the signer may wish to shake the head while signing CAN'T.

What's the Sign?

Athletes

Some verbs can be made into a noun by adding the AGENT-sign at the end of the verb sign. The sign ATHLETE is made by adding the AGENT-sign to the verb sign COMPETE to get COMPETE + AGENT-sign = ATHLETE. This sign is also used for COMPETITOR.

FLY-to

FLY-to is a directional verb sign. The locations of the starting and ending positions of this sign show the subject and object of the sentence.

me-FLY-to-there

The sign for me-FLY-to-there begins in front of the signer's chest to show that the signer ("me") is the subject. The hand then moves out to a position off to the right or left side of the signing space, which will then represent the place referred to as "there."

FOR-FOR

The meaning of the FOR-FOR sign is the same as for the sign WHY. There is no rule for determining when to use FOR-FOR or WHY because both are interchangeable. As you improve in your signing, you will use FOR-FOR in certain situations and WHY in others.

GAMES

There is no difference in the way GAME and GAMES are signed because the singular form (GAME) is signed with a repeated motion. Repeated motion can be used to show the plural form of a noun only if the singular form of the noun is not already made with a repeated motion. The reason for using GAMES in the phrase WORLD GAMES DEAF is because that is the appropriate English gloss for the sign given the meaning of the phrase.

NEXT-WEEK

The NEXT-WEEK sign is an example of how the signing space is used to indicate time. The body represents the present time, movement of the hand to the front of the body can be used to indicate the future, and movement to the back shows that something has happened in the past. In the sign NEXT-WEEK, the hand moves to the front of the body.

WORLD GAMES DEAF (W-G-D)

When introducing an abbreviation, you give the name or phrase first, followed by the initials or letters of the abbreviation.

ASL Synonyms

Sign	Also used for
ATHLETES	COMPETITOR
HEARING	PUBLIC
HOST	ADOPT

Practice Activities

1. MODEL FOR INFORMATION-SEEKING QUESTIONS AND RHETORICAL QUESTIONS

| Signer A: | 1. Describe the topic; |
| | 2. ask a question about the topic. |

| Topic: | YOU EXCITED |
| Question: | WHY? |

| Signer B: | 1. Repeat the wh-question to form a rhetorical wh-question; |
| | 2. answer the question. |

| Rhetorical question: | ME EXCITED WHY? |
| Answer: | NEXT-WEEK JAPAN me-FLY-to-there. |

Practice

| Signer A: | YOU EXCITED WHY? |
| Signer B: | ME EXCITED WHY? NEXT-WEEK JAPAN me-FLY-to-there. |

2. MODEL FOR INFORMATION-SEEKING QUESTIONS, ORDERING OF SIMPLE SENTENCES, AND ABBREVIATIONS

| Signer A: | 1. Describe the topic; |
| | 2. ask a question about the topic using the sign FOR-FOR. |

| Topic: | JAPAN you-FLY-to-there, |
| Question: | FOR-FOR? |

Signer B:	1. Sign the subject;
	2. sign the verb;
	3. sign the object;
	4. give the abbreviations for the object named in the sentence.

Subject:	JAPAN
Verb:	HOST
Object:	WORLD GAMES DEAF,
Abbreviation:	W-G-D.

Practice

Signer A:	JAPAN you-FLY-to-there, FOR-FOR?
Signer B:	JAPAN HOST WORLD GAMES DEAF, W-G-D.

3. MODEL FOR INFORMATION-SEEKING QUESTIONS AND FOR PREPOSITION EXCEPT

Signer A:
1. Describe the topic;
2. ask a question about the topic.

Topic:	W-G-D
Question:	MEAN?

Signer B:
1. Sign the first phrase that is joined by a preposition;
2. sign the preposition EXCEPT;
3. sign the phrase following the preposition.

First phrase:	W-G-D SIMILAR OLYMPICS
Preposition:	EXCEPT
Second phrase:	ATHLETE ALL DEAF.

Practice

Signer A:	W-G-D MEAN?
Signer B:	W-G-D SIMILAR OLYMPICS EXCEPT ATHLETE ALL DEAF.

4. MODEL FOR TOPIC/COMMENT AND CONDITIONAL SENTENCES

Signer A:
1. Describe the topic;
2. make a comment about the topic.

Topic:	ATHLETE ALL DEAF,
Comment:	INTERESTING.

Signer B:
1. Describe the condition;
2. describe the outcome of this condition.

Condition:	SUPPOSE YOU HEARING,
Outcome:	YOU COMPETE W-G-D, CAN'T.

Practice

Signer A:	ATHLETE ALL DEAF, INTERESTING.
Signer B:	SUPPOSE YOU HEARING, YOU COMPETE W-G-D, CAN'T.

5. MASTERY LEARNING

When you feel comfortable signing these phrases, practice signing the entire dialogue shown at the beginning of this lesson. Practice the dialogue until you can sign it comfortably.

6. FURTHER PRACTICE

Practice your fingerspelling skills by fingerspelling an abbreviation and having a partner fingerspell the entire name for it. Use abbreviations for organizations, states, provinces, or anything else. For example:

Signer A:	O-R
Signer B:	O-R-E-G-O-N
Signer A:	U-S
Signer B:	U-N-I-T-E-D S-T-A-T-E-S

In the following dialogue, (1) replace the sign EXCITED with other descriptive terms from Lesson 4 or other lessons, and (2) replace the sign NEXT-WEEK with other time adverbs found in Lessons 20–22.

Signer A:	HELLO, YOU EXCITED WHY?
Signer B:	ME EXCITED WHY? NEXT-WEEK JAPAN me-FLY-to-there.

LESSON 28: SOCIALIZING AND THE WORLD GAMES FOR THE DEAF

Signing Dialogue

1. **Jazmine:** **YOU W-G-D ARRIVE-there, YOU DO-what?**

    What do you do when you arrive at the World Games for the Deaf?

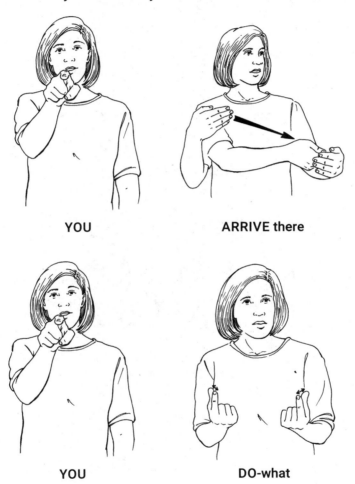

YOU	ARRIVE there

YOU	DO-what

2. **Tyrone:**   **ME WATCH COMPETITION.**

I watch the competition.

ME   WATCH

COMPETITION

3. **Tyrone**   **ME ENJOY WATCH MOST WHAT? SWIMMING.**

I enjoy watching swimming the most.

ME   ENJOY

WATCH   MOST

WHAT   SWIMMING

4. **Jazmine:** **SUPPOSE GAMES BORING, DO-what YOU?**

What do you do if the Games are boring?

SUPPOSE   GAMES

BORING   DO-what

YOU

5. **Tyrone:** **GAMES BORING, NEVER!**

The Games are never boring!

GAMES   BORING

NEVER

6. **Tyrone**   **DEAF PEOPLE COUNTRIES VARIOUS cl-55:FLOCK-to-Games.**

Deaf people from many countries come to the Games.

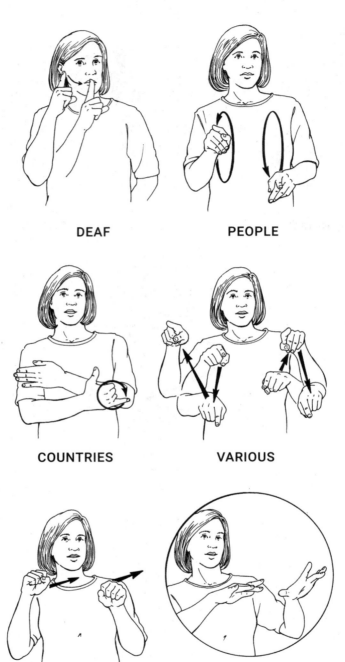

DEAF   PEOPLE

COUNTRIES   VARIOUS

FLOCK-to-Games

7. **Jazmine:** **NEAT!**

Hey, that's neat!

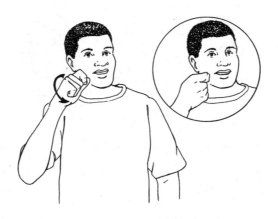

NEAT

8. **Tyrone:** **YOU W-G-D GO-to SHOULD.**

You should go to the Games.

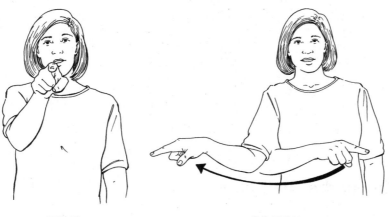

YOU   GO-TO

SHOULD

9.　**Jazmine:**　**YES, ME SHOULD.**

Yes, I should.

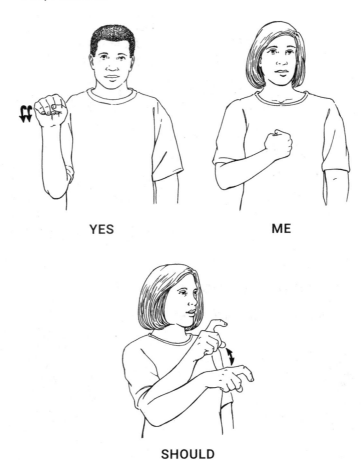

YES　　　　　　　ME

SHOULD

Breaking Down the Dialogue

Information-seeking Questions and the Directional Verb ARRIVE

The opening sentence of the dialogue is the wh-question

YOU W-G-D ARRIVE-there, YOU DO-what?

The topic is described first followed by the wh-question. The sentence makes use of the directional verb ARRIVE to place the noun W-G-D in the signing space. You can either move the sign ARRIVE toward the left side of your signing space or the right side. After you have done this, you can refer to the World Games for the Deaf by merely pointing to that location.

Ordering of Simple Sentences and Classifier CL-55

The following sentences use the subject-verb-object (SVO) ordering:

1. ME WATCH COMPETITION.
2. DEAF PEOPLE COUNTRIES VARIOUS cl-55:FLOCK-to-Games.

The SVO ordering is obvious in sentence 1. In sentence 2, the subject is clearly signed (DEAF PEOPLE COUNTRIES VARIOUS or Deaf people from various countries), but the object is incorporated into the movement of the classifier cl-55:FLOCK-to-Games. This incorporation is represented by the phrase FLOCK-to-Games, which is telling you to move the classifier cl-55: to the same location where the Games (i.e., the World Games for the Deaf) were located in the signing space in the first sentence of the dialogue. That is, if Jazmine signed ARRIVE-there to the right side of the signing space, then the classifier cl-55: will also move to the right side.

Rhetorical Questions

The following rhetorical question was used in the dialogue:

ME ENJOY WATCH MOST WHAT? SWIMMING.

Conditional Sentences

The conditional sentence

SUPPOSE GAMES BORING, DO-what YOU?

was translated as "What do you do if the Games are boring?" This is not the only possible translation. Other acceptable translations are "If the Games are boring, what do you do?" and "Suppose the Games are boring, what do you do?" How a sentence gets translated depends upon your command of language and your customary use of words and signs.

Negation

In the sentence

GAMES BORING, NEVER!

the emphasis is placed on NEVER. The emphasis can be reinforced (1) *by shaking your head* and (2) *by raising your eyebrows* as you sign NEVER!

Topic/Comment and the Directional Verb GO-to

In the following sentence, Tyrone is urging Jazmine to go to the Games:

YOU W-G-D GO-to SHOULD.

Because Tyrone wishes to emphasize that Jazmine *should* go to the Games, she signs SHOULD at the end of the sentence. This sentence could also be signed YOU SHOULD GO-to-GAMES. The movement of the directional verb GO-to is to the same location in which the GAMES were placed in the signing space in the first sentence of the dialogue.

What's the Sign?

ARRIVE-there

The "there" in this sign is telling you to move the sign ARRIVE to a particular place in the signing space. Where this particular place is has to be decided by you. To what is "there" referring? The sign ARRIVE-there comes after the noun W-G-D; therefore, the concept "there" represents is the World Games for the Deaf. Because this is the first sentence of the dialogue, you must decide where in the signing space you are going to place the W-G-D.

NEAT

This sign is used to express a feeling about something and is typically translated as "Hey, that's cool," "Cool," "That's neat," and "Neat." It is *not* to be used to mean *orderly* as in "The room looked neat and tidy."

ASL Synonyms

Some signs can be used to mean other things.

Sign	Also used for
NEAT	COOL
SHOULD	NECESSARY, NEED
SWIMMING	SWIM
VARIOUS	DIVERSE, DIVERSITY, ET CETERA (ETC.), VARY

 Practice Activities

1. MODEL FOR INFORMATION-SEEKING QUESTIONS, RHETORICAL QUESTIONS, AND ORDERING OF SIMPLE SENTENCES

    Signer A: 1. Describe the topic and sign ARRIVE-there to either the right or left side of the signing space;

    2. ask a question about the topic.

    Topic: YOU W-G-D ARRIVE-there,

    Question: YOU DO-what?

Signer B:
1. Sign the subject;
2. sign the verb;
3. sign the object.

Subject:	ME
Verb:	WATCH
Object:	COMPETITION.

1. Ask a rhetorical question;
2. answer the question.

Rhetorical question:	ME ENJOY WATCH MOST WHAT?
Answer:	SWIMMING.

Practice

Signer A:	YOU W-G-D ARRIVE-there, YOU DO-what?
Signer B:	ME WATCH COMPETITION.
	ME ENJOY WATCH MOST WHAT? SWIMMING.

2. MODEL FOR ORDERING OF SIMPLE SENTENCES, CONDITIONAL SENTENCES, AND NEGATION

Signer A:
1. Describe the condition;
2. ask a wh-question about the condition.

Condition:	SUPPOSE GAMES BORING,
Question:	DO-what YOU?

Signer B:
1. Describe the topic;
2. sign the negative sign NEVER.

Topic:	GAMES BORING,
Negation:	NEVER!

1. Sign the subject;
2. sign the classifier that includes the verb and object of the sentence (sign cl-55 to the same location where the hands moved for the sign ARRIVE-there).

Subject:	DEAF PEOPLE COUNTRIES VARIOUS
Verb & object:	cl-55:FLOCK-to-Games.

Practice

Signer A:	SUPPOSE GAMES BORING, DO-what YOU?
Signer B:	GAMES BORING, NEVER!
	DEAF PEOPLE COUNTRIES VARIOUS cl-55:FLOCK-to-Games.

3. MODEL FOR TOPIC/COMMENT

Signer A: 1. Describe the topic;
2. make a comment about the topic.

Topic:	YOU W-G-D GO-to
Comment:	SHOULD.

Signer B: 1. Respond affirmatively to the comment just made;
2. repeat the comment.

Response:	YES,
Comment:	ME SHOULD.

Practice

Signer A:	YOU W-G-D GO-to SHOULD.
Signer B:	YES, ME SHOULD.

4. MASTERY LEARNING

When you feel comfortable signing these phrases, practice signing the entire dialogue shown at the beginning of this lesson. Practice the dialogue until you can sign it comfortably.

5. FURTHER PRACTICE

Join the dialogue with the one in a previous lesson, and practice signing both until you are comfortable signing them. Note that you must select a location for the World Games for the Deaf in the signing space and maintain it throughout both dialogues.

LESSON 29: SIGNING AND THE WORLD GAMES FOR THE DEAF

Signing Dialogue

1. **Huy:**   **DEAF PEOPLE W-G-D cl-55:FLOCK-to-Games, YOU SOCIALIZE?**

Do you socialize with the Deaf people who go to the World Games for the Deaf?

DEAF   PEOPLE

FLOCK-to-Games

YOU   SOCIALIZE

2. **Chelsea:** **YES WHY? DEAF PEOPLE DIFFERENT+ COUNTRIES SIGN DIFFERENT.**

Yes I do, because Deaf people from various countries sign differently.

YES   WHY

DEAF   PEOPLE

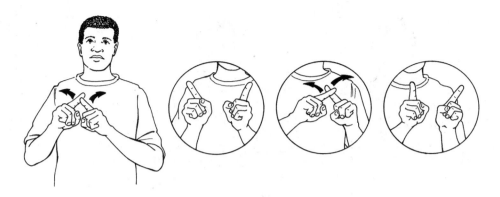

DIFFERENT+

COUNTRIES   SIGN   DIFFERENT

3. **Huy:**   **ASL NOT UNIVERSAL?**

You mean that ASL is not universal?

ASL

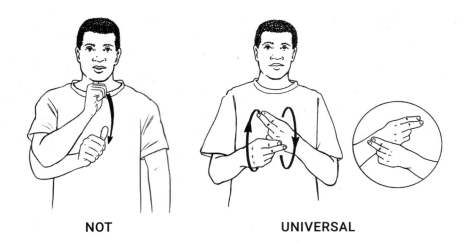

NOT   UNIVERSAL

4. **Chelsea:** **RIGHT. ASL USE WHERE? UNITED-STATES CANADA.**

     That's right. ASL is used in the United States and Canada.

RIGHT

ASL   USE

ASL TIP

USE/USED

The sign USE/USED can also be signed with the U handshape facing in toward your body as well as facing out.

| WHERE | UNITED-STATES | CANADA |

5. **Huy:**   **OH-I-see. W-G-D COUNTRIES INVOLVED, HOW-MANY?**

I see. How many countries are involved in the WGD?

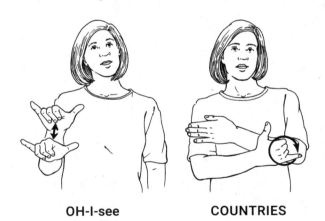

OH-I-see   COUNTRIES

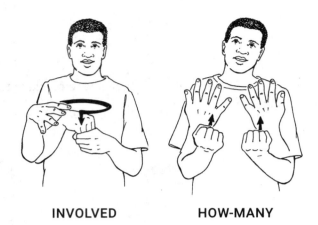

INVOLVED HOW-MANY

6.   **Chelsea:**   **COUNTRIES 57.**

Fifty-seven countries.

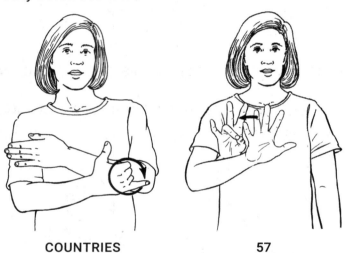

COUNTRIES 57

ASL TIP

The sign for country/countries can also be signed in the same position, but with a flat hand rubbing the elbow.

Breaking Down the Dialogue

Long Yes/No Questions and Classifier CL-55

In the following sentence, the topic is first described followed by a yes/no question about the topic.

topic:	DEAF PEOPLE W-G-D cl-55:FLOCK-to-Games
question:	YOU SOCIALIZE?

Because of the length of the sentence, the nonmanual signals would be used only when the question is signed.

The classifier cl-55:FLOCK-to-Games will be moved to the right or left of the signing space. Because this dialogue is a continuation of the two previous dialogues, you should practice moving the classifier to the location where the Games were initially placed in the signing space in the previous lesson. Also, although the noun W-G-D is inserted in this sentence, it would not have been necessary to do so if this dialogue was signed as a continuation of the dialogue in the Lessons.

Rhetorical Questions

In the following sentence, the signer is responding to a question and then turning the response into a rhetorical question:

YES WHY? DEAF PEOPLE DIFFERENT+ COUNTRIES SIGN DIFFERENT.

Note that a topic/comment word ordering is used to respond to the WHY question—the topic is DEAF PEOPLE DIFFERENT+ COUNTRIES, and the comment is SIGN DIFFERENT.

Another rhetorical question in the dialogue was

ASL USE WHERE? UNITED-STATES CANADA.

This sentence is an example of how the sign WHERE is commonly used.

Simple Yes/No Questions

The question

ASL NOT UNIVERSAL?

is distinguished from the declarative sentence "ASL is not universal" by the nonmanual signals that accompany the sentence. For yes/no questions, the nonmanual signals are (1) *the raised eyebrows* and (2) *the head tilting forward*.

Information-seeking Questions

The following question is asked about the number of countries involved in the WGD.

W-G-D COUNTRIES INVOLVED, HOW-MANY?

This was translated to "How many countries are involved in the WGD?" The sign INVOLVED could also be translated as "How many countries take part in the WGD?" The response to this question was COUNTRIES 57, which is an example of a noun-adjective word ordering commonly used in ASL.

What's the Sign?

UNITED-STATES

The sign UNITED-STATES is the same one used for America or American. That is, this sign would be used to sign AMERICA as in NORTH AMERICA and American as in AMERICAN SIGN LANGUAGE. If you wanted to ensure that the addressee understood that the meaning of the sign is United States and not America, then you could fingerspell U-S or U-S-A.

SOCIALIZE

The movement of the SOCIALIZE sign represents people interacting with one another. It is *not* used to mean *social* or *society*.

DIFFERENT+

Recall that the plus symbol (+) means to repeat a sign. When the sign DIFFERENT is re-peated, its meaning is similar to the sign VARIOUS. When you sign DIFFERENT the second time, you should move both hands over to the side slightly.

ASL Synonyms

Some signs can be used to mean other things.

Sign	Also used for
DIFFERENT	BUT
DIFFERENT+	VARIOUS
SOCIALIZE	ACQUAINT, ASSOCIATE, BROTHERHOOD, EACH-OTHER, FELLOWSHIP, FRATERNITY, INTERACT, INTERACTION, INTERACTIVE, MINGLE, ONE-ANOTHER
UNITED-STATES	AMERICA, AMERICAN
INVOLVED	INCLUDE, TAKE-PART
HOW-MANY	HOW-MUCH

Practice Activities

1. MODEL FOR LONG YES/NO QUESTIONS AND RHETORICAL QUESTIONS

Signer A: 1. Describe the topic;
              2. ask a yes/no question about the topic.

       Topic: DEAF PEOPLE W-G-D cl-55:FLOCK-to-Games,

       Question: YOU SOCIALIZE?

Signer B: 1. Respond affirmatively;
              2. ask a rhetorical question using WHY;
              3. describe the topic;
              4. make a comment about the topic.

       Response: YES

       Rhetorical question: WHY?

       Topic: DEAF PEOPLE DIFFERENT+ COUNTRIES

       Comment: SIGN DIFFERENT.

Practice

Signer A: DEAF PEOPLE W-G-D cl-55:FLOCK-to-Games, YOU SOCIALIZE?

Signer B: YES WHY? DEAF PEOPLE DIFFERENT+ COUNTRIES SIGN DIFFERENT.

2. MODEL FOR SIMPLE YES/NO QUESTIONS, INFORMATION-SEEKING QUESTIONS, AND RHETORICAL QUESTIONS

Signer A: 1. Describe the topic;
              2. ask a yes/no question about the topic.

       Topic: ASL

       Question: NOT UNIVERSAL?

Signer B: 1. Respond affirmatively to the yes/no question;
              2. ask a rhetorical question;
              3. answer the question.

       Response: RIGHT.

       Rhetorical question: ASL USE WHERE?

       Answer: UNITED-STATES CANADA.

Signer A:	1. Acknowledge that you understand what was just said;
	2. describe a topic;
	3. ask a question about the topic.

Acknowledgment:	OH-I-see.
Topic:	W-G-D COUNTRIES INVOLVED,
Question:	HOW-MANY?

| Signer B: | 1. Respond to the question using a noun-adjective phrase. |

| Response: | COUNTRIES 57. |

Practice

Signer A:	ASL NOT UNIVERSAL?
Signer B:	RIGHT. ASL USE WHERE? UNITED-STATES CANADA.
Signer A:	OH-I-see. W-G-D COUNTRIES INVOLVED, HOW-MANY?
Signer B:	COUNTRIES 57.

3. MASTERY LEARNING

When you feel comfortable signing these phrases, practice signing the entire dialogue shown at the beginning of this lesson. Practice the dialogue until you can sign the part of each character smoothly.

4. FURTHER PRACTICE

Sign all the dialogues in this chapter together. Remember that after you have established a place in the signing space for the World Games for the Deaf, you should refer to this location when using the classifier cl-55:FLOCK-to-Games and the directional verbs ARRIVE-there and GO-to-Games.

LESSON 30: PLANS FOR A BALL GAME

Signing Dialogue

1. **Alan:** **BASEBALL GAME TWO TICKETS, ME BUY FINISH.**

   YOU WANT GO-TO YOU?

   I have bought two tickets to a baseball game. Do you want to go?

BASEBALL	GAME	TWO

TICKETS	ME	BUY

FINISH YOU WANT

GO-TO YOU

2. **Mary:** **BASEBALL ME ENJOY, NOT. ME DECLINE.**

I don't enjoy baseball. I will decline.

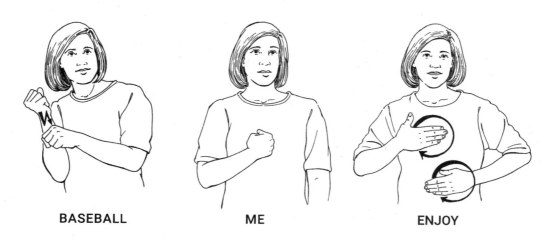

BASEBALL ME ENJOY

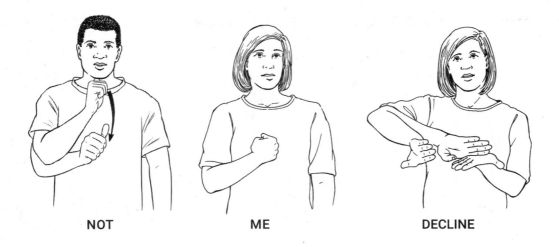

NOT   ME   DECLINE

3. **Alan:** **ME TICKETS HAVE.**

      I have the tickets.

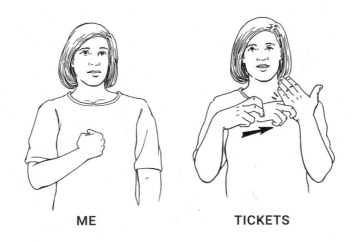

ME   TICKETS

HAVE

4. **Mary:** **O-H W-E-L-L. TICKETS SELL, YOU CAN.**

Oh, well. You can sell the tickets.

TICKETS   SELL

YOU   CAN

ASL TIP

OH WELL

OH WELL is a form of expression. This can be fingerspelled for emphasis, or shown by the use of body language with a shrug and matching facial expression.

5. **Alan:**   **FINE. TONIGHT, RESTAURANT GO OKAY?**

That's fine. How about going to a restaurant tonight?

FINE   TONIGHT   RESTAURANT

GO   OKAY

6. **Mary:**   **MYSELF, RESTAURANT GO?**

Go to a restaurant by myself?

MYSELF   RESTAURANT

GO

7. **Alan:**   **FUNNY. you-TEASE-me FINISH.**

That's funny. Stop teasing me.

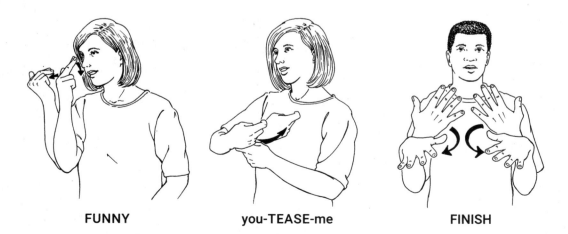

FUNNY   you-TEASE-me   FINISH

8.   **Mary:**   **RESTAURANT, EXPENSIVE CHEAP WHICH?**

Is the restaurant expensive or cheap?

RESTAURANT   EXPENSIVE

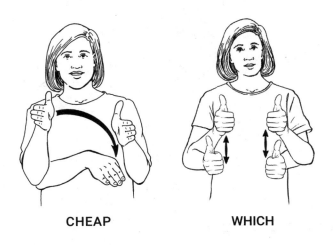

CHEAP   WHICH

9.   **Alan:**   **FOR YOU? CHEAP.**

For you, it will be cheap.

FOR   YOU   CHEAP

10. **Mary:** **THANK-YOU. ME ACCEPT.**

Thank you. I accept.

THANK-YOU ME

ACCEPT

Breaking Down the Dialogue

Topic/Comment

Three sentences used the topic/comment format.

1. BASEBALL GAME TWO TICKETS, ME BUY FINISH.
2. TICKETS SELL, YOU CAN.
3. you-TEASE-ME FINISH.

Note that in sentence 1 the sign FINISH determines the tense of the sentence but that in sentence 3 FINISH is used to mean *stop*.

Simple Yes/No Questions

Two sentences asked yes/no questions.

1. TONIGHT, RESTAURANT GO OKAY?
2. MYSELF, RESTAURANT GO?

In sentence 1, the tense with time adverbs rule is also used because the tense is established directly with the use of the sign TONIGHT. Although the nonmanual signals for yes/no questions apply to both questions, the flavor of the dialogue is such that Mary asks question 2 with a tongue-in-cheek mannerism. You can reflect this mannerism by (1) *smiling slightly* while (2) *tilting your head* and (3) *raising your eyebrows* when signing the question.

Long Yes/No Questions

The question YOU WANT GO YOU? can stand alone as a simple yes/no question, or it can be thought of as part of a long yes/no question because it is asking a question about the previous sentence.

BASEBALL GAME TWO TICKETS, ME BUY FINISH. YOU WANT GO YOU?

Information-seeking Questions

The question

RESTAURANT, EXPENSIVE CHEAP WHICH?

is an example of a question that specifies two of the possible answers. Notice that no sign for the concept "or" is in the sentence. The concept "or" is expressed in the meaning of the sign WHICH.

Rhetorical Questions

The following sentence is another example of how the mood of the signer will influence the nonmanual signals when signing:

FOR YOU? CHEAP.

The sentence does contain a rhetorical question, but there are several options for the type of nonmanual signals when signing CHEAP. It could be signed with a hint of humor, with a bland look, with a look of mock seriousness, and so forth.

Ordering of Simple Sentences

1. ME DECLINE,
2. ME TICKETS HAVE.
3. ME ACCEPT.

Sentences 1 and 3 use a simple subject-verb format. The objects of both sentences are implied from the dialogue. It is readily understood that in sentence 1 Mary is declining the invitation to go to a baseball game, and in sentence 3 she is accepting the invitation to go to a restaurant.

Negation

The negation rule was applied in the following sentence:

BASEBALL ME ENJOY, NOT.

The topic is first described, followed by the negative sign NOT.

What's the Sign?

FUNNY

The English gloss of a sign is only the best approximation for a sign. Your facial grammar provides the clues necessary to determine the exact meaning of a sign. In the dialogue, Alan signs FUNNY, but it is clear that he does not mean that what Mary had just said is very funny or it is something to laugh at. Rather, Alan's intended meaning is more like "Yeah right, funny" or "I could almost laugh at that." Study the dialogue and decide how you might sign it. With a deadpan expression? With an exasperated look?

you-TEASE-me

TEASE is a directional verb. The dominant hand moves toward the signer to indicate that the subject is "you" and the object is "me."

GO

Compare the formation of this sign with GO-to. Although the signs can sometimes be used interchangeably, there are instances when one sign feels more appropriate than the other. The sign GO-to is a directional verb and is always used when the signer wishes to indicate movement to a specific location in the signing space. The sign GO is often used when movement to a particular point in the signing space is not necessary. For example, GO is best used when the meaning of the sentence is along the lines of "Let's go" and "He's gone."

ASL Synonyms

Some signs can be used to mean other things.

Sign	Also used for
ACCEPT	APPROVE
BASEBALL	BAT
BUY	PURCHASE
CHEAP	BARGAIN, INEXPENSIVE
DECLINE	REJECT, WAIVE, LAID-OFF
FUNNY	COMEDY, HUMOR, JOKE
LET'S-GO	GO, GONE, GO OUT

Practice Activities

1. MODEL FOR TOPIC/COMMENT, LONG YES/NO QUESTIONS, ORDERING OF SIMPLE SENTENCES, AND NEGATION

Signer A:
1. Describe the topic;
2. say something about the topic;
3. ask a yes/no question about the topic.

Topic: BASEBALL GAME TWO TICKETS,

Comment: ME BUY FINISH.

Question: YOU WANT GO YOU?

Signer B:
1. Describe the topic;
2. negate the topic with a negative sign;
3. describe an action with a simple sentence structure.

Topic: BASEBALL ME ENJOY,

Negative: NOT.

Action: ME DECLINE.

Practice

Signer A: BASEBALL GAME TWO TICKETS, ME BUY FINISH.
YOU WANT GO YOU?

Signer B: BASEBALL ME ENJOY, NOT. ME DECLINE.

2. MODEL FOR TOPIC/COMMENT AND ORDERING OF SIMPLE SENTENCES

Signer A:
1. Create a simple subject-verb-object sentence.
SVO: ME TICKETS HAVE.

Signer B:
1. Make a comment about the previous sentence;
2. describe the topic;
3. make a comment about the topic.

Comment: O-H W-E-L-L.

Topic: TICKETS SELL,

Comment: YOU CAN.

Practice

Signer A: ME TICKETS HAVE.

Signer B: O-H W-E-L-L. TICKETS SELL, YOU CAN.

3. MODEL FOR TOPIC/COMMENT, TENSE WITH TIME ADVERBS, AND SIMPLE YES/NO QUESTIONS

Signer A:
1. Establish the tense with a time adverb;
2. describe the topic;
3. ask a yes/no question about the topic.

Tense:	TONIGHT,
Topic:	RESTAURANT GO
Question:	OKAY?

Signer B:
1. Describe the topic;
2. ask a question about the topic.

Topic:	MYSELF,
Question:	RESTAURANT GO?

Signer A:
1. Respond to the question with a comment;
2. describe an action as a topic;
3. indicate that the action is to stop by using FINISH to make a comment about the topic.

Comment:	FUNNY.
Topic (action)	you-TEASE-me,
Comment:	FINISH.

Practice

Signer A: TONIGHT, RESTAURANT GO OKAY?

Signer B: MYSELF, RESTAURANT GO?

Signer A: FUNNY. you-TEASE-ME, FINISH.

4. MODEL FOR INFORMATION-SEEKING QUESTIONS, RHETORICAL QUESTIONS, AND ORDERING OF SIMPLE SENTENCES

Signer A: 1. Describe the topic;
             2. ask a question about the topic.

             Topic: RESTAURANT,
             Question: EXPENSIVE CHEAP WHICH?

Signer B: 1. Ask a rhetorical question;
             2. answer the question.

             Rhetorical question: FOR YOU?
             Answer: CHEAP.

Signer A: 1. Make a courteous response;
             2. describe an action with a simple sentence structure.

             Response: THANK-you.
             Action: ME ACCEPT.

Practice

Signer A: RESTAURANT, EXPENSIVE CHEAP WHICH?

Signer B: FOR YOU? CHEAP.

Signer A: THANK-you. ME ACCEPT.

5. MASTERY LEARNING

When you feel comfortable signing these phrases, practice signing the entire dialogue shown at the beginning of this lesson. Practice the dialogue until you can sign the part of each character smoothly while using the appropriate nonmanual signals. Try to assume the mannerism that you think each character in the dialogue is portraying.

6. FURTHER PRACTICE

Create five alternative responses for Signer B in the following dialogue:

Signer A: BASEBALL GAME, YOU WANT GO YOU?

Signer B: BASEBALL ME ENJOY, NOT. ME DECLINE.

Practice signing the dialogue and the alternative responses with a partner.

LESSON 31: SPORTS AND LEISURE

Signing Dialogue

1. **Lily:** **YOU PLAY SPORTS?**

    Do you play sports?

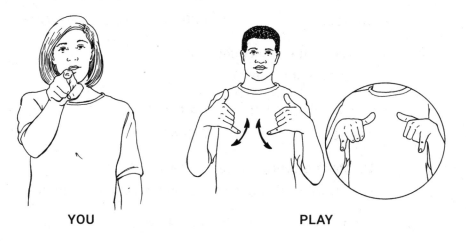

YOU   PLAY

SPORTS

2. **Lee:** **YES. MANY SPORTS, ME INVOLVE.**

Yes. I'm involved in many sports.

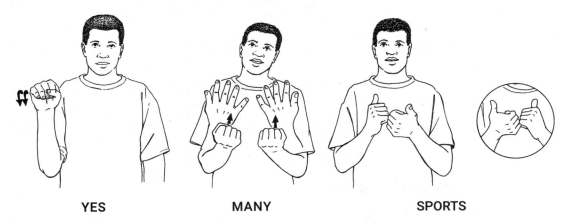

YES   MANY   SPORTS

ME   INVOLVE

3. **Lily:** **YOUR FAVORITE SPORT, WHAT?**

What's your favorite sport?

YOUR   FAVORITE   SPORT

WHAT

4. **Lee:**   **VOLLEYBALL, TENNIS.**

   Volleyball and tennis.

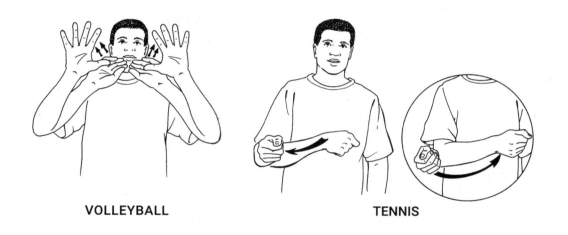

VOLLEYBALL   TENNIS

Sports

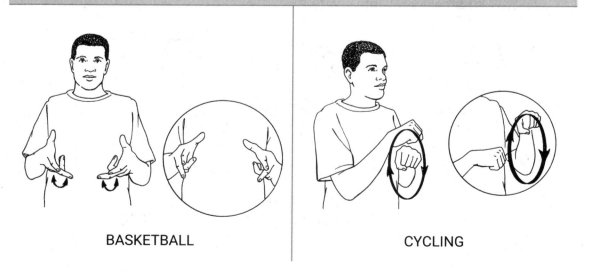

BASKETBALL   CYCLING

Sports

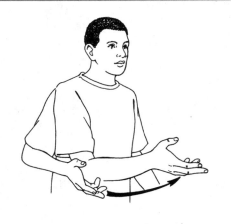

BOWLING

FOOTBALL

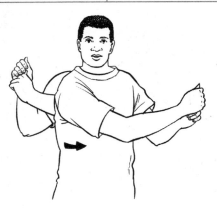

GOLF

HOCKEY

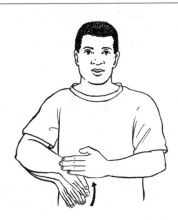

SOCCER

GOLF   SOCCER   SKIING

WRESTLING   SOFTBALL

Signing Dialogue

5. **Jin:**   **SPORTS, YOU LIKE?**

Do you like sports?

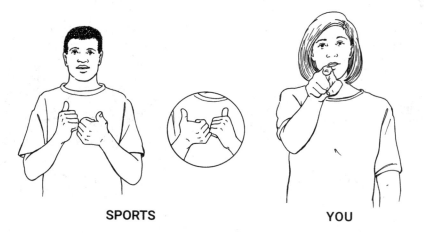

SPORTS   YOU

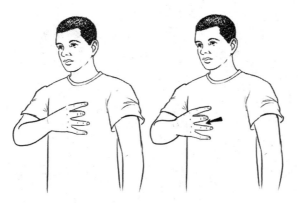

LIKE (to like something)

6. **Alyiah:** **SPORTS ME DON'T-LIKE. ME PREFER EASY-GOING ACTIVITIES.**

I don't like sports. I prefer easy-going activities.

SPORTS ME

DON'T-LIKE ME PREFER

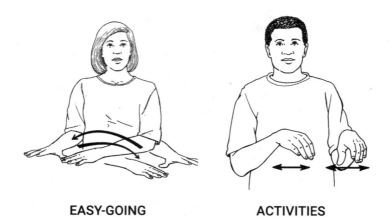

EASY-GOING   ACTIVITIES

ASL TIP

LEISURE

An alternate sign for EASY-GOING is LEISURE, which indicates pleasure. You may see this sign in the video quiz for the chapter.

LEISURE

7. **Jin:** **EASY-GOING ACTIVITIES, WHAT KIND?**

What kind of easy-going activities?

EASY-GOING   ACTIVITIES

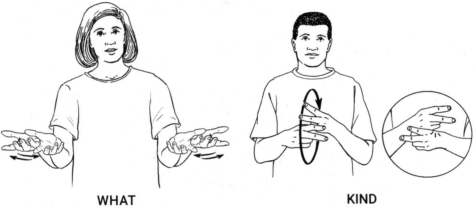

WHAT   KIND

8. **Alyiah:** **HORSEBACK RIDING, JOGGING.**

Horseback riding and jogging.

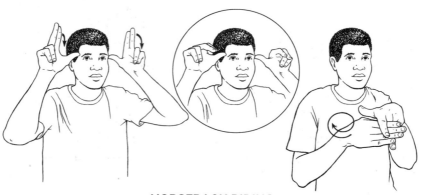

HORSEBACK RIDING

RUNNING/JOGGING

Leisure

BILLIARDS/POOL

EXERCISE

Leisure

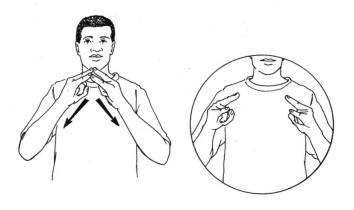

CAMPING

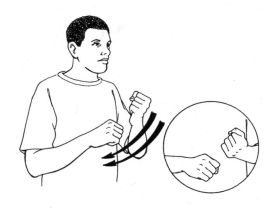

CANOEING

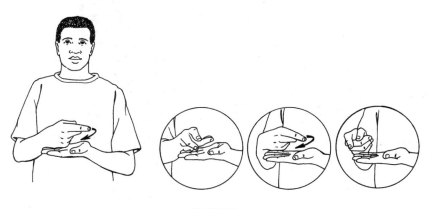

CARDS

Leisure

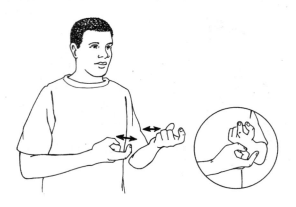

ICE-SKATING

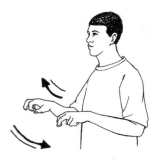

ROLLER-SKATING

HIKING

ARCHERY

Breaking Down the Dialogue

Topic/Comment

The sentence

MANY SPORTS, ME INVOLVE.

illustrates a common use of the sign INVOLVE. Possible translations include "I'm involved in many sports" and "I participate in many sports."

Simple Yes/No Questions

Two simple yes/no questions were used in the dialogues:

1. YOU PLAY SPORTS?
2. SPORTS, YOU LIKE?

Simple questions can have variable ordering of the signs. Question 1 uses a subject-verb-object (SVO) sentence structure, and question 2 uses an object-subject-verb (OSV) order.

Information-seeking Questions

1. YOU FAVORITE SPORT, WHAT?
2. EASY-GOING ACTIVITIES, WHAT KIND?

In both questions, the wh-sign comes after the topic is described. Question 2 could have been signed without KIND in it.

Ordering of Simple Sentences

An SVO sentence order is used in the following sentence:

ME PREFER EASY-GOING ACTIVITIES.

Negation

The negative sign follows the topic in this example of how the negation rule is applied:

SPORTS ME DON'T-LIKE.

What's the Sign?

LIKE/DON'T-LIKE

The sign DON'T-LIKE is an example of negative incorporation. It is similar to the sign LIKE except that the hand is opened up and turned away from the body. Thus, there is no sign DON'T in the sign DON'T-LIKE.

EASY-GOING

It is also common practice to sign the word "easy-going" and then sign an explanation to ensure that the intended meaning of the sign is understood clearly.

KIND

The meaning of the sign KIND is *type*. Avoid using this sign for the other meaning of KIND, which is *generous*.

ASL Synonyms

Some signs can be used to mean other things.

Sign	Also used for
ACTIVITIES	ACTIVE, DO
KIND	TYPE
SPORT	COMPETE, COMPETITION, RACE
MANY	MANIFOLD, MULTIPLE, PLURAL
INVOLVE	INVOLVED, INCLUDE, PARTICIPATE
FAVORITE	PREFER
SOCCER	KICK
SOFTBALL	BALL
EASY-GOING	RELAXED, CHILL, CASUAL, LAID-BACK

 Practice Activities

1. MODEL FOR TOPIC/COMMENT, YES/NO QUESTIONS, AND INFORMATION-SEEKING QUESTIONS

   Signer A: 1.   Use the SVO sentence structure to ask a simple yes/no question.

   SVO: YOU PLAY SPORT?

   Signer B: 1.   Respond affirmatively to the question;
                2.   describe a topic;
                3.   make a comment about the topic.

   Response: YES.
   Topic: MANY SPORTS,
   Comment: ME INVOLVE.

Signer A: 1. Describe a topic;
              2. ask a wh-question about the topic.

              Topic: YOUR FAVORITE SPORT,

              Question: WHAT?

Signer B: 1. Respond to the question with the names of sports.

              Response: VOLLEYBALL, TENNIS.

Practice

Signer A: YOU PLAY SPORT?

Signer B: YES. MANY SPORTS, ME INVOLVE.

Signer A: YOUR FAVORITE SPORT, WHAT?

Signer B: VOLLEYBALL, TENNIS.

2. MODEL FOR SIMPLE YES/NO QUESTIONS, INFORMATION-SEEKING QUESTIONS, ORDERING OF SIMPLE SENTENCES, AND NEGATION

Signer A: 1. Describe a topic;
              2. ask a yes/no question about the topic.

              Topic: SPORTS,

              Question: YOU LIKE?

Signer B: 1. Describe a topic:
              2. negate the topic with the negative sign DON'T-LIKE;
              3. describe a preference for something by using an SVO sentence structure.

              Topic: SPORTS

              Negative: ME DON'T-LIKE.

              SVO: ME PREFER EASY-GOING ACTIVITIES.

Signer A: 1. Describe a topic;

                  2. ask a wh-question about the topic.

                  Topic: EASY-GOING ACTIVITIES,

                  Question: WHAT KIND?

Signer B: 1. Respond to the question with the names of leisure activities.

                  Response: HORSEBACK RIDING, JOGGING.

Practice

Signer A: SPORTS, YOU LIKE?

Signer B: SPORTS ME DON'T-LIKE. ME PREFER LEISURE ACTIVITIES.

Signer A: EASY-GOING ACTIVITIES, WHAT KIND?

Signer B: HORSEBACK RIDING, JOGGING.

3. MASTERY LEARNING

Practice the two dialogues until you feel comfortable with them.

4. FURTHER PRACTICE

Substitute signs in the dialogues with other signs for sports and leisure activities that are shown in the list of signs. If you do not see the sport or activity you like, use the Internet to help you find if there is an ASL sign; if not, fingerspell it.

 Video Quiz Visit online.barronsbooks.com for scored practice on ASL expressions related to sports and leisure.

Grammar Practice

Write an English translation for each of the following ASL sentences.

Note that there may be other ways of translating these sentences than the ones shown here.

1. W-G-D, you-GO-to-there FOR-FOR?

2. W-G-D PEOPLE cl-55:FLOCK-to-Games, WHEN?

3. W-G-D DEAF PEOPLE COMPETE HOW-MANY?

4. YOU COMPETITION INVOLVE HOW-MANY?

5. YOU DIFFERENT+ LANGUAGE UNDERSTAND, HOW-MANY?

6. NEXT-YEAR, GAMES WHERE?

7. IN-THREE-YEARS GAMES WHERE? CANADA.

8. EVERY DAY TIME 7:00, MAN cl-1:WALK-past-me.

9. FOUR-WEEKS-AGO, GAME you-CHALLENGE-him WHAT?

10. SUPPOSE YOUR CLASS me-JOIN, you-HELP-me STUDY DON'T-MIND YOU?

CHAPTER 14

Health

> **Learning Objectives**
>
> In this chapter, you will learn:
> - How to apply the following grammar rules to create sentences: topic/comment, simple yes/no questions, long yes/no questions, ordering of simple sentences, negation, and information-seeking questions
> - The verb OPEN to indicate the location of an action on the body
> - The directional verbs SHOW, GIVE, ACCOMPANY, and PULL-OUT
> - The sign PAIN to indicate the location of pain on the body
> - How to use LIKE as a conjunction

LESSON 32: GOING TO THE DENTIST

Signing Dialogue

1. **Dentist:** **HELLO D-E-N-I-S-E, FEEL+ YOU?**

   Hello Denise, how are you feeling?

HELLO

FEEL

YOU

2. **Denise:** **TODAY ME SO-SO TOOTH PAIN-in-mouth.**

Today, I am feeling so-so. My tooth hurts.

| TODAY | ME | SO-SO |

TOOTH   PAIN-in-mouth

3. **Dentist:** **YOUR TOOTH PAIN? you-SHOW-me, OPEN-mouth-wide.**

Your tooth is sore? Open your mouth wide and show me.

YOUR   TOOTH

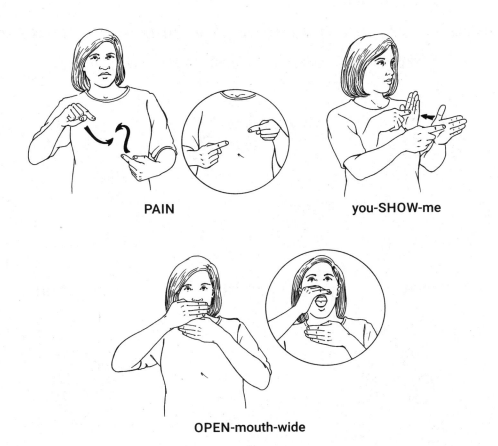

PAIN

you-SHOW-me

OPEN-mouth-wide

4.   **Denise:**   **YOU SEE WHAT?**

What do you see?

YOU

SEE

WHAT

5. **Dentist:** **TOOTH ROTTEN INFECTION HAVE YOU. ME PULL-OUT HAVE-TO.**

You have an infected rotten tooth. I will have to pull it out.

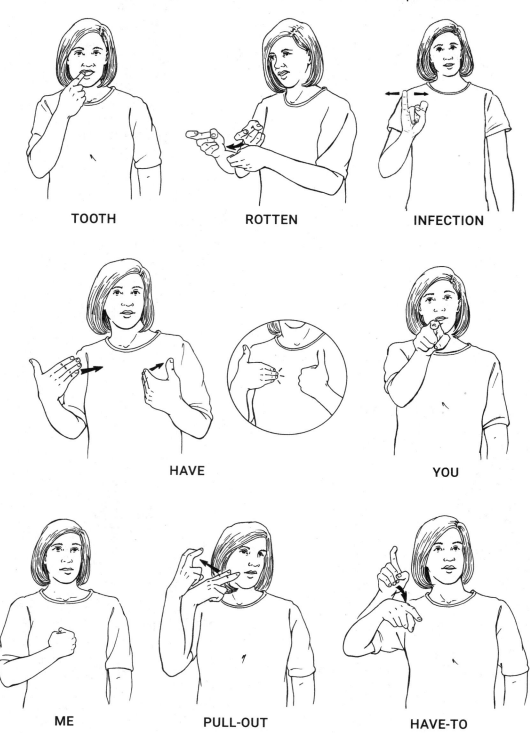

TOOTH	ROTTEN	INFECTION

HAVE		YOU

ME	PULL-OUT	HAVE-TO

6. **Denise:** **YOU DENTIST EXPERIENCE MANY YEAR FINISH YOU?**

Do you have many years of experience as a dentist?

YOU   DENTIST   EXPERIENCE

MANY   YEAR

FINISH   YOU

7. **Dentist:** **RELAX, ME GOOD.**

Relax, I'm good.

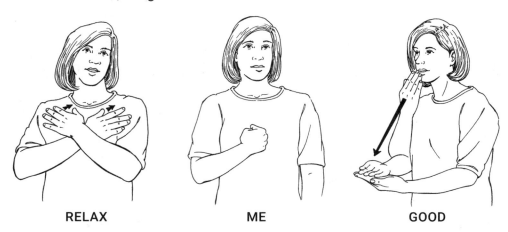

RELAX   ME   GOOD

8. **Denise:** **YOU SURE?**

Are you sure about that?

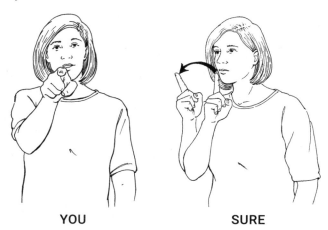

YOU   SURE

Breaking Down the Dialogue

Greeting

The dentist begins the dialogue with the greeting

HELLO D-E-N-I-S-E, FEEL+YOU?

The ASL phrase FEEL+YOU? translates to "How are you feeling?" in English. There is no verb *to-be* in ASL. Recall that a hyphenated word means to fingerspell that word.

SO-SO

TODAY ME SO-SO, MY TOOTH PAIN-in-mouth.

This ASL sentence states an average or fair feeling, then follows up with why.

Simple Yes/No Questions

In the question

YOUR TOOTH PAIN?

the sign PAIN is placed at the end of the sentence because it asks a question about the tooth. In the dialogue, the dentist doesn't wait for an answer, which is not an uncommon procedure used in many conversations. A person will simply ask a question to establish what is going to be said next.

OPEN and SHOW

In the sentence

you-SHOW-me, OPEN-mouth-wide.

two signs make use of the signing space. First, the sign OPEN is made by the mouth to show the location of the action *open* or what is to be opened. Second, the sign SHOW is made from the addressee toward the signer. In the dialogue, the dentist makes the sign from Denise toward herself or himself.

Information-seeking Questions

In the dialogue, Denise asks the following wh-question:

YOU SEE WHAT?

This is a short sentence and the ordering of the signs can vary. For example, you could also sign WHAT YOU SEE? and SEE WHAT YOU?

Topic/Comment

The dialogue contains two consecutive sentences that follow the topic/comment rule.

	Topic	Comment
	YOU TOOTH ROTTEN INFECTION	HAVE YOU.
	ME PULL-OUT	HAVE-TO.

Note that HAVE and HAVE-TO are two different signs. The phrase HAVE YOU refers to the possession or ownership of something, whereas the phrase HAVE-TO refers to a requirement to do something.

Long Yes/No Questions

The question

YOU DENTIST EXPERIENCE MANY YEAR FINISH YOU?

can be thought of as consisting of two parts. The first part describes the topic of the question, whereas the second part asks a yes/no question about the topic.

topic:	YOU DENTIST EXPERIENCE
yes/no question:	MANY YEAR FINISH YOU?

What's the Sign?

DENTIST

The sign DENTIST is a combination of the sign TOOTH + AGENT-sign. It is not uncommon to simply sign TOOTH alone to mean DENTIST.

OPEN-mouth-wide

There are several ways to sign OPEN and each one of them depends upon what object is being opened. In this sign, the hands mimic the action of the mouth opening wide. This sign is an example of a verb that shows the location of an action because of where it is made in the signing space.

PAIN-in-mouth

The sign PAIN is made by the mouth to show the location of the pain.

PULL-OUT

The dentist in the dialogue signed PULL-OUT by the cheeks to show that one of the back teeth (a molar) will be pulled out. If this sign is made by the throat, it becomes TONSILITIS or throat pain. If it is made by the right side of the stomach, it becomes APPENDECTOMY or stomach pain.

ASL Synonyms

Some signs can be used to mean other things.

Sign	Also used for
HAVE	POSSESS
HAVE-TO	MUST
PAIN	HURT, SORE
RELAX	REST
ROTTEN	ROT, RUIN, RUINED, SPOIL, SPOILED
INFECTION	INFECTED, INFECT, INSURANCE
SO-SO	FAIR, OK, SORT-OF, KIND OF
TOOTH	DENTIST, TEETH

Practice Activities

1. MODEL FOR GREETINGS AND PREPOSITION BUT

| Signer A: | 1. Greet the person; |
| | 2. ask how she is. |

| Greeting: | HELLO D-E-N-I-S-E, |
| Question: | FEEL+YOU? |

Signer B:	1. Respond to greeting;
	2. indicate the preposition BUT by moving your body to the side and tilting your head with a facial expression;
	3. describe the exception relating to the body movements that indicate BUT.

Response:	TODAY ME SO-SO,
Preposition:	body, head movement, facial expression (NMS) indicating BUT
Exception:	TOOTH PAIN-in-mouth.

Practice

| Signer A: | HELLO D-E-N-I-S-E, FEEL+YOU? |
| Denise: | TODAY ME SO-SO, TOOTH PAIN-in-mouth. |

2. MODEL FOR SIMPLE YES/NO QUESTIONS, USING OPEN TO SHOW THE LOCATION OF THIS ACTION AND DIRECTIONAL VERB SHOW

| Signer: | 1. Describe the topic; |
| | 2. ask a question about the topic using the sign PAIN. |

| Topic: | YOUR TOOTH |
| Question: | PAIN? |

| Signer: | 1. Sign SHOW moving the hands from the addressee to yourself; |
| | 2. indicate the location of the action by signing OPEN in front of the mouth. |

| Directional verb: | you-SHOW-me, |
| Location: | OPEN-mouth-wide. |

Practice

Signer:	YOUR TOOTH PAIN? you-SHOW-me, OPEN-mouth-wide.

3. MODEL FOR SIMPLE YES/NO QUESTIONS AND INFORMATION-SEEKING QUESTIONS

Signer A:
1. Describe the topic;
2. ask a question about the topic.

Topic:	YOU SEE
Question:	WHAT?

Signer B:
1. Describe the topic;
2. make a comment about the topic;
3. repeat steps 1 and 2.

Topic:	TOOTH ROTTEN INFECTION
Comment:	HAVE YOU.
Topic:	ME PULL-OUT
Comment:	HAVE-TO.

Practice

Signer A:	YOU SEE WHAT?
Signer B:	TOOTH ROTTEN INFECTION HAVE YOU. ME PULL-OUT HAVE-TO.

4. MODEL FOR LONG YES/NO QUESTIONS

Signer A:
1. Describe the topic;
2. ask a yes/no question about the topic.

Topic:	YOU DENTIST EXPERIENCE
Question:	MANY YEAR FINISH YOU?

Signer B:
1. Respond to the question.

Response:	RELAX, ME GOOD.

Practice

| Signer A: | YOU DENTIST EXPERIENCE MANY YEAR FINISH YOU? |
| Signer B: | RELAX, ME GOOD. |

5. MASTERY LEARNING

When you feel comfortable signing these phrases, practice signing the entire dialogue shown at the beginning of this lesson. Practice the dialogue until you can sign it comfortably.

6. FURTHER PRACTICE

Create five simple dialogues where one person tells another person about a pain in the shoulder, stomach, knee, nose, and forehead. Practice signing each of the dialogues with a partner. Make the sign PAIN in the area mentioned. Note that when PAIN is signed by the stomach, you have produced the sign STOMACHACHE; when PAIN is signed by the forehead, you have the sign HEADACHE.

LESSON 33: PULLING THE TOOTH

Signing Dialogue

1. **Dentist:** **FEEL YOU? CHEEK NUMB?**

   How do you feel? Is your cheek numb?

FEEL YOU CHEEK

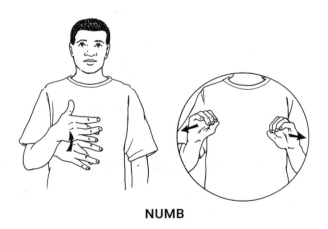

NUMB

2. **Denise:**   **YES, ME FEEL NOTHING.**

                 Yes, I feel nothing.

3. **Dentist:**   **GOOD. OPEN-mouth-wide YOUR TOOTH ME PULL-OUT.**

                 Good, open your mouth wide and I will pull your tooth out.

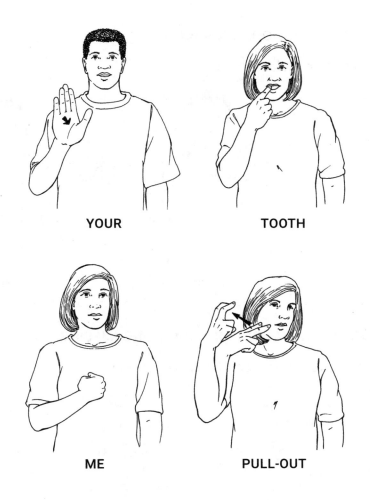

YOUR   TOOTH

ME   PULL-OUT

4.   **Denise:**   **PULL-OUT-by-cheek, FINISH YOU?**

Have you finished pulling out my tooth?

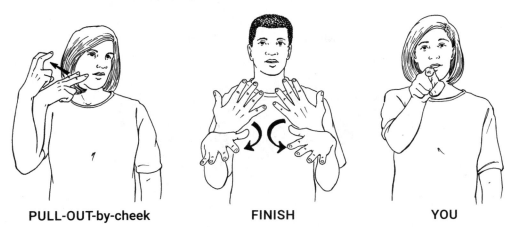

PULL-OUT-by-cheek   FINISH   YOU

5. **Dentist:** **YES. YOUR M-O-L-A-R HUGE.**

Yes. Your molar is huge.

YES   YOUR   HUGE

6. **Denise:** **ME FEEL STRANGE LIKE SOMETHING MISSING.**

I feel strange as if something is missing.

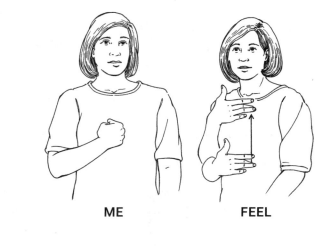

ME   FEEL

STRANGE

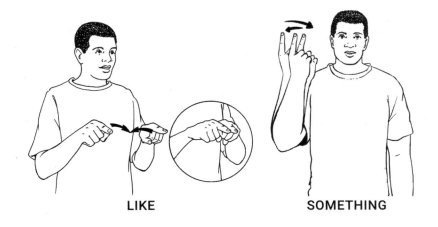

LIKE   SOMETHING

MISSING

7. **Dentist:** **YOUR TOOTH MISSING. RELAX, YOU FEEL BETTER SOON.**

Your tooth is missing. Relax and you will feel better soon.

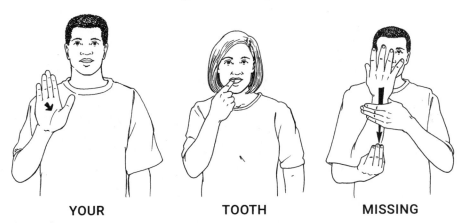

YOUR   TOOTH   MISSING

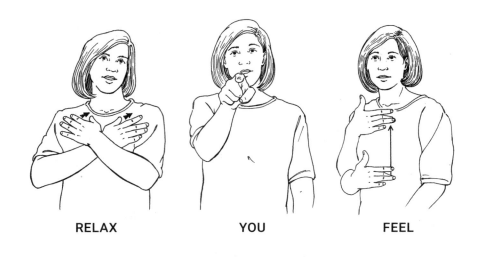

RELAX   YOU   FEEL

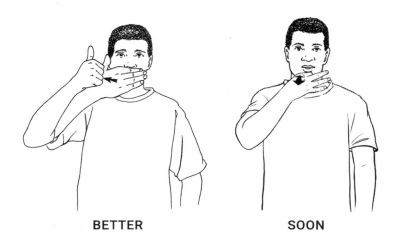

BETTER   SOON

8.   **Denise:**   **ME HOPE.**

     I hope!

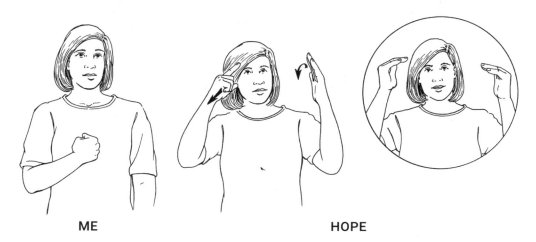

ME   HOPE

Breaking Down the Dialogue

Information-seeking Questions and Simple Yes/No Questions

The dialogue begins with two different types of questions:

FEEL YOU? CHEEK NUMB?

The first question seeks information about how a person (Denise) is feeling. The second question asks for a yes or no response. Both types of questions require a different set of nonmanual signals. Review Chapter 3 for a reminder of which nonmanual signals go with which question.

Negation

The sentence

ME FEEL NOTHING

is an example of using the negation rule. The negative sign NOTHING is placed at the end of the sentence to represent what it was that Denise felt.

Topic/Comment and the Directional Verb PULL-OUT

The following sentence makes use of the signing space in two ways:

OPEN-mouth-wide YOUR TOOTH ME PULL-OUT.

First, the sign OPEN is made by the mouth to get OPEN-mouth-wide to show the location of an action. Second, the sign PULL-OUT can be made in a neutral position in the signing space. Alternatively, it can start with the hand held in the direction of Denise's tooth and then pulled back to show whose tooth is being pulled out.

There are two more examples of a topic/comment sentence in the dialogue.

Topic	Comment
YOUR M-O-L-A-R	HUGE.
YOUR TOOTH	MISSING.

Simple Yes/No Questions and the Directional Verb PULL-OUT

In the sentence

PULL-OUT-by-cheek, FINISH YOU?

the starting position of the sign PULL-OUT-by-cheek is by the cheek on the side from which the tooth is pulled. The subject of the sentence is implied in the context of the dialogue, and the object of the sentence, tooth, is incorporated into the movement of the sign. The phrase FINISH YOU? asks a yes/no question about PULL-OUT-by-cheek.

LIKE as a Conjunction

In the sentence

ME FEEL STRANGE LIKE SOMETHING MISSING.

the sign LIKE is used to mean *as if*, and it joins the phrases ME FEEL STRANGE and SOME-THING MISSING.

Ordering of Simple Sentences

Ordering of some sentences can be highly variable. The sentence

RELAX, YOU FEEL BETTER SOON.

could also be signed RELAX, SOON YOU FEEL BETTER or SOON YOU FEEL BETTER, RELAX.

What's the Sign?

CHEEK

Some parts of the anatomy are signed by pointing to them.

HUGE

The size and intensity of this sign indicates the relative degree of largeness. To emphasize that something is very large, you should (1) *squeeze the eyebrows together* and (2) *purse your lips together tightly*.

NUMB

The sign for NUMB is a compound sign made up of the signs FEEL and NONE.

SOMETHING

This compound sign is made up of the signs SOME and THING.

ASL Synonyms

Some signs can be used to mean other things.

Sign	Also used for
HUGE	ENORMOUS, GIGANTIC, LARGE
LIKE	AS-IF, ALIKE, SIMILAR, SAME
MISSING	ABSENCE, ABSENT, GONE
SOON	SHORTLY, IN THE NEAR FUTURE

Practice Activities

1. MODEL FOR SIMPLE YES/NO QUESTIONS, INFORMATION-SEEKING QUESTIONS, AND NEGATION

| Signer A: | 1. Ask a simple information-seeking question; |
| | 2. ask a yes/no question. |

| Information-seeking question: | FEEL YOU? |
| Yes/no question: | CHEEK NUMB? |

| Signer B: | 1. Respond to the yes/no question; |
| | 2. use the negation rule to state how you feel. |

| Response: | YES, |
| Negative: | ME FEEL NOTHING. |

Practice

| Signer A: | FEEL YOU? CHEEK NUMB? |
| Signer B: | YES, ME FEEL NOTHING. |

2. MODEL FOR VERBS THAT SHOW THE LOCATION OF AN ACTION OPEN, TOPIC/ COMMENT, DIRECTIONAL VERB PULL-OUT, AND SIMPLE YES/NO QUESTIONS

Signer A:	1. Describe the location of an action with the verb OPEN;
	2. describe the topic;
	3. make a comment about the topic using the directional verb PULL-OUT.

Location:	OPEN-mouth-wide
Topic:	YOUR TOOTH
Comment:	ME PULL-OUT.

| Signer B: | 1. Describe the topic; |
| | 2. ask a yes/no question about the topic. |

| Topic: | PULL-OUT-by-cheek |
| Question: | FINISH YOU? |

Signer A:
1. Respond to the yes/no question;
2. describe the topic;
3. make a comment about the topic.

Response: YES.

Topic: YOUR M-O-L-A-R

Comment: HUGE.

Practice

Signer A: OPEN-mouth-wide YOUR TOOTH ME PULL-OUT.

Signer B: PULL-OUT-by-cheek, FINISH YOU?

Signer A: YES. YOUR M-O-L-A-R HUGE.

3. MODEL FOR CONJUNCTION LIKE, TOPIC/COMMENT, AND ORDERING OF SIMPLE SENTENCES

Signer A:
1. Sign a simple SVO phrase;
2. sign the conjunction LIKE;
3. sign another simple phrase.

Phrase: ME FEEL STRANGE.

Conjunction: LIKE

Phrase: SOMETHING MISSING.

Signer B:
1. Describe a topic;
2. make a comment about the topic.

Topic: YOUR TOOTH

Comment: MISSING.

1. Create a simple sentence.

Sentence: RELAX, YOU FEEL BETTER SOON.

Practice

Signer A: ME FEEL STRANGE LIKE SOMETHING MISSING.

Signer B: YOUR TOOTH MISSING. RELAX, YOU FEEL BETTER SOON.

4. MASTERY LEARNING

When you feel comfortable signing these phrases, practice signing the entire dialogue shown at the beginning of this lesson. Practice the dialogue until you can sign it comfortably.

5. FURTHER PRACTICE

Join the dialogue with one in a previous lesson, and practice signing both until you are comfortable signing them.

LESSON 34: A VISIT WITH THE DOCTOR

Signing Dialogue

1. **Rain:** **EXCUSE-me, ME APPOINTMENT WITH DOCTOR. HAVE**

   Excuse me, I have an appointment with the doctor.

EXCUSE-me   ME

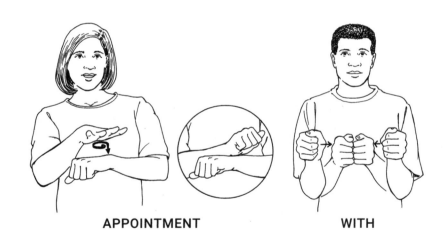

APPOINTMENT   WITH

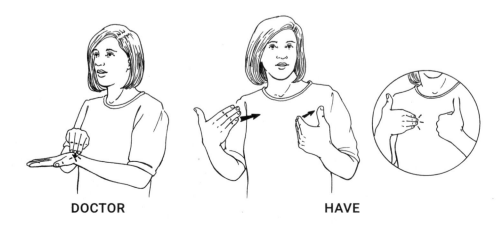

DOCTOR   HAVE

2. **Nurse:** **APPOINTMENT TIME?**

What time is your appointment?

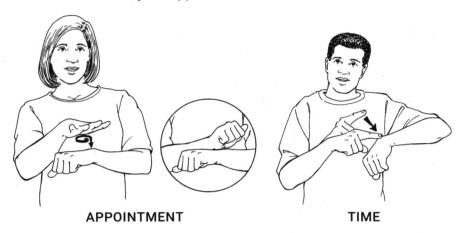

APPOINTMENT   TIME

3. **Rain:** **APPOINTMENT TIME 11:30.**

My appointment is at 11:30.

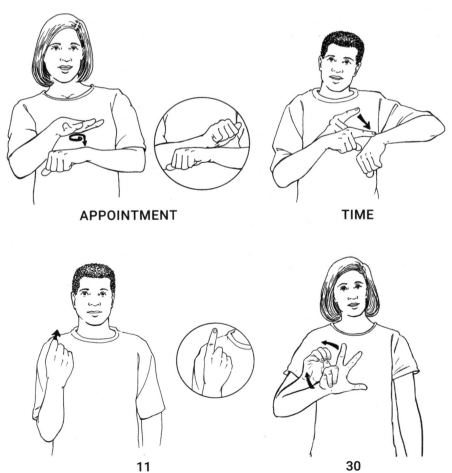

APPOINTMENT   TIME

11   30

4. **Nurse:** **RIGHT. ME NURSE ACCOMPANY-me PLEASE.**

That's right. I'm the nurse, could you please come with me?

RIGHT   ME   NURSE

ACCOMPANY-me   PLEASE

5. **Rain:** **O-K, me-ACCOMPANY-you.**

Okay, I will come with you.

me-ACCOMPANY-you

6. **Nurse:** **SIT PLEASE. YOU MEDICATION ALLERGY HAVE?**

Please have a seat. Do you have an allergy to medication?

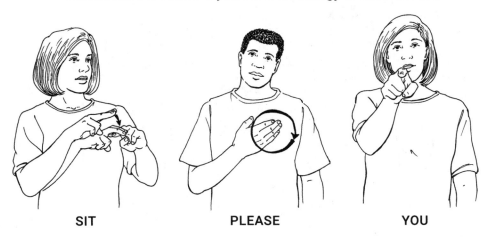

SIT	PLEASE	YOU

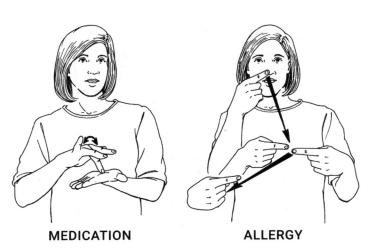

MEDICATION	ALLERGY

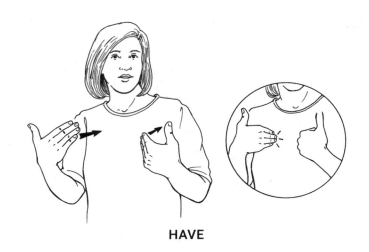

HAVE

7. **Rain:** **NO, ME ALLERGY NONE.**

No, I have no allergies.

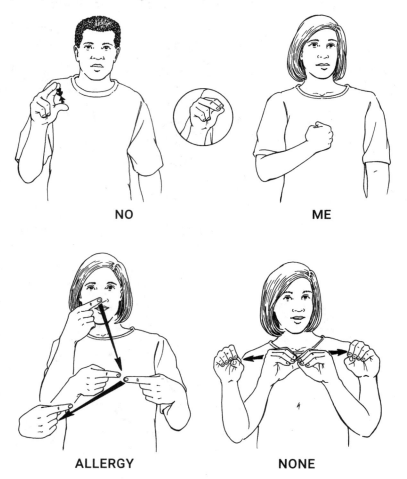

NO   ME

ALLERGY   NONE

8. **Nurse:** **YOU SMOKE?**

Do you smoke?

YOU   SMOKE

9. **Rain:** **NO, ME SMOKE NEVER.**

No, I never smoke.

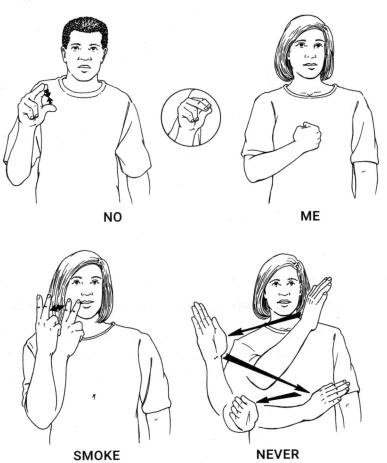

NO   ME

SMOKE   NEVER

10. **Nurse:** **GOOD. DOCTOR COME SOON. WAIT PLEASE.**

Good for you. The doctor will come soon. Please wait.

| GOOD | DOCTOR | COME |

| SOON | WAIT | PLEASE |

Breaking Down the Dialogue

Ordering of Simple Sentences

The dialogue begins with a simple sentence structure:

EXCUSE-me, ME APPOINTMENT WITH DOCTOR. HAVE

The WITH in this sentence is not necessary. The sentence ME APPOINTMENT DOCTOR is acceptable because the meaning can be implied from the situation. This sentence would be readily understood if it came from a person walking up to a reception desk in a doctor's office.

Four more simple sentences in the dialogue are:

1. ME NURSE ACCOMPANY-me PLEASE.
2. SIT PLEASE.
3. DOCTOR COME SOON.
4. WAIT PLEASE.

Sentence 1 is organized by the nurse introducing herself or himself followed by a command and the sign PLEASE. In English, you could have said, "Please come with me, I am the nurse." In ASL, it is common to set up the situation first and in the case of this sentence to introduce oneself before giving a command. Hence, in sentences 3 and 4 the nurse first informs Rain that the doctor is coming soon and then tells her to please wait. Sentence 2 could be translated as "Please have a seat" or "Sit down please" or some other variation. A key factor in translating is to ensure that the conventions of one language, such as those with regard to politeness, are accounted for. In English, we would not normally say "Sit please" to a patient in a doctor's office because it is too curt and may be seen as impolite.

One further example of a simple sentence is

O-K, me-ACCOMPANY-you.

The subject and object of the sentence are incorporated into the directional verb ACCOMPANY.

Topic/Comment

Telling the time for something can be done by following the topic/comment rule. You first describe what sort of time you are about to tell and then tell the time. An example of this is found in one sentence in the dialogue:

MY APPOINTMENT TIME 11:30.

Information-seeking Questions

To ask a time-related question, you follow the rule for information-seeking questions. This occurred in the following sentence:

APPOINTMENT TIME?

As with all questions, nonmanual signals are necessary to show that the sentence is a question and not a statement. In the response to this question

MY APPOINTMENT TIME 11:30.

the sign TIME is not translated as such. It is used because it shows that the numbers following it tell the time.

Simple Yes/No Questions

The dialogue contained the following two simple yes/no questions:

1. YOU MEDICATION ALLERGY HAVE?
2. YOU SMOKE?

Both questions are dependent upon the nonmanual signals to indicate that they are asking a question. Without these signals, you would get "You are allergic to medication" and "You do smoke."

Negation

The dialogue contained one example of a sentence using the rule for negation.

Answers a previous question	Topic	Negation
NO,	ME ALLERGY	NONE.
NO,	ME SMOKE	NEVER.

In both sentences, the signer uses two negative signs: one to answer a question and the other to negate a topic.

What's the Sign?

ACCOMPANY-me and me-ACCOMPANY-you

The sign for ACCOMPANY-me starts in a neutral position and then moves to the side to indicate that the person being addressed should accompany the person signing. A proper translation is dependent upon the context of the dialogue, but it is usually just as appropriate to say "come with me" as it is to say "accompany me." The dialogue also has the sign me-ACCOMPANY-you. This sign directly incorporates the subject (me) and the object (you) because of its starting location (by the body of the signer) and its ending position (toward the body of the addressee).

ALLERGY

The sign for ALLERGY consists of the two signs NOSE + OPPOSITE.

NONE

The sign for NONE is also used to mean "no" as in "No more games for you" or "There are no rules for being lazy." Beginning signers often substitute this sign for the other sign NO, which is only to be used to express a negation as in "No, you may not go."

11:30

Time is indicated by first signing TIME and then adding the correct numbers, which in this case are the signs for 11 and 30.

ASL Synonyms

Some signs can be used to mean other things.

Sign	Also used for
APPOINTMENT	ASSIGNMENT, BOOK, RESERVATION
ALLERGY	ALLERGIC
MEDICATION	MEDICINE
NONE	NO
PLEASE	APPRECIATE
SMOKE	SMOKING
SIT	SIT-DOWN

 Practice Activities

1. MODEL FOR TOPIC/COMMENT, SIMPLE YES/NO QUESTIONS, AND ORDERING OF SIMPLE SENTENCES

   Signer A: 1. Initiate the conversation;
   2. describe something about yourself.

   Initiate: EXCUSE-me,

   Description: ME APPOINTMENT WITH DOCTOR.

   Signer B: 1. Describe the topic;
   2. ask a question about the topic using the sign TIME.

   Topic: APPOINTMENT

   Question: TIME?

Signer A: 1. Describe the topic;

2. make a comment about the topic.

Topic:	MY APPOINTMENT
Comment:	TIME 11:30.

Practice

Signer A: EXCUSE-me, ME APPOINTMENT WITH DOCTOR.

Signer B: APPOINTMENT TIME?

Signer A: MY APPOINTMENT TIME 11:30.

2. MODEL FOR ORDERING OF SIMPLE SENTENCES

Signer A: 1. Introduce self;

2. give a command.

Introduction:	ME NURSE
Command:	ACCOMPANY-me PLEASE.

Signer B: 1. Acknowledge command;

2. describe the action that you will do.

Acknowledgment:	O-K
Action:	me-ACCOMPANY-you.

Signer A: 1. Give a command.

Command:	SIT PLEASE.

Practice

Signer A: ME NURSE ACCOMPANY-me PLEASE.

Signer B: O-K, me-ACCOMPANY-you.

Signer A: SIT PLEASE.

3. MODEL FOR SIMPLE YES/NO QUESTIONS AND NEGATION

Signer A: 1. Describe the topic;
2. ask a question about the topic.

Topic: YOU MEDICATION ALLERGY

Question: HAVE?

Signer B: 1. Respond to the question;
2. describe the topic;
3. use a negative sign to negate the topic.

Response: NO,

Topic: ME ALLERGY

Negation: NONE.

Signer A: 1. Ask a simple yes/no question.

Question: YOU SMOKE?

Signer B: 1. Respond to the question;
2. describe the topic;
3. use a negative sign to negate the topic.

Response: NO,

Topic: ME SMOKE

Negation: NEVER.

Practice

Signer A: YOU MEDICATION ALLERGY HAVE?

Signer B: NO, ME ALLERGY NONE.

Signer A: YOU SMOKE?

Signer B: NO, ME SMOKE NEVER.

4. MODEL FOR ORDERING OF SIMPLE SENTENCES

Signer A: 1. Describe an action;
2. give a command.

Action: DOCTOR COME SOON.

Command: WAIT PLEASE.

Practice

Signer A: DOCTOR COME SOON. WAIT PLEASE.

5. MASTERY LEARNING

When you feel comfortable signing these phrases, practice signing the entire dialogue shown at the beginning of this lesson. Practice the dialogue until you can sign the part of each character smoothly.

6. FURTHER PRACTICE

Create five simple dialogues using various signs for time adverbs to discuss the time of an appointment. For example:

Signer A: YOU DOCTOR APPOINTMENT TIME?

What time is your doctor appointment?

Signer B: ME DOCTOR APPOINTMENT TOMORROW AFTERNOON TIME 4:30.

My doctor appointment is tomorrow afternoon at 4:30.

Signer A: YOU ARRIVE-there EARLY, YOU SHOULD.

You should arrive there early.

Signer B: ME EARLY ALWAYS.

I'm always early.

LESSON 35: WHAT THE DOCTOR SAID

Signing Dialogue

1.   **Doctor:**   **HELLO A-L-I -S-O-N, YOU SICK YOU?**

   Hello Alison, are you sick?

HELLO   YOU

SICK   YOU

2. **Alison:** **YES, SINCE THREE-DAYS ME STOMACHACHE.**

Yes, I have had a stomachache for three days.

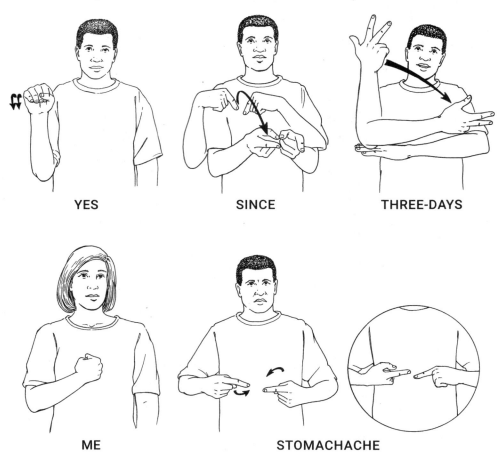

YES   SINCE   THREE-DAYS

ME   STOMACHACHE

3. **Doctor:** **SINCE THREE-DAYS VOMIT YOU?**

Have you been vomiting for three days?

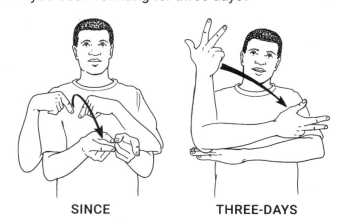

SINCE   THREE-DAYS

VOMIT   YOU

4. **Alison:**   **YES, ME VOMIT OCCASIONALLY.**

Yes, I have been vomiting occasionally.

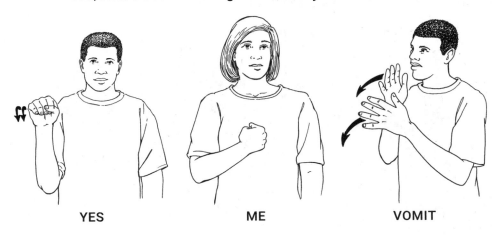

YES   ME   VOMIT

OCCASIONALLY

5. **Doctor:** **YOU FEEL HOT, COLD?**

Do you feel hot and cold?

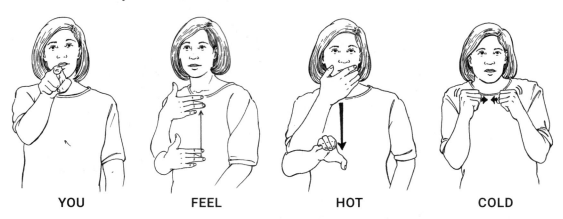

| YOU | FEEL | HOT | COLD |

6. **Alison:** **(nods) BUT MOST FEEL HOT.**

Yes, but mostly I feel hot.

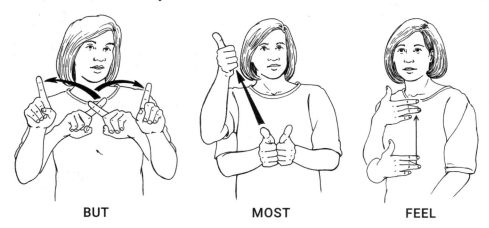

| BUT | MOST | FEEL |

HOT

7. **Doctor:** **OH-I-see. YOU F-E-V-E-R HAVE.**

I see. You have a fever.

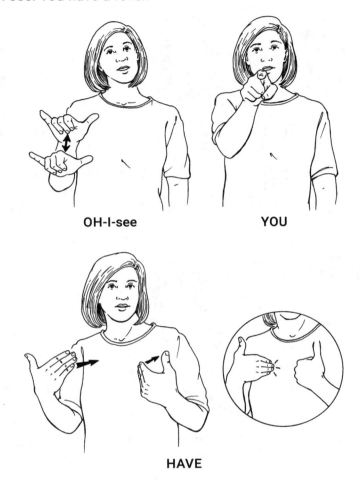

OH-I-see   YOU

HAVE

8. **Alison:** **YOU THINK?**

Do you think so?

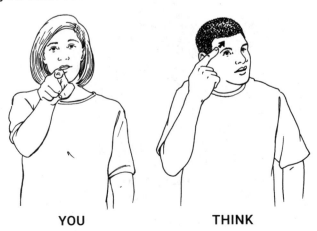

YOU   THINK

9. **Doctor:** **YES. YOU REST MUST. MEDICATION me-GIVE-you.**

Yes. You must rest. I will give you medication.

YES   YOU   REST

MUST   MEDICATION   me-GIVE-you

10. **Alison:** **THANK-YOU.**

Thank you.

THANK-YOU

Breaking Down the Dialogue

Simple Yes/No Questions

As with doctors in general, the doctor in the dialogue relied on yes/no questions to get information from Alison.

1. YOU SICK YOU?
2. SINCE THREE-DAYS VOMIT YOU?
3. YOU FEEL HOT, COLD?

Sentence 2 includes the phrase SINCE THREE-DAYS, which translates to "for the past three days," "since three days ago," or "from three days ago until now."

Alison also used a yes/no question:

4. YOU THINK?

This question can also be signed THINK YOU? Note that the nonmanual signals are critical with question 4. The signals for a yes/no question are (1) *a raised eyebrow* and (2) *the head tilted forward.* If you signed this question with a squeezed eyebrow, then you are asking for information and the meaning of the question changes from "Do you think so?" to "What do you think about that?"

Tense with Time Adverbs

The phrase SINCE THREE-DAYS is used in the sentence

SINCE THREE-DAYS ME STOMACHACHE.

It can be translated in several ways such as "I have had a stomachache for three days," "I have had a stomachache for the past three days," or "For three days now, I have had a stomachache." All the translations indicate that something took place in the past and continues to the present time.

Topic/Comment

It is common in ASL to place signs for time (or time adverbs) at the beginning of the sentence. When the time adverb is not used to establish the tense of a sentence but rather to comment on the occurrences of a particular event, it usually follows the action sign. This is seen in the following sentence:

YES, ME VOMIT OCCASIONALLY.

The sign MUST often comes at the end of a sentence when it is the emphasis of the sentence, as in the following:

YOU REST MUST.

This sentence can be signed YOU MUST REST without any change in the meaning. However, placing MUST at the end of the sentence in this dialogue fits well with what a doctor would sign when admonishing a patient.

BUT as a Conjunction

A head nod can take the place of the sign YES. Thus, in the following sentence, the sign BUT is used to join an affirmative thought (indicated by the head nod) and an exception.

(nods) BUT MOST FEEL HOT.

Ordering of Simple Sentences

The simple sentence

MEDICATION me-GIVE-you.

has the subject (me) and object (you) incorporated into the movement of the directional sign GIVE. The movement begins in front of the body and moves toward the addressee. Another simple sentence in the dialogue was

YOU F-E-V-E-R HAVE.

What's the Sign?

me-GIVE-you

This is a directional sign whereby the subject and object are incorporated into the movement of the sign.

STOMACHACHE

The sign for PAIN is made by the stomach to show the location of the pain.

THREE-DAYS

The 3 sign is used to make the sign DAY. This is an example of number incorporation, which is common in ASL.

ASL Synonyms

Some signs can be used to mean other things.

Sign	Also used for
MEDICATION	MEDICINE
BUT	EXCEPT
OCCASIONALLY	ONCE-IN-A-WHILE, PERIODICALLY, SOMETIMES
REST	RELAX
SICK	ILL
SINCE	ALL-ALONG, BEEN, EVER-SINCE, SO-FAR, UP-TO-NOW
VOMIT	THROW-UP

 Practice Activities

1. MODEL FOR TOPIC/COMMENT, TENSE WITH TIME ADVERBS, SIMPLE YES/NO QUESTIONS, AND FOR CONJUNCTION BUT

   Signer A:
   1. Initiate the conversation with a greeting;
   2. describe the topic;
   3. ask a yes/no question about the topic.

Initiate:	HELLO A-L-I-S-O-N.
Topic:	YOU SICK
Question:	YOU?

   Signer B:
   1. Respond to the question;
   2. describe the time that something took place;
   3. describe what took place.

Response:	YES,
Time:	SINCE THREE-DAYS
Describe:	ME STOMACHACHE

Signer A:	1. Describe the time that something took place;
	2. describe the action;
	3. ask a yes/no question.

Time:	SINCE THREE-DAYS
Action:	VOMIT
Question:	YOU?

Signer B:	1. Respond affirmatively to the question;
	2. describe the action;
	3. describe the time of the action.

Response:	YES,
Action:	ME VOMIT
Time:	OCCASIONALLY.

| Signer A: | 1. Describe the topic; |
| | 2. ask a question about the topic. |

| Topic: | YOU FEEL |
| Question: | HOT, COLD? |

Signer B:	1. Respond affirmatively to the question with a head nod;
	2. sign the conjunction BUT;
	3. describe the exception.

Response:	(nods)
Conjunction:	BUT
Exception:	MOST FEEL HOT.

Practice

Signer A:	HELLO A-L-I-S-O-N, YOU SICK YOU?
Signer B:	YES, SINCE THREE-DAYS ME STOMACHACHE.
Signer A:	SINCE THREE-DAYS VOMIT YOU?
Signer B:	YES, ME VOMIT OCCASIONALLY.
Signer A:	YOU FEEL HOT, COLD?
Signer B:	(nods) BUT MOST FEEL HOT.

2. MODEL FOR TOPIC/COMMENT, SIMPLE YES/NO QUESTIONS, AND ORDERING OF SIMPLE SENTENCES

Signer A:
1. Demonstrate you understood something;
2. sign the subject;
3. sign the object;
4. sign the verb.

Understanding:	OH-I-see.
Subject:	YOU
Object:	F-E-V-E-R
Verb:	HAVE.

Signer B:
1. Ask a yes/no question relating to Signer A's statement.

Question:	YOU THINK?

Signer A:
1. Respond affirmatively to the question;
2. describe a topic;
3. make a comment about the topic.

Response:	YES.
Topic:	YOU REST
Comment:	MUST.

1. Name the object that is given;
2. sign the verb.

Object:	MEDICATION
Verb:	me-GIVE-you.

Signer B:
1. Respond by expressing your gratitude.

Response:	THANK-YOU.

Practice

Signer A:	OH-I-see. YOU F-E-V-E-R HAVE YOU.
Signer B:	YOU THINK?
Signer A:	YES. YOU REST MUST. MEDICATION me-GIVE-you.
Signer B:	THANK-YOU.

3. MASTERY LEARNING

When you feel comfortable signing these phrases, practice signing the entire dialogue shown at the beginning of this lesson. Practice the dialogue until you can sign the part of each character smoothly.

4. FURTHER PRACTICE

Join this dialogue with the one in a previous lesson and sign them together.

LESSON 36: HEALTH AND SYMPTOMS

Signing Dialogue

1. **Kristian:** **YOU SICK?**

   Are you sick?

| YOU | SICK |

2. **Laine:** **ME RASH-ON-FACE HAVE.**

   I have a rash on my face.

| ME | RASH-ON-FACE |

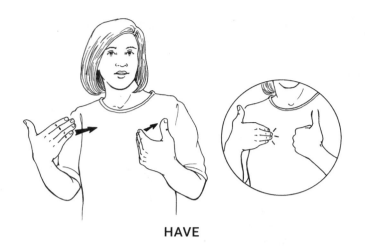

HAVE

3. **Kristian:** **SIGN RASH-ON-FACE, ME DON'T UNDERSTAND. FINGERSPELL PLEASE.**

I don't understand the sign RASH. Please fingerspell it.

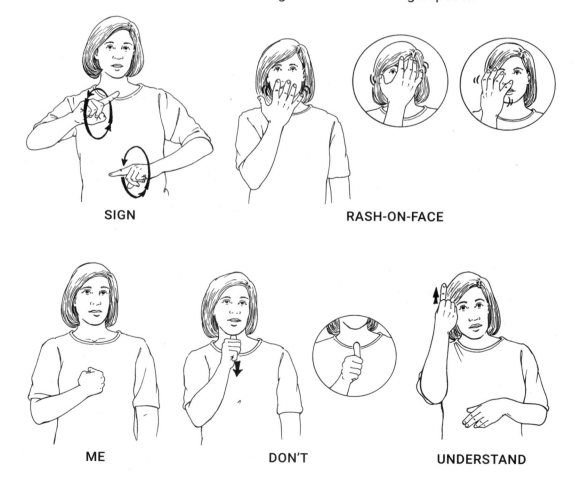

SIGN   RASH-ON-FACE

ME   DON'T   UNDERSTAND

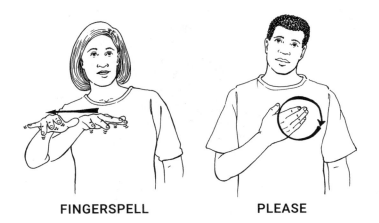

FINGERSPELL   PLEASE

4. **Laine:** **R-A-S-H.**

 Rash.

5. **Kristian:** **OH-I-see. SORRY. YOU GET-WELL QUICK, GOOD-LUCK.**

 I see. I'm sorry. I hope you get well quickly, good luck.

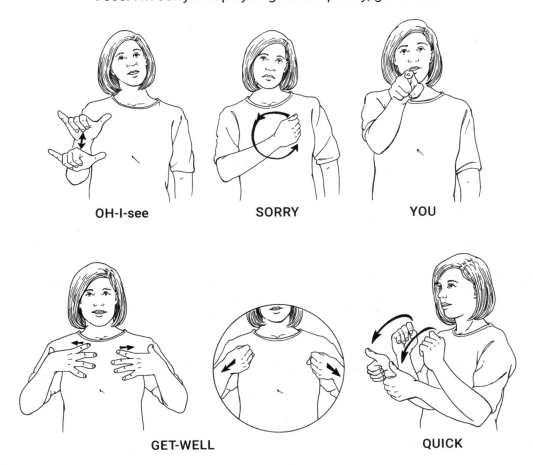

OH-I-see   SORRY   YOU

GET-WELL   QUICK

GOOD-LUCK

6. **Laine:** **THANK-YOU.**

Thank you.

THANK-YOU

Breaking Down the Dialogue

Topic/Comment

A topic/comment sentence structure used in the dialogue was

YOU GET-WELL QUICK, GOOD-LUCK.

Simple Yes/No Questions

A simple structure can be used to inquire about a person's condition:

YOU SICK?

Although this is a simple question, in the absence of appropriate nonmanual signals it would mean "You are sick."

Ordering of Simple Sentences

The following two simple sentence structures were illustrated in the dialogue:

a. ME RASH HAVE.
b. FINGERSPELL PLEASE.

Sentence a is an example of a subject-object-verb (SOV) sentence order. Sentence b is an example of what you can say when you do not understand the meaning of a sign.

Negation

In the sentence

SIGN RASH, ME DON'T UNDERSTAND.

the phrase ME DON'T UNDERSTAND is in reference to the phrase SIGN RASH. When expressing a negative thought, it is always important to first describe the topic that is not understood.

What's the Sign?

GET-WELL

You must avoid falling into the trap of trying to find a sign for each English word. The sign GET-WELL is a single sign and not a compound sign made of the signs GET and WELL.

ASL Synonyms

Some signs can be used to mean other things.

Sign	Also used for
GET-WELL	HEALTHY, ROBUST
GOOD-LUCK	SENDING LUCK, POSITIVE VIBES

Additional Health-related Signs

Sign: Also used for:

DIZZY   LIGHT-HEADED

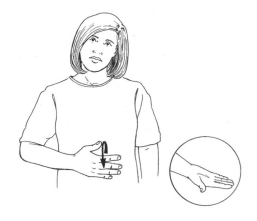

UPSET

PALE

Sign: **Also used for:**

HEART-ATTACK

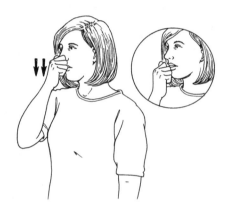

COLD (SICK)   SNEEZE

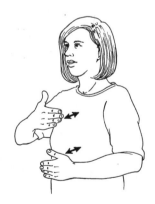

BREATH   BREATHE

Sign: **Also used for:**

| TEMPERATURE | DEGREE |

THERMOMETER

OPERATION   CUT, DISSECTION, SURGERY

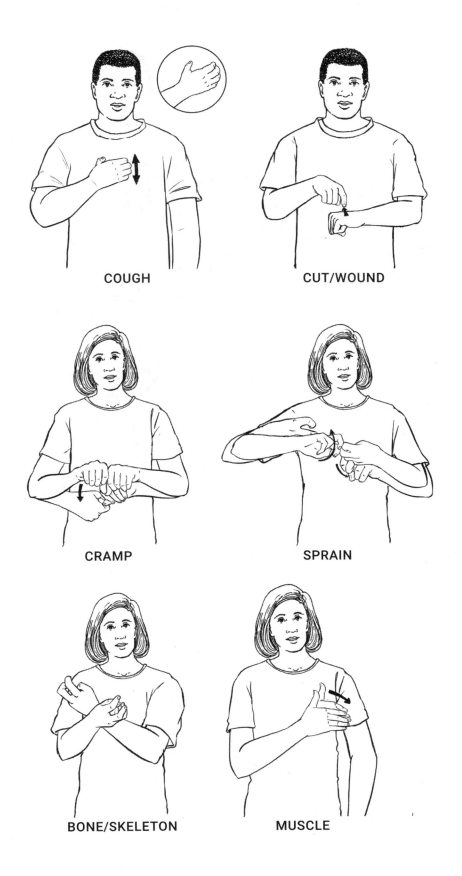

COUGH

CUT/WOUND

CRAMP

SPRAIN

BONE/SKELETON

MUSCLE

BREAK (to separate)   BLOOD/BLEEDING

PANDEMIC

Practice Activities

1. MODEL FOR TOPIC/COMMENT, SIMPLE YES/NO QUESTIONS, ORDERING OF SIMPLE SENTENCES, AND NEGATION

Signer A: 1. Ask a simple yes/no question.

   Question: YOU SICK?

Signer B: 1. Respond to the question with an SOV sentence.

   SOV: ME RASH HAVE.

Signer A: 1. Describe a topic;
   2. sign a negative phrase about the topic.

   Topic: SIGN RASH,

   Negative: ME DON'T UNDERSTAND.

   1. Use a simple sentence to make a request.

   Request: FINGERSPELL PLEASE.

Signer B: 1. Fingerspell the name of the sign that Signer A did not understand.

   Fingerspell: R-A-S-H.

Signer A: 1. Indicate that you understand;
   2. sign a sympathetic remark;
   3. describe a topic;
   4. make a comment about the topic.

   Indication: OH-I-see.

   Remark: SORRY

   Topic: YOU GET-WELL QUICK,

   Comment: GOOD-LUCK.

Signer B: 1. Express your appreciation.

   Appreciation: THANK-you.

Practice

Signer A:	YOU SICK?
Signer B:	ME RASH HAVE. (SIGN ON FACE)
Signer A:	SIGN RASH, ME DON'T UNDERSTAND. FINGERSPELL PLEASE.
Signer B:	R-A-S-H.
Signer A:	OH-I-see. SORRY. YOU GET-WELL QUICK, GOOD-LUCK.
Signer B:	THANK-you.

2. MASTERY LEARNING

Practice the above dialogue until you feel comfortable signing it.

3. FURTHER PRACTICE

Create dialogues using the health-related signs in this chapter. Write the English gloss and translation for your dialogue and practice signing it with a partner.

 Video Quiz Visit online.barronsbooks.com for scored practice on ASL phrases related to health.

Grammar Practice

Write an English translation for each of the following ASL sentences.

Note that there may be other ways of translating these sentences than the ones shown here.

1. FOOTBALL GAME ME WATCH FINISH.

2. TOMORROW NIGHT RESTAURANT TWO-of-us GO-to, TIME?

3. YOU PREFER SPORTS, LEISURE ACTIVITIES WHICH?

4. ME LIKE WHAT? HOCKEY, GOLF, CYCLING.

5. SUPPOSE YOU PAIN-in-mouth, YOU APPOINTMENT DOCTOR DENTIST WHICH?

6. ME FEEL AWFUL WHY? MY TOOTH ROTTEN.

7. YOU HURT WHERE? you-SHOW-me.

8. ME ALLERGY WHAT? P-E-N-I-C-I-L-L-I-N.

9. ME SICK, ME FEEL HOT.

10. MORNING YOU HOCKEY PLAY, AFTERNOON YOU FOOTBALL WATCH, NOW SICK YOU?

CHAPTER 15

Traveling

Learning Objectives

In this chapter, you will learn:

- How to apply the following grammar rules to create sentences, topic/comment, tense with time adverbs, information-seeking questions, ordering of simple sentences, negation, pronominalization, and conditional sentences
- The directional verbs HELP, FLY, and JOIN
- The question WHAT'S-WRONG?
- New signs for countries and cities
- How to use signs TRAIN, CAR, MOTORCYCLE, and BUS as vehicles to travel in
- The months of the year and numbers for the days of the months

LESSON 37: TAKING A TRIP

Signing Dialogue

1. **John:**   **HELLO, DO-what YOU?**

    Hello, what are you doing?

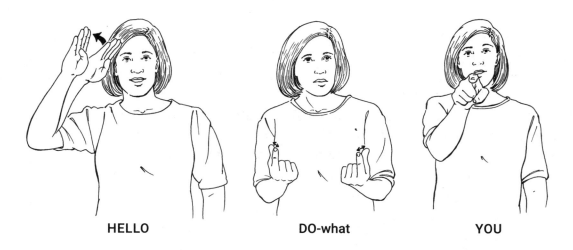

| HELLO | DO-what | YOU |

2. **Jenny:**   **ME NEED VACATION. GO-to POLAND ME WANT.**

    I need a vacation. I want to go to Poland.

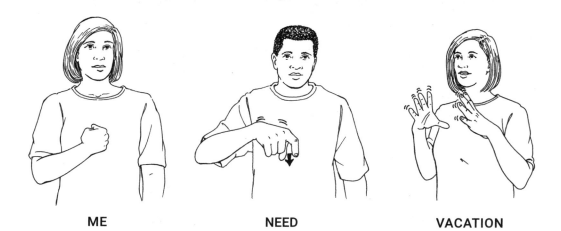

| ME | NEED | VACATION |

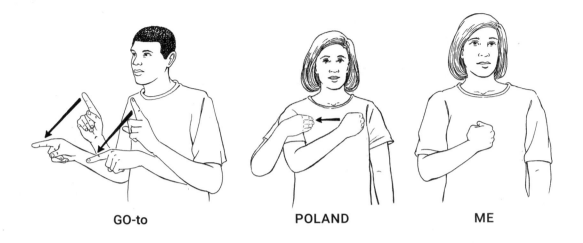

GO-to   POLAND   ME

WANT

3. **Jenny:**   **NOW INTERNET ME CHECK.**

I am checking the Internet now.

NOW   INTERNET   ME

CHECK

4.   **John:**   **INTERNET CHECK FOR-FOR?**

Why are you checking out the Internet?

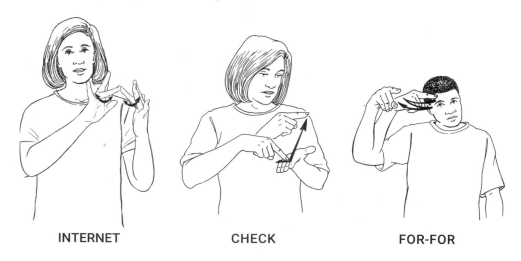

INTERNET   CHECK   FOR-FOR

5. **Jenny:**   **PAST, SUPPOSE ME WANT TRAVEL, SLOW PROCESS PLAN ALWAYS.**

In the past if I wanted to travel, it always took a long time to plan.

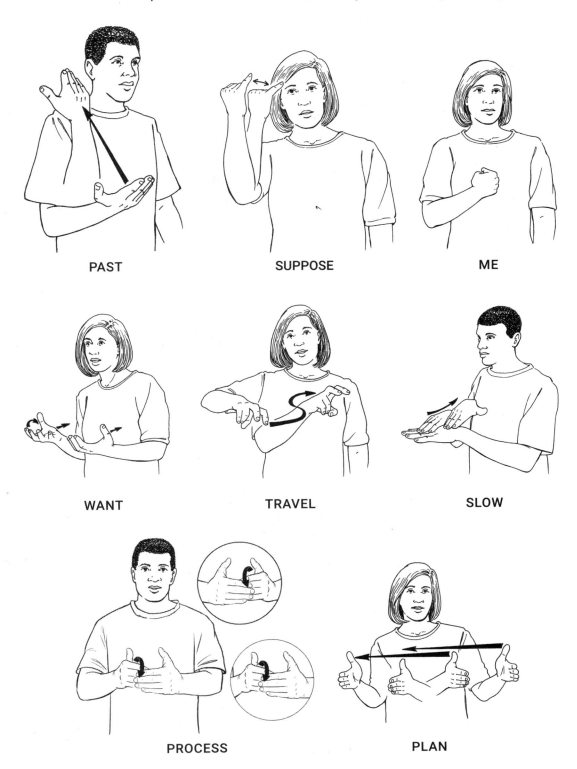

PAST   SUPPOSE   ME

WANT   TRAVEL   SLOW

PROCESS   PLAN

ALWAYS

6. **Jenny:** **TODAY, ME TRAVEL MYSELF PLAN, INTERNET HELP-me.**

Today, I do my own travel planning and the Internet helps me.

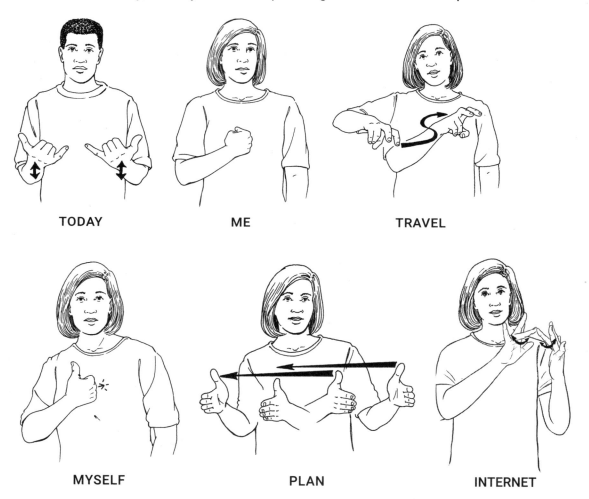

TODAY   ME   TRAVEL

MYSELF   PLAN   INTERNET

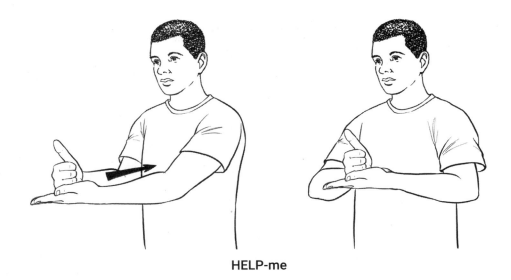

HELP-me

7. **John:** **AWESOME! TECHNOLOGY TODAY, IMPROVED (BIG IMPROVEMENT/ ADVANCEMENT).**

Hey, that's awesome! Today's technology has really improved.

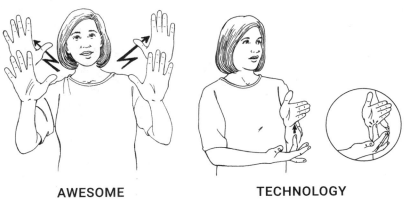

AWESOME   TECHNOLOGY

TODAY   IMPROVE (BIG
                           IMPROVEMENT/
                           ADVANCEMENT)

8. **John:** **YOU VACATION HOW LONG?**

How long will your vacation be?

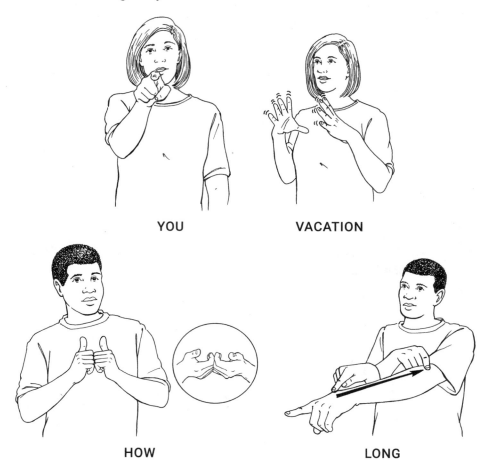

YOU   VACATION

HOW   LONG

9. **Jenny:** **FOUR-WEEKS.**

Four weeks.

FOUR-WEEKS

10. John: **me-JOIN-you, DON'T-MIND YOU?**

Do you mind if I join you?

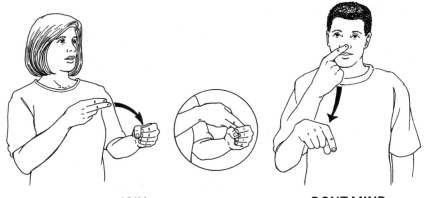

me-JOIN-you   DONT-MIND

YOU

11. Jenny: **SURE!**

Sure, please do!

SURE

Breaking Down the Dialogue

Greeting

The dialogue begins with the following greeting:

HELLO, DO-what YOU?

The phrase DO-what YOU? is commonly used to initiate a conversation.

Topic/Comment

The following phrases follow the topic/comment rule:

Topic	Comment
GO-to POLAND	ME WANT.
INTERNET	ME CHECK.
TECHNOLOGY TODAY,	IMPROVED.
ME TRAVEL	MYSELF PLAN,
INTERNET	HELP-me.

Tense with Time Adverbs

Each of the following sentences relies on a time adverb to establish the tense of the sentence. The time adverb is placed at the beginning of the sentence.

1. NOW INTERNET ME CHECK.
2. PAST, SUPPOSE ME WANT TRAVEL, SLOW PROCESS PLAN ALWAYS.
3. TODAY, ME TRAVEL MYSELF PLAN, INTERNET HELP-me.

In the dialogue, sentences 2 and 3 follow one another and demonstrate how a signer uses time adverbs to change the tense of a conversation. If the sign TODAY was left out of sentence 3, then the sentence TRAVEL PLAN MYSELF INTERNET HELP-me would be in the past tense in the dialogue because the sentence before it contained the time adverb, PAST.

Simple Yes/No Questions

In the question

me-JOIN-you, DON'T-MIND YOU?

the topic is described (me-JOIN-you) followed by a yes/no question about the topic (DON'T-MIND YOU?).

Information-seeking Questions

In the sentences

INTERNET CHECK FOR-FOR?

YOU VACATION HOW LONG?

the questions FOR-FOR? and HOW LONG? follow the description of the topic. Recall that FOR-FOR means Yes and is interchangeable with the sign WHY.

Ordering of Simple Sentences

The sentence

ME NEED VACATION.

follows a subject-verb-object (SVO) word ordering.

Conditional Sentences

In the following conditional sentence

PAST, SUPPOSE ME WANT TRAVEL, SLOW PROCESS PLAN ALWAYS.

the time adverb is placed at the beginning of the sentence and before the sign SUPPOSE. This sentence is modeled on a topic/comment format. The topic is ME WANT TRAVEL, and the comment is SLOW PROCESS PLAN ALWAYS.

The Directional Verbs JOIN and HELP

The dialogue contained the following two examples of directional verbs or verbs that change the meaning of a sentence in the signing space:

me-JOIN-you

HELP-me

In the dialogue, HELP-me is used in a sentence, and the subject of that sentence is the Internet. The subject of the sentence is implied in the signing. That is, the sign HELP-me begins in a neutral position and then moves toward the signer. It would also be proper to sign it-HELP-me, which would more clearly indicate the subject of the sentence. But before you can sign this, you must first place the Internet in your signing space and then begin the sign it-HELP-me from that location.

What's the Sign?

FOUR-WEEKS

The sign for 4 is incorporated into the sign for WEEK.

JOIN

This sign is not to be used to mean to join things together, as in "join the two ropes together." It is to be used only when referring to the concept of becoming a member of something or to participate in something. In the dialogue, John wants to join Jenny on her trip to Poland.

MYSELF

The pronoun MYSELF and all other pronouns containing -self are made with the A handshape replacing the pointing finger, which is used to make the pronouns ME, YOU, SHE, IT, THEM, and so forth. The sign is also used to mean self- as in self-esteem and self-concept.

ASL Synonyms

Some signs can be used to mean other things.

Sign	Also used for
AWESOME	EXCELLENT, FABULOUS, FANTASTIC, SUPERB, WONDERFUL, GREAT IMPROVEMENT, IMPROVED, GREATLY INCREASED, ADVANCED
IMPROVE	FORWARD
CHECK	EXPLORE, INVESTIGATE
INTERNET	NETWORK, ONLINE, OUTREACH
MYSELF	SELF-
PLAN	ARRANGE, PREPARE
PROCESS	PROCEDURE, PACE, PROGRESS, TAKE STEPS, SEQUENCE
TECHNOLOGY	TECHNICAL, TECH
TRAVEL	TOUR, TRIP
VACATION	HOLIDAY

Practice Activities

1. MODEL FOR GREETINGS, TOPIC/COMMENT, TIME ADVERBS, AND ORDERING OF SIMPLE SENTENCES

Signer A: 1. Greet the person;

        2. ask what the person is doing.

    Greeting: HELLO,

    Question: DO-what YOU?

Signer B: 1. Respond to the question with an SOV sentence.

    Response: ME NEED VACATION.

    1. Describe a topic;

    2. make a comment about the topic.

    Topic: GO-to POLAND

    Comment: ME WANT.

    1. Use a time adverb to establish the time frame of a sentence;

    2. describe a topic;

    3. make a comment about the topic.

    Tense: NOW

    Topic: INTERNET

    Comment: ME CHECK.

Practice

Signer A: HELLO, DO-what YOU?

Signer B: ME NEED VACATION. GO-to POLAND ME WANT. NOW INTERNET ME CHECK.

2. MODEL FOR TENSE WITH TIME ADVERBS, INFORMATION-SEEKING QUESTIONS, AND CONDITIONAL SENTENCES

Signer A: 1. Describe a topic;

               2. ask a question about the topic using the sign FOR-FOR.

Topic:	INTERNET CHECK
Wh-question:	FOR-FOR?

Signer B: 1. Indicate the tense with a time adverb;

               2. describe the condition;

               3. describe an outcome of the condition using the directional verb HELP.

Tense:	PAST,
Condition:	SUPPOSE ME WANT TRAVEL,
Outcome:	SLOW PROCESS ALWAYS.

               1. Change the tense by placing the time adverb TODAY at the beginning of a sentence;

               2. describe a topic;

               3. make a comment about the topic;

               4. describe another topic;

               5. make a comment about the topic.

Tense:	TODAY,
Topic:	ME TRAVEL
Comment:	MYSELF PLAN,
Topic:	INTERNET
Comment:	HELP-me.

Practice

Signer A: W-E-B S-I-T-E CHECK FOR-FOR?

Signer B: PAST, SUPPOSE ME WANT TRAVEL, SLOW PROCESS ALWAYS. TODAY, ME TRAVEL MYSELF PLAN, INTERNET HELP-me.

3. MODEL FOR TOPIC/COMMENT AND INFORMATION-SEEKING QUESTIONS

Signer A:
1. Use the sign AWESOME to make a comment relating to the use of Internet technologies to help a person make travel plans;
2. describe the topic;
3. add another comment.

Comment: AWESOME!

Topic: TECHNOLOGY TODAY, IMPROVED (BIG IMPROVEMENT/ADVANCED).

1. Describe a topic;
2. ask a question about the topic.

Topic: YOU VACATION

Comment: HOW LONG?

Signer B:
1. Respond to the question.

Response: FOUR-WEEKS.

Practice

Signer A: AWESOME! TECHNOLOGY TODAY, IMPROVED. YOU VACATION HOW LONG?

Signer B: FOUR-WEEKS.

4. MODEL FOR SIMPLE YES/NO QUESTIONS

Signer A:
1. Describe the topic;
2. ask a yes/no question about the topic.

Topic: me-JOIN-you,

Question: DON'T-MIND YOU?

Signer B:
1. Respond to the question.

Response: SURE.

Practice

Signer A:	me-JOIN-you, DON'T-MIND YOU?
Signer B:	SURE.

5. MASTERY LEARNING

When you feel comfortable signing these phrases, practice signing the entire dialogue shown at the beginning of this lesson. Practice the dialogue until you can sign it comfortably.

6. FURTHER PRACTICE

Create ten ASL sentences about traveling that use time adverbs and descriptive terms for feelings. Write the English gloss for these sentences; then practice signing them to a partner. The partner should write the English translation of your ASL sentences.

LESSON 38: TRAVEL PLANS

Signing Dialogue

1. **Paul:** **ENGLAND point-right TWO-of-us FLY-to-right WHEN?**

   When do the two of us fly to England?

ENGLAND   point-right   TWO-of-us

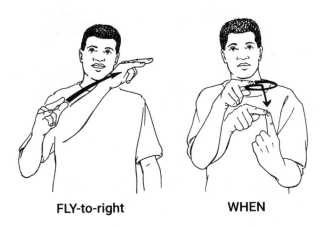

FLY-to-right   WHEN

2. **Jessica:** **J-U-L-Y 21.**

July 21st.

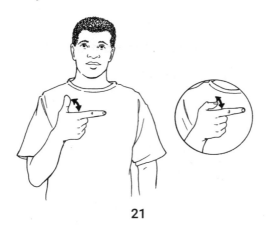

21

3. **Paul:** **right-FLY-back WHEN?**

When do we fly back?

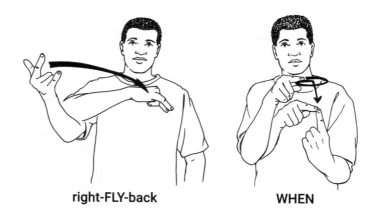

right-FLY-back   WHEN

4. **Jessica:** **A-U-G-U-S-T 18.**

August 18th.

18

5. **Paul:** **TWO-of-us ARRIVE-there DO-what?**

What do we do when we get there?

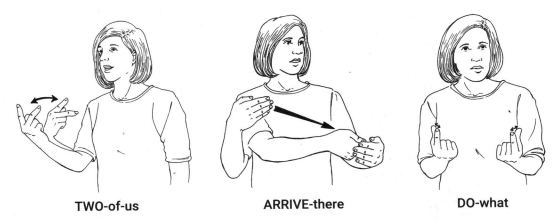

TWO-of-us   ARRIVE-there   DO-what

6. **Jessica:** **FIRST, LONDON VISIT. THEN TRAIN GET-on COUNTRY TRAVEL-AROUND.**

First we visit London. Then we get on a train and travel around the country.

FIRST   LONDON   VISIT

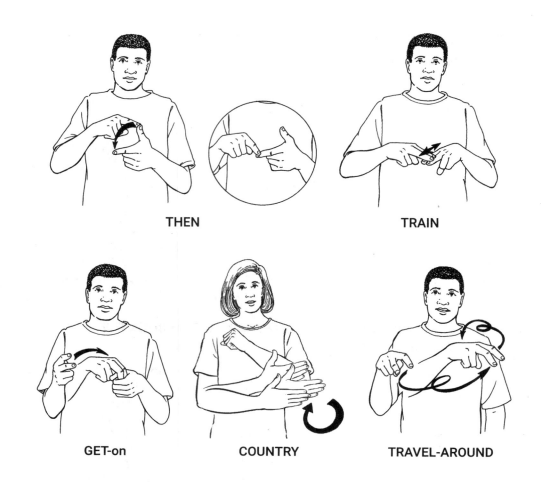

THEN   TRAIN

GET-on   COUNTRY   TRAVEL-AROUND

7.   **Paul:**   **TRAIN RIDE-on WILL?**

              We will ride on a train?

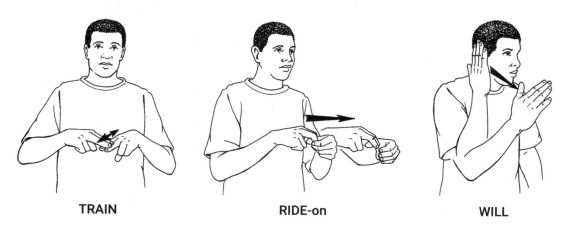

TRAIN   RIDE-on   WILL

8. **Jessica:** **YES. WHAT'S-WRONG?**

Yes. What's wrong?

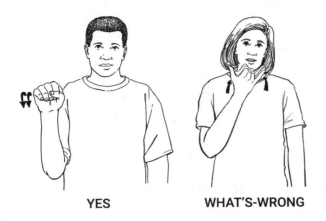

YES WHAT'S-WRONG

9. **Paul:** **BEFORE ME TRAIN RIDE-on, NEVER. NERVOUS ME.**

I have never been on a train before. I'm nervous.

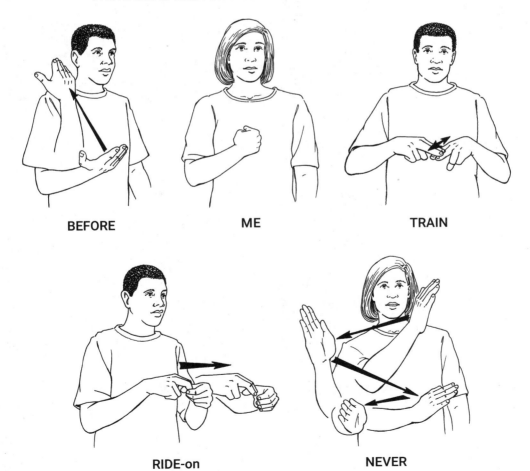

BEFORE ME TRAIN

RIDE-on NEVER

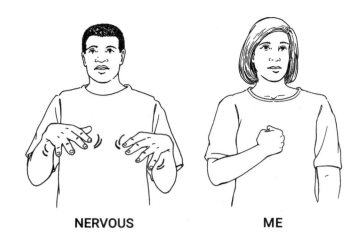

NERVOUS   ME

10. **Jessica:** **REALLY? TRAIN RIDE-on NOTHING-to-it. YOU ENJOY, WILL.**

Really? Riding on a train is nothing to worry about. You will enjoy it.

REALLY   TRAIN   RIDE-on

NOTHING-to-it   YOU

ENJOY   WILL

11. **Paul:**   **PROMISE?**

Do you promise?

PROMISE

12. **Jessica:**   **YES. TRUST ME.**

Yes. Trust me.

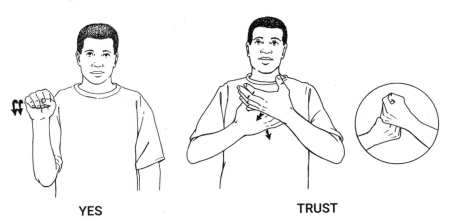

YES   TRUST

ME

Breaking Down the Dialogue

Information-seeking Questions and Pronominalization

In the first sentence of the dialogue, England is placed to the right side of the signing space:

ENGLAND point-right TWO-of-us FLY-to-right WHEN?

The sign FLY-to-right moves from a neutral point in the signing space to the right side where England was placed. The sign FLY-to-right starts in a neutral position because it is referring to both people in the dialogue.

The sentence is also an example of a wh-question, in which the first part of the sentence describes the topic and the sign WHEN asks a question about the topic. Another example of a wh-question that includes pronominalization is

TWO-of-us ARRIVE-there DO-what?

The sign ARRIVE-there moves from a position in front of the body to the right side of the signing space, which is where England was placed.

In the following sentence:

right-FLY-back WHEN?

the sign right-FLY-back starts in the same location in the signing space where England was placed, which was in the right side of the signing space. The topic of this question is right-FLY-back and the wh-question sign is WHEN?

Ordering of Simple Sentences

The sentence

FIRST, LONDON VISIT.

is translated to "First, we will visit London." This ASL sentence does not contain a sign for a pronoun because it is readily implied from the context of the dialogue. The second sentence provides an example of how sentences can be organized by laying out events in the way that they occurred:

THEN TRAIN GET-on COUNTRY TRAVEL-AROUND.

Two more examples of simple sentences found in the dialogue are

NERVOUS ME.

TRUST ME.

Simple Yes/No Questions

In the sentence

TRAIN RIDE-on WILL?

the topic is first described followed by a yes/no question about it. Signing WILL at the end of the sentence highlights the sentence as a question. Another yes/no question in the dialogue is

PROMISE?

Negation

There are two points to consider in the following sentence:

BEFORE ME TRAIN RIDE-on, NEVER.

First, it is an example of the negation rule: A topic is described and then negated by a negative sign (NEVER). The second point is the use of the sign BEFORE. This sign is made in the same manner as PAST because its meaning is related to what a person has done in the past.

Topic/Comment

The sign NOTHING-to-it is either signed alone or placed at the end of a sentence, as in the following:

TRAIN RIDE-on NOTHING-to-it.

It is always used to make a comment about something. Another topic/comment sentence in the dialogue was

YOU ENJOY, WILL.

The sign WILL is often used to emphasize that a person is going to do something, and that is why it fulfills the role of a comment in the foregoing sentence.

What's the Sign?

FLY-to/FLY-back

FLY is a directional verb because its movement tells about the subject and object of a sentence. The sign FLY-to moves toward the outside of the signing space, and the sign FLY-back moves from the outside of the signing space toward the inside. The exact starting and ending positions of both signs are dependent upon who is flying: the signer or someone whom the signer is talking about.

GET-on/RIDE-on

The difference between the signs for GET-on and RIDE-on is that the hand does not move forward in the sign GET-on, whereas in the sign RIDE-on the hand moves forward to represent going someplace.

WRONG-WRONG/WRONG-WHAT

The common English gloss for this sign is "What's wrong?" or "What's the matter?" It is often signed by itself as a means of inquiring about something.

WILL

Although the sign WILL is used to indicate the future time, it is also commonly used to emphasize that a person will do something.

ASL Synonyms

Some signs can be used to mean other things.

Sign	Also used for
NOTHING-TO-IT	INSIGNIFICANT, PUNY, TRIVIAL, NOT A BIG DEAL
TRUST	CONFIDENT

Practice Activities

1. MODEL FOR INFORMATION-SEEKING QUESTIONS AND PRONOMINALIZATION

Signer A:
1. Sign the object of the sentence, ENGLAND;
2. place England in the signing space by pointing to the right (note that you could also point to the left);
3. describe the topic;
4. ask a question about the topic.

Object:	ENGLAND
Placement of object:	point right
Topic:	TWO-of-us FLY-to-right
Question:	WHEN?

Signer B:
1. Respond to the question.

Response:	J-U-L-Y 21.

Signer A:
1. Describe the topic;
2. ask a question about the topic.

Topic:	right-FLY-back
Question:	WHEN?

Signer B:
1. Respond to the wh-question.

Response:	A-U-G-U-S-T 18.

Practice

Signer A: ENGLAND-point-right TWO-of-us FLY-to-right WHEN?

Signer B: J-U-L-Y 21.

Signer A: right-FLY-back WHEN?

Signer B: A-U-G-U-S-T 18.

2. MODEL FOR INFORMATION-SEEKING QUESTIONS AND ORDERING OF SIMPLE SENTENCES

Signer A:
    1. Describe the topic;
    2. ask a question about the topic.

Topic:	TWO-of-us ARRIVE-there
Question:	DO-what?

Signer B:
    1. Establish the initial sequence of events by signing FIRST;
    2. describe an action;
    3. establish the next sequence of events by signing THEN;
    4. describe an action.

Initial sequence:	FIRST,
Action:	LONDON VISIT.
Next sequence:	THEN
Action:	TRAIN GET-on COUNTRY TRAVEL-AROUND.

Practice

Signer A: TWO-of-us ARRIVE-there DO-what?

Signer B: FIRST, LONDON VISIT. THEN TRAIN GET-on COUNTRY TRAVEL-AROUND.

3. MODEL FOR SIMPLE YES/NO QUESTIONS, INFORMATION-SEEKING QUESTIONS, ORDERING OF SIMPLE SENTENCES, AND NEGATION

Signer A:
    1. Describe the topic;
    2. ask a yes/no question using the sign WILL.

Topic:	TRAIN RIDE-on
Question:	WILL?

Signer B:
    1. Answer the question affirmatively with the sign YES;
    2. ask a question using the sign WHAT'S-WRONG?

Response:	YES.
Question:	WHAT'S-WRONG?

Signer A: 1. Describe the topic;

2. use a negative sign to negate the topic;

3. use a simple sentence structure to describe how you feel.

Topic: BEFORE ME TRAIN RIDE-on,

Negation: NEVER.

Simple sentence: NERVOUS ME.

Practice

Signer A: TRAIN RIDE-on WILL?

Signer B: YES. WHAT'S-WRONG?

Signer A: BEFORE ME TRAIN RIDE-on, NEVER. NERVOUS ME.

4. MODEL FOR TOPIC/COMMENT, SIMPLE YES/NO QUESTIONS, AND USING WILL IN ITS EMPHATIC SENSE

Signer A: 1. Describe the topic;

2. make a comment about the topic;

3. describe an action;

4. emphasize the action with the sign WILL.

Topic: TRAIN RIDE-on

Comment: NOTHING-to-it.

Action: YOU ENJOY,

Emphasis: WILL.

Signer B: 1. Ask a simple yes/no question.

Question: PROMISE?

Signer A: 1. Respond affirmatively to the yes/no question;

2. use a simple sentence to make a command.

Response: YES.

Simple sentence: TRUST ME.

Practice

Signer A:	TRAIN RIDE-on NOTHING-to-it. YOU ENJOY, WILL.
Signer B:	PROMISE?
Signer A:	YES. TRUST ME.

5. MASTERY LEARNING

When you feel comfortable signing these phrases, practice signing the entire dialogue shown at the beginning of this lesson. Practice the dialogue until you can sign it comfortably.

6. FURTHER PRACTICE

Join the dialogue in this lesson with the one in a previous lesson. Practice signing both until you are comfortable signing them.

LESSON 39: COUNTRIES

This lesson is a repeat dialogue of Lesson 38 with different character names for added fingerspelling practice. In this lesson, you will sign the short sections of dialogue and replace the bolded word. For the first section, you will replace the country with one of the provided countries or fingerspell one of your choosing.

The country signs we have provided may have other signs as well. We picked the most popular sign for each country, whether it be what we use here in North America or what someone may use in her or his home country.

Cities

Most major cities have signs; however, they are sometimes regional. Because they are proper nouns, play it safe and fingerspell major cities until you learn the regional sign. Refer to Chapter 9: Relations, Lesson 18, pp. 384–387.

Muhammad: HELLO, DO-what YOU?
Ariana: ME NEED VACATION. GO-to **ENGLAND** ME WANT.

ITALY   ROME

BARRON'S AMERICAN SIGN LANGUAGE

FRANCE

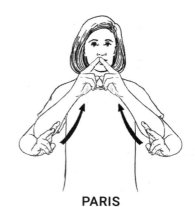

PARIS

This is also the sign for the language FRENCH.

BRAZIL

**SAO PAULO
RIO DE JANEIRO**

AUSTRALIA

**CANBERRA
SYDNEY**

NETHERLANDS

AMSTERDAM

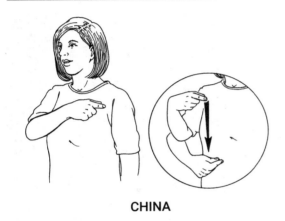

CHINA

BEIJING
SHANGHAI

ISRAEL

TEL AVIV
JERUSALEM

EGYPT   CAIRO

GREECE   ATHENS

FINLAND   HELSINKI

KOREA   SEOUL

POLAND   WARSAW

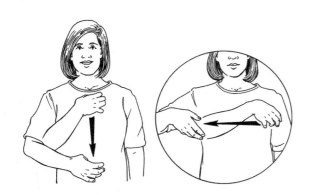

SWITZERLAND   ZURICH

RUSSIA   MOSCOW

SPAIN   BARCELONA
                                               MADRID

This is also the sign for the language SPANISH.

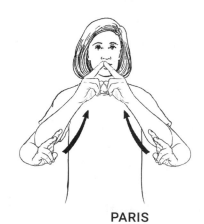   

PARIS   ROME

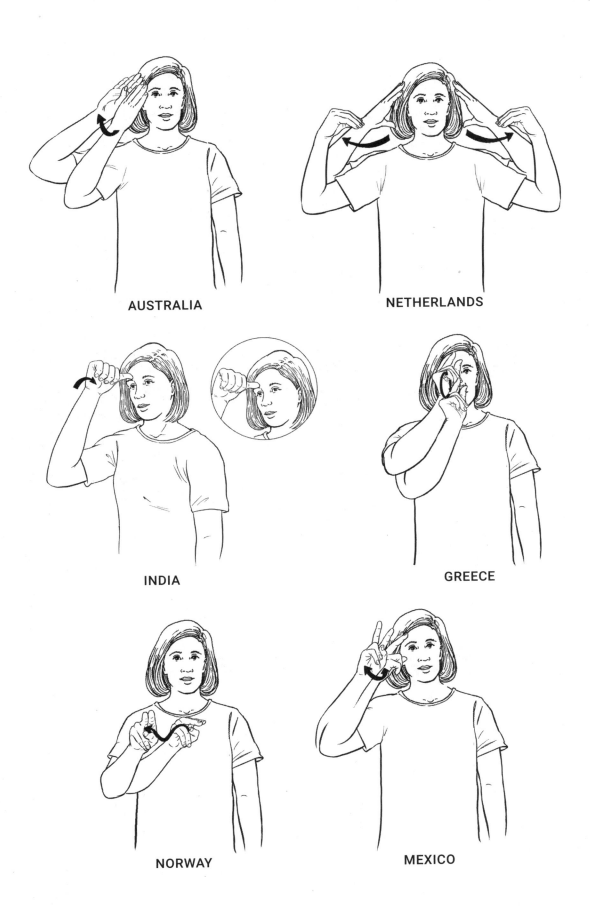

AUSTRALIA

NETHERLANDS

INDIA

GREECE

NORWAY

MEXICO

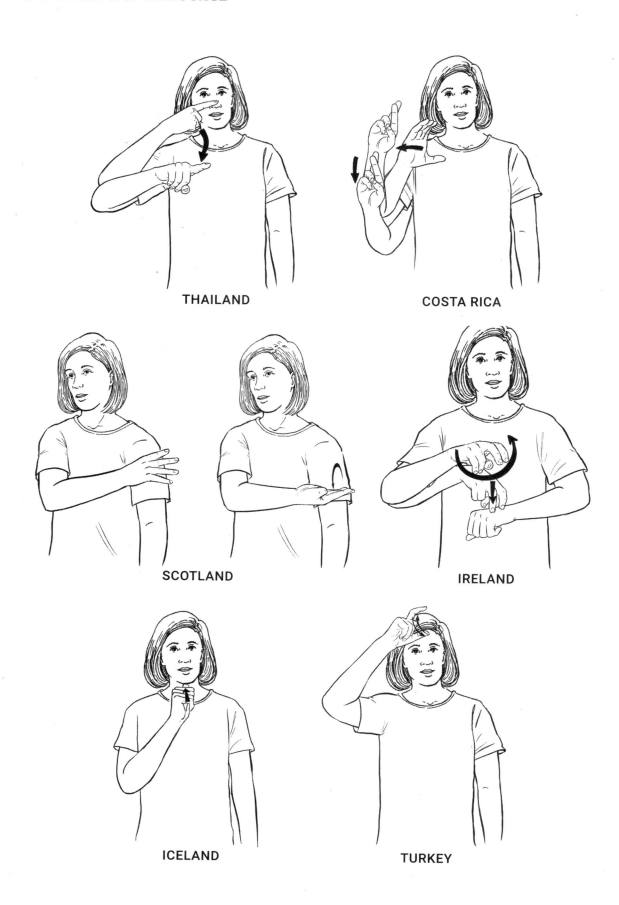

THAILAND

COSTA RICA

SCOTLAND

IRELAND

ICELAND

TURKEY

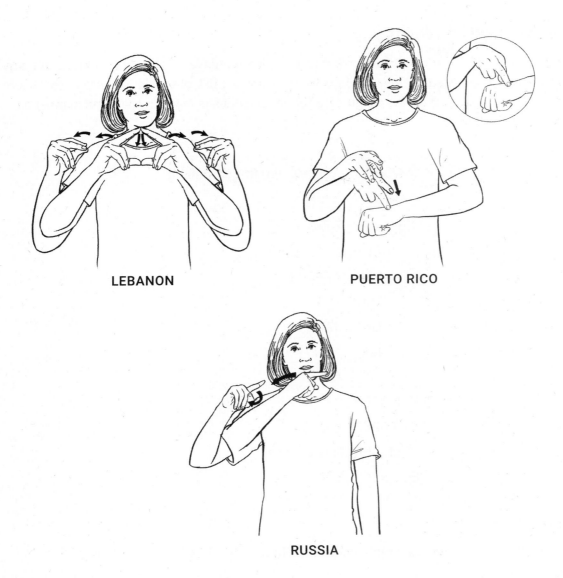

LEBANON

PUERTO RICO

RUSSIA

Months, Dates, and Countries

1. Marcus: **ITALY** point-right TWO-of-us FLY-to-right WHEN?

    Danielle: **A-P-R-I-L 10**.

2. Marcus: right-FLY-back WHEN?

    Danielle: **M-A-Y 8**.

Substitute signs from the list of countries already shown.

Fingerspelled Words

All months of the year can be fingerspelled completely; however, the abbreviations of many of the months can also be fingerspelled. In the following list, abbreviations are noted where they are appropriate. There is a sign for September, which is made in the same manner as the sign AUTUMN.

Months	Abbreviated fingerspelling
JANUARY	J-A-N
FEBRUARY	F-E-B
MARCH	M-A-R-C-H
APRIL	A-P-R-I-L
MAY	M-A-Y
JUNE	J-U-N-E
JULY	J-U-L-Y
AUGUST	A-U-G
SEPTEMBER	S-E-P-T
OCTOBER	O-C-T
NOVEMBER	N-O-V
DECEMBER	D-E-C

Numbers

For the dates, substitute any numbers from 1 through 30 or 31.

Cities and Vehicles

Patrick: TWO-of-us ARRIVE-there-right DO-what?

Ronnie: FIRST, **ROME** VISIT. THEN **TRAIN** GET-on COUNTRY TRAVEL-AROUND.

Cities

Although there are signs for the names of all the major cities listed previously, almost all of them are unknown to most Deaf people in the United States and Canada. They are typically known only by Deaf people who travel to international conferences and international Deaf sporting events. Therefore, in this lesson you will practice fingerspelling the names of some of the major cities of each of the countries listed. Fingerspelling is a complex art, and all beginning signers are advised to seek instruction from ASL instructors.

Vehicles

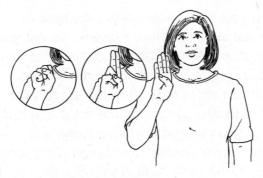

B-U-S

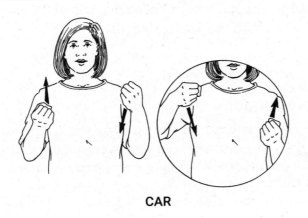

CAR

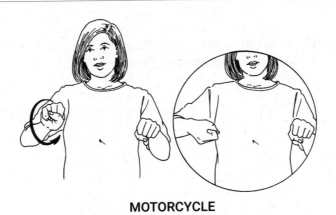

MOTORCYCLE

Practice Activities

For practice in expanding your sign vocabulary, substitute the signs learned in this lesson for various signs learned in previous lessons. Do not attempt to learn all the new signs in this lesson in one day. Divide up the signs and learn them over a period of a few days. Because you will not use some of these signs in your everyday conversations, you may find it more difficult to remember them when you do need to use them. Refer back to this lesson from time to time to refresh your memory of these signs. Do keep in mind that at any time during a signed conversation, you can always fingerspell the proper nouns. This lesson will also provide practice in fingerspelling the months of the year, numbers for the days of the month, and names of cities in various countries.

In each of the proceeding chapter lesson dialogues, substitute the word in bold with a sign or fingerspelled word from the appropriate list.

When in Doubt—Fingerspell

Each country has its own signs, which may be local, regional, or national. The signs we are showing are the ones most commonly recognized in the United States and Canada for that country. When the name of a country is in doubt, it should be fingerspelled.

 Video Quiz Visit online.barronsbooks.com for scored practice on ASL expressions related to travel.

Grammar Practice

Write an English translation for each of the following ASL sentences.

Note that there may be other ways of translating these sentences than the ones shown here.

1. SUPPOSE YOU VACATION NEED, YOU TRAVEL WHERE?

2. YOU SWITZERLAND GO-to, FOR-FOR?

3. ME VACATION HOW-LONG? THREE-WEEKS.

4. LAST-YEAR YOU TRAVEL WHERE?

5. YOU VACATION PLAN, COMPUTER HELP-you HOW?

6. POLAND YOU ARRIVE-there, DO-what YOU?

7. YOU RIDE-on TRAIN, YOU NERVOUS YOU?

8. B-U-S TICKET, ME BUY FINISH.

9. you-FLY-to SPAIN WHEN?

10. IN-TWO-YEARS ME NEW-YORK VISIT WILL.

FINAL EXAM

For a scored, cumulative exam on the ASL topics you've learned in this book, visit Barron's Online Learning Hub:

online.barronsbooks.com

There are 30 video questions that cover:

- Fingerspelling
- Numbering
- ASL grammar rules
- Signs and phrases

To prepare for the final exam, review practice activities and video quizzes throughout the book.

Appendix

Chapter Review and Grammar Practice Answers

Index

Chapter Review and Grammar Practice Answers

Chapter 1 Review

1. Individual response.

2. Requires an Internet search based on your location. For example, Michigan School for the Deaf and Blind in Flint, Michigan.

3. ASL is American Sign Language. It is the language of the American Deaf community. Many people can use ASL to communicate, including hearing people as well.

4. Two of the following: Gently tap on someone's shoulder. Flick the lights. Do the "Deaf wave" (a low, light wave within someone's eyesight). Get in someone's line of vision and make eye contact. Stomp on the floor close to someone's feet.

5. Sources: Laurent Clerc (Deaf teacher from France), Thomas Hopkins Gallaudet, and the Deaf community (Deaf students and families).

6. 1. The *handshape* is the shape of the hands when the sign is formed.
   2. The *orientation* is the position of the hand(s) relative to the body.
   3. The *location* is the place in the signing space where a sign is formed.
   4. The *movement* of a sign is the direction in which the hand moves relative to the body.
   5. *Nonmanual markers* add to signs to create meaning. They consist of various facial expressions, head tilting, shoulder movement, and mouthing.

7. *Name signs* or *sign names* are signs that represent your name in ASL. A name sign can only be given to you by a Deaf person, and the gift of a name sign carries a cultural importance.

Chapter 2 Review

1. 1. Having a hearing loss
   2. Using American Sign Language
   3. Having shared experiences

2. One example from this chapter: "Let's say you had a young friend who has acquired a hearing loss and was fitted with hearing aids. Would we say that he was Deaf? No, we say that he is hard of hearing because speaking is still his main means of communication."

3. Deaf people who have nondeaf parents will likely have developed their ties with the Deaf community away from home, learning ASL from other Deaf children they meet in school programs, and especially in schools for the Deaf.

4. Individual response.

5. Individual response.

6. Use the Internet to find Deaf organizations.

7. Use the Internet to research your chosen organization. Send an email or message to the organization to gather more information if desired.

8. The National Association of the Deaf (NAD) has helped protect Deaf and hard-of-hearing persons against discrimination in employment, education, telecommunication, television, and other services by involving the U.S. Congress in passing legislation like the Americans with Disabilities Act, the Television Decoder Circuitry Act of 1990, telecommunication rules and regulations, etc. NAD has been the voice of Deaf and hard-of-hearing citizens.

9. Suggested questions:

   1. What does the organization do? (People need to know what services they provide.)

   2. Where is the office? (Office location is needed so that people can visit or write to the organization.)

   3. What is the video-relay phone number, email address, and website? (People need this information to contact individuals and departments at these organizations.)

   4. What, when, and where is the next activity? (The public will need to know how and where they can participate in the group's activities.)

   5. Who can become a member? (This question is necessary because each organization has different rules.)

Chapter 3 Review

1. Rule #5: Information-seeking questions.

2. Rule #4: Long yes/no questions.

3. Rule #10: Negation.

4. Rule #1: Topic/comment.

5. Rule #6: Pronominalization.

6. Rule #2: Tense with time adverbs.

7. Rule #9: Conditional sentences.

8. Rule #8: Ordering of simple sentences.

9. Rule #7: Rhetorical questions.

10. Rule #3: Simple yes/no questions.

13. **Yes/no question:** raised eyebrows and forward tilting head
Question-seeking information: squeezed eyebrows and forward tilting head
Rhetorical question: raised eyebrows, forward tilting head, and holding last sign longer
Topic/comment sentence structure: raised eyebrows, forward tilting head, pause between sentences, and holding last sign longer
Conditional sentence: raised eyebrows, forward tilting head, and holding last sign longer

Chapter 5 Review

2. When signing phone numbers, addresses, or anything that is more than a single number from 1 to 5, your palm faces away from you.

3. You sign large numbers in the same way that you say them in English. As you practice signing large numbers, say them out loud in English first, then sign them while quietly saying the English in your head.

Chapter 6 Grammar Practice

1. GEOGRAPHY, YOU TAKE-UP?

2. COMPUTER CLASS START WHEN? TIME 6. or COMPUTER CLASS START, TIME 6.

3. YOU DISCOURAGED? or DISCOURAGED YOU?

4. FEEL+ YOU?

5. YOU LEARN ASL, WHEN?

6. ME FEEL LUCKY, YOU?

7. NOW, ASL NUMBERS ME LEARN.

8. YOU TIRED, ALWAYS.

9. MORNING, BUSINESS CLASS YOU GO-to.

10. DRAMA ROOM, WHERE?

Chapter 8 Grammar Practice

1. YOU STUDY FINISH? ME DON'T-CARE.

2. YESTERDAY, SNOW.

3. TOMORROW AFTERNOON, TIME ONE, me-MEET-you HERE.

4. SUPPOSE TOMORROW SNOW, DO-what YOU?

5. SUPPOSE YOUR NAME ME FORGET, me-CONTACT-you HOW?

6. VIDEO NAME?

7. ASL PRACTICE, ME MUST?

8. HE CLASS SHOW-UP, NOT-YET.

9. INTERPRETER SIGN HOW? ASL.

10. SIGN, SHE SKILL.

Chapter 11 Grammar Practice

1. YOUR BOOK, you-BORROW-me?

2. EVERY DAY ME STUDY ASL WHY? MY SISTER, DEAF.

3. MONDAY MORNING, ME START WORK, TIME 7.

4. YOU FEEL HOT COLD WHICH?

5. ME LIVE WHERE? PHILADELPHIA.

6. MY COUSIN, SHE COMPUTER-ANALYST.

7. MY ROOM, DARK QUIET.

8. YOU POEM WRITE FINISH, TIME?

9. YOUR UNCLE, NAME?

10. WOMAN THERE, SHE ENGINEER DOCTOR WHICH?

Chapter 13 Grammar Practice

1. Why are you going to the WGD?

2. When are people going to the WGD?

3. How many Deaf people compete in the WGD?

4. How many competitions are you involved with?

5. How many different languages do you understand?

6. Where are the Games next year?

7. In three years, the Games will be in Canada.

8. Every day at seven o'clock, a man walks past me.

9. In what game did you challenge him four weeks ago?

10. If I join your class, would you mind helping me study?

Chapter 14 Grammar Practice

1. I watched the football game.

2. What time are we going to the restaurant tomorrow night?

3. Do you prefer sports or leisure activities? or Which do you prefer, sports or leisure activities?

4. I like hockey, golf, and cycling.

5. If you have a pain in your mouth, do you make an appointment to see the dentist or the doctor?

6. I feel awful because I have a rotten tooth.

7. Show me where you are hurt.

8. I have an allergy to penicillin.

9. I am sick and I feel hot.

10. You played hockey in the morning, watched football in the afternoon, and now you are sick?

Chapter 15 Grammar Practice

1. If you needed a vacation, where would you travel? or Where would you travel if you needed a vacation?

2. Why are you going to Switzerland?

3. My vacation is three weeks long.

4. Where did you travel last year?

5. How does the computer help you plan your vacation?

6. What are you going to do when you arrive in Poland?

7. Are you nervous when you ride on a train?

8. I have bought the bus ticket.

9. When are you flying to Spain?

10. I will visit New York in two years.

Index